Bismarck

And the Foundation of the German Empire

by James Wycliffe Headlam

Originally published in 1899.

PREFACE.

The greater portion of the following pages were completed before the death of Prince Bismarck; I take this opportunity of apologising to the publishers and the editor of the series, for the unavoidable delay which has caused publication to be postponed for a year.

During this period, two works have appeared to which some reference is necessary. The value of Busch's Memoirs has been much exaggerated; except for quite the last years of Bismarck's life they contain little new information which is of any importance. Not only had a large portion of the book already been published in Busch's two earlier books, but many of the anecdotes and documents in those parts which were new had also been published elsewhere.

Bismarck's own Memoirs have a very different value: not so much because of the new facts which they record, but because of the light they throw on Bismarck's character and on the attitude he adopted towards men and political problems. With his letters and speeches, they will always remain the chief source for our knowledge of his inner life.

The other authorities are so numerous that it is impossible here to enumerate even the more important. I must, however, express the gratitude which all students of Bismarck's career owe to Horst Kohl; in his Bismarck-Regesten he has collected and arranged the material so as infinitely to lighten the labours of all others who work in the same field. His Bismarck-Jahrbuch is equally indispensable; without this it would be impossible for anyone living in England to use the innumerable letters, documents, and anecdotes which each year appear in

German periodicals. Of collections of documents and letters, the most important are those by Herr v. Poschinger, especially the volumes containing the despatches written from Frankfort and those dealing with Bismarck's economic and financial policy. A full collection of Bismarck's correspondence is much wanted; there is now a good edition of the private letters, edited by Kohl, but no satisfactory collection of the political letters.

For diplomatic history between 1860 and 1870, I have, of course, chiefly depended on Sybel; but those who are acquainted with the recent course of criticism in Germany will not be surprised if, while accepting his facts, I have sometimes ventured to differ from his conclusions.

J.W.H.

September, 1899.

CONTENTS.

CHAPTER I.

BIRTH AND PARENTAGE.

Otto Eduard Leopold Von Bismarck was born at the manor-house of Schoenhausen, in the Mark of Brandenburg, on April 1, 1815. Just a month before, Napoleon had escaped from Elba; and, as the child lay in his cradle, the peasants of the village, who but half a year ago had returned from the great campaign in France, were once more called to arms. A few months passed by; again the King of Prussia returned at the head of his army; in the village churches the medals won at Waterloo were hung up by those of Grossbehren and Leipzig. One more victory had been added to the Prussian flags, and then a profound peace fell upon Europe; fifty years were to go by before a Prussian army again marched out to meet a foreign foe.

The name and family of Bismarck were among the oldest in the land. Many of the great Prussian statesmen have come from other countries: Stein was from Nassau, and Hardenberg was a subject of the Elector of Hanover; even Blücher and Schwerin were Mecklenburgers, and the Moltkes belong to Holstein. The Bismarcks are pure Brandenburgers; they belong to the old Mark, the district ruled over by the first Margraves who were sent by the Emperor to keep order on the northern frontier; they were there two hundred years before the first Hohenzollern came to the north.

The first of the name of whom we hear was Herbort von Bismarck, who, in 1270, was Master of the Guild of the

Clothiers in the city of Stendal. The town had been founded about one hundred years before by Albert the Bear, and men had come in from the country around to enjoy the privileges and security of city life. Doubtless Herbort or his father had come from Bismarck, a village about twenty miles to the west, which takes its name either from the little stream, the Biese, which runs near it, or from the bishop in whose domain it lay. He was probably the first to bear the name, which would have no meaning so long as he remained in his native place, for the von was still a mark of origin and had not yet become the sign of nobility. Other emigrants from Bismarck seem also to have assumed it; in the neighbouring town of Prenzlau the name occurs, and it is still found among the peasants of the Mark; as the Wends were driven back and the German invasion spread, more adventurous colonists migrated beyond the Oder and founded a new Bismarck in Pomerania.

Of the lineage of Herbort we know nothing [1] ; his ancestors must have been among the colonists who had been planted by the Emperors on the northern frontier to occupy the land conquered from the heathen. He seems himself to have been a man of substance and position; he already used the arms, the double trefoil, which are still borne by all the branches of his family. His descendants are often mentioned in the records of the Guild; his son or grandson, Rudolph or Rule, represented the town in a conflict with the neighbouring Dukes of Brunswick. It was his son Nicolas, or Claus as he is generally called, who founded the fortunes of the family; he attached himself closely to the cause of the Margrave, whom he supported in his troubles with the Duke of Brunswick, and whose interests he represented in the Town Council. He was amply rewarded for his fidelity. After a quarrel between the city and the Prince, Bismarck left his native home and permanently entered the service of the Margrave. Though probably hitherto only a simple citizen, he was enfiefed with the castle of Burgstall, an important post, for it was situated on the borders of the Mark and the bishopric of Magdeburg; he was thereby admitted into the privileged class of the Schlossgesessenen, under the Margrave, the highest order in the feudal hierarchy. From that day the Bismarcks have held their own among the nobility of Brandenburg. Claus eventually became Hofmeister of Brandenburg, the chief officer at the Court; he had his quarrels with the Church, or rather with the spiritual lords, the bishops of Havelburg and Magdeburg, and was once excommunicated, as his father had been before him, and as two of his sons were after him.

Claus died about the year 1385. For two hundred years the Bismarcks continued to live at Burgstall, to which they added many other estates. When Conrad of Hohenzollern was appointed Margrave and Elector, he found sturdy supporters in the lords of Burgstall; he and his successors often came there to hunt the deer and wild boars, perhaps also the wolves and bears, with which the forests around the castle abounded; for the Hohenzollerns were keen sportsmen then as now, as their vassals found to their cost. In 1555, Hans George, son of the reigning Elector, Albert Achilles, bought the neighbouring estate of Letzlingen from the Alvenslebens; there he built a house which is still the chief hunting-lodge of the Kings of Prussia. Soon he cast envious eyes on the great woods and preserves which belong to Burgstall, and intimated that he wished to possess them. The Bismarcks resisted long. First they were compelled to surrender their hunting rights; this was not sufficient; the appetite of the Prince grew; in his own words he wished "to be rid of the Bismarcks from the moor and the Tanger altogether." He offered in exchange some of the monasteries which had lately been suppressed; the Bismarcks (the family was represented by two pairs of brothers, who all lived together in the great castle) long refused; they represented that their ancestors had been faithful vassals; they had served the Electors with blood and treasure; they wished "to remain in the pleasant place to which they had been assigned by God Almighty." It was all of no use; the Prince insisted, and his wrath was dangerous. The Bismarcks gave in; they surrendered Burgstall and received in exchange Schoenhausen and Crevisse, a confiscated nunnery, on condition that as long as the ejected nuns lived the new lords should support them; for which purpose the Bismarcks had annually to supply a certain quantity of food and eighteen barrels of beer.

Of the four co-proprietors, all died without issue, except Friedrich, called the Permutator, in whose hands the whole of the family property was again collected; he went to live at Schoenhausen, which since then has been the home of the family. No remains of the old castle exist, but the church, built in the thirteenth century, is one of the oldest and most beautiful in the land between the Havel and the Elbe. House and church stand side by side on a small rising overlooking the Elbe. Here they took up their abode; the family to some extent had come down in the world. The change had been a disadvantageous one; they had lost in wealth and importance. For two hundred years they played no very prominent part; they married with the neighbouring country gentry and fought in all the wars. Rudolph, Friedrich's son, fought in France in behalf of the Huguenots, and then under the Emperor against the Turks. His grandson, August, enlisted under Bernhard of Saxe-Weimar; afterwards he fought in the religious wars in

France and Germany, always on the Protestant side; lastly, he took service under the Elector of Brandenburg.

It was in his lifetime that a great change began to take place which was to alter the whole life of his descendants. In 1640, Frederick William, known as the great Elector, succeeded his father. He it was who laid the foundations for that system of government by which a small German principality has grown to be the most powerful military monarchy in modern Europe. He held his own against the Emperor; he fought with the Poles and compelled their King to grant him East Prussia; he drove the Swedes out of the land. More than this, he enforced order in his own dominions; he laid the foundation for the prosperity of Berlin; he organised the administration and got together a small but efficient military force. The growing power of the Elector was gained to a great extent at the expense of the nobles; he took from them many of the privileges they had before enjoyed. The work he began was continued by his son, who took the title of King; and by his grandson, who invented the Prussian system of administration, and created the army with which Frederick the Great fought his battles.

The result of the growth of the strong, organised monarchy was indeed completely to alter the position of the nobles. The German barons in the south had succeeded in throwing off the control of their territorial lords; they owned no authority but the vague control of the distant Emperor, and ruled their little estates with an almost royal independence; they had their own laws, their own coinage, their own army.

In the north, the nobles of Mecklenburg Holstein, and Hanover formed a dominant class, and the whole government of the State was in their hands; but those barons whose homes fell within the dominion of the Kings of Prussia found themselves face to face with a will and a power stronger than their own; they lost in independence, but they gained far more than they lost. They were the basis on which the State was built up; they no longer wasted their military prowess in purposeless feuds or in mercenary service; in the Prussian army and administration they found full scope for their ambition, and when the victories of Frederick the Great had raised Prussia to the rank of a European Power, the nobles of Brandenburg were the most loyal of his subjects. They formed an exclusive caste; they seldom left their homes; they were little known in the south of Germany or in foreign countries; they seldom married outside their own ranks. Their chief amusement was the chase, and their chief occupation was war. And no king has ever had under his orders so fine a race of soldiers; they commanded the armies of Frederick and won his battles. Dearly did they pay for the greatness of Prussia; of one family alone, the Kleists, sixty-four fell on the field of battle during the Seven Years' War.

They might well consider that the State which they had helped to make, and which they had saved by their blood, belonged to them. But if they had become Prussians, they did not cease to be Brandenburgers; their loyalty to their king never swerved, for they knew that he belonged to them as he did to no other of his subjects. He might go to distant Königsberg to assume the crown, but his home was amongst them; other provinces might be gained or lost with the chances of war, but while a single Hohenzollern lived he could not desert his subjects of the Mark. They had the intense local patriotism so characteristic of the German nation, which is the surest foundation for political greatness; but while in other parts the Particularists, as the Germans called them, aimed only at independence, the

Brandenburger who had become a Prussian desired domination.

Among them the Bismarcks lived. The family again divided into two branches: one, which became extinct about 1780, dwelling at Crevisse, gave several high officials to the Prussian Civil Service; the other branch, which continued at Schoenhausen, generally chose a military career. August's son, who had the same name as his father, rebuilt the house, which had been entirely destroyed by the Swedes during the Thirty Years' War; he held the position of Landrath, that is, he was the head of the administration of the district in which he lived. He married a Fräulein von Katte, of a well-known family whose estates adjoined those of the Bismarcks. Frau von Bismarck was the aunt of the unfortunate young man who was put to death for helping Frederick the Great in his attempt to escape. His tomb is still to be seen at Wust, which lies across the river a few miles from Schoenhausen; and at the new house, which arose at Schoenhausen and still stands, the arms of the Kattes are joined to the Bismarck trefoil. The successor to the estates, August Friedrich, was a thorough soldier; he married a Fräulein von Diebwitz and acquired fresh estates in Pomerania, where he generally lived.

He rose to the rank of colonel, and fell fighting against the Austrians at Chotusitz in 1742. "Ein ganzer Kerl" (a fine fellow), said the King, as he stood by the dying officer. His son, Carl Alexander, succeeded to Schoenhausen; the next generation kept up the military traditions of the family; of four brothers, all but one became professional officers and fought against France in the wars of liberation. One fell at Möckern in 1813; another rose to the rank of lieutenant-general; the third also fought in the war; his son, the later Count Bismarck-Bohlen, was wounded at Grossbehren, and the father at once came to take his place during his convalescence, in order that the Prussian army might not have fewer Bismarcks. When the young Otto was born two years later, he would often hear of the adventures of his three uncles and his cousin in the great war. The latter, Bismarck-Bohlen, rose to very high honours and was to die when over eighty years of age, after he had witnessed the next great war with France. It is a curious instance of the divisions of Germany in those days that there were Bismarcks fighting on the French side throughout the war. One branch of the family had settled in South Germany; the head of it, Friedrich Wilhelm, had taken service in the Wurtemburg army; he had become a celebrated leader of cavalry and was passionately devoted to Napoleon. He served with distinction in the Russian campaign and was eventually taken prisoner by the Germans in the battle of Leipzig.

The youngest of the four brothers, Karl Wilhelm Friedrich v. Bismarck, had retired from the army at an early age: he was a quiet, kindly man of domestic tastes; on the division of the estates, Schoenhausen fell to his lot, and he settled down there to a quiet country life. He took a step which must have caused much discussion among all his friends and relations, for he chose as wife not one of his own rank, not a Kleist, or a Katte, or a Bredow, or an Arnim, or an Alvensleben, or any other of the neighbouring nobility; he married a simple Fräulein Mencken. She was, however, of no undistinguished origin. Her father, the son of a professor at the University of Leipzig, had entered the Prussian Civil Service; there he had risen to the highest rank and had been Cabinet Secretary to both Frederick William II. and Frederick III. He was a man of high character and of considerable ability; as was not uncommon among the officials of those days, he was strongly affected by the liberal and even revolutionary doctrines of France.

Fräulein Mencken, who was married at the age of sixteen, was a clever and ambitious woman. From her her son inherited his intellect; from his father he derived what the Germans call Gemüth, geniality, kindliness, humour. By his two parents he was thus connected with the double foundation on which Prussia had been built: on his father's side he had sprung from the fighting nobles; on his mother's, from the scholars and officials. In later life we shall find that while his prejudices and affections are all enlisted on the side of the noble, the keen and critical intellect he had inherited from his mother enabled him to overcome the prejudices of his order.

The early life of the young pair was not altogether fortunate. Several children died at a very early age; the defeat of Prussia brought foreign occupation; Schoenhausen was seized by French troopers; the marks of their swords are still to be seen in a beam over one of the doors, and Rittmeister v. Bismarck had to take his wife away into the woods in order to escape their violence.

Of all the children of the marriage only three lived: Bernhard, who was born in 1810, Otto, and one sister, Malvina, born in 1827.

Otto did not live at Schoenhausen long; when he was only a year old, his father moved to Pomerania and settled on the estates Kniephof and Kulz, which had come into the family on his grandfather's marriage. Pomerania was at that time a favourite residence among the Prussian nobility; the country was better wooded than the Mark, and game more plentiful; the rich meadows, the wide heaths and forests were more attractive than the heavy corn-lands and the sandy wastes of the older province. Here, in the deep seclusion of country life, the boy passed his first years; it was far removed from the bustle and turmoil of civilisation. Naugard, the nearest town, was five miles distant; communication was bad, for it was not till after 1815 that the Prussian Government began to construct highroads. In this distant province, life went on as in the olden days, little altered by the changes which had transformed the State. The greater portion of the land belonged to large proprietors; the noble as in old days was still all-powerful on his own estate; in his hands was the administration of the law, and it was at his manorial court that men had to seek for justice, a court where justice was dealt not in the name of the King but of the Lord of the Manor. He lived among his people and generally he farmed his own lands. There was little of the luxury of an English country-house or the refinement of the French noblesse; he would be up at daybreak to superintend the work in the fields, his wife and daughters that of the household, talking to the peasants the pleasant Platt Deutsch of the countryside. Then there would be long rides or drives to the neighbours' houses; shooting, for there was plenty of deer and hares; and occasionally in the winter a visit to Berlin; farther away, few of them went. Most of the country gentlemen had been to Paris, but only as conquerors at the end of the great war.

They were little disturbed by modern political theories, but were contented, as in old days, to be governed by the King. It was a religious society; among the peasants and the nobles, if not among the clergy, there still lingered something of the simple but profound faith of German Protestantism; they were scarcely touched by the rationalism of the eighteenth or by the liberalism of the nineteenth century; there was little pomp and ceremony of worship in the village church, but the natural periods of human life—birth, marriage, death—called for the blessing of the Church, and once or twice a year came the solemn confession and the sacrament.

Religious belief and political faith were closely joined, for the Church was but a department of the State; the King was chief bishop, as he was general of the army, and the sanctity of the Church was transferred to the Crown; to the nobles and peasants, criticism of, or opposition to, the King had in it something of sacrilege; the words "by the Grace of God" added to the royal title were more than an empty phrase. Society was still organised on the old patriarchal basis: at the bottom was the peasant; above him was the gnädiger Herr; above him, Unser allergnädigste Herr, the King, who lived in Berlin; and above him, the Herr Gott in Heaven.

To the inhabitants of South Germany, and the men of the towns, these nobles of Further Pomerania, the Junker as they were called, with their feudal life, their medieval beliefs, their simple monarchism, were the incarnation of political folly; to them liberalism seemed another form of atheism, but in this solitude and fresh air of the great plain was reared a race of men who would always be ready, as their fathers had been, to draw their sword and go out to conquer new provinces for their King to govern.

CHAPTER II.

EARLY LIFE. 1821-1847.

Of the boy's early life we know little. His mother was ambitious for her sons; Otto from his early years she designed for the Diplomatic Service; she seems to have been one of those women who was willing to sacrifice the present happiness of her children for their future advancement. When only six years old the boy was sent away from home to a school in Berlin. He was not happy there; he pined for the free life of the country, the fields and woods and animals; when he saw a plough he would burst into tears, for it reminded him of his home. The discipline of the school was hard, not with the healthy and natural hardships of life in the open air, but with an artificial Spartanism, for it was the time when the Germans, who had suddenly awoke to feelings of patriotism and a love of war to which they had long been strangers, under the influence of a few writers, were throwing all their energies into the cultivation of physical endurance. It was probably at this time that there was laid the foundation of that dislike for the city of Berlin which Bismarck never quite overcame; and from his earliest years he was prejudiced against the exaggerated and affected Teutonism which was the fashion after the great war. A few years later his parents came to live altogether in the town; then the boy passed on to the Gymnasium, boarding in the house of one of the masters. The teaching in this school was supplemented by private tutors, and he learned at this time the facility in the use of the English and French languages which in after years was to be of great service to him. The education at school was of course chiefly in the classical languages; he acquired a sufficient mastery of Latin. There is no evidence that in later life he continued the study of classical literature. In his seventeenth year he passed the Abiturienten examination, which admitted him as a student to the university and entitled him to the privilege of serving in the army for one instead of three years. His leaving certificate tells us that his conduct and demeanour towards his comrades and teachers were admirable, his abilities considerable, and his diligence fair.

The next year he passed in the ordinary course to the university, entering at Göttingen; the choice was probably made because of the celebrity which that university had acquired in law and history. It is said that he desired to enter at Heidelberg, but his mother refused her permission, because she feared that he would learn those habits of beer-drinking in which the students of that ancient seat of learning have gained so great a proficiency; it was, however, an art which, as he found, was to be acquired with equal ease at Göttingen. The young Bismarck was at this time over six feet high, slim and well built, of great physical strength and agility, a good fencer, a bold rider, an admirable swimmer and runner, a very agreeable companion; frank, cheerful, and open-hearted, without fear either of his comrades or of his teachers. He devoted his time at Göttingen less to learning than to social life; in his second term he entered the Corps of the Hanoverians and was quickly noted for his power of drinking and fighting; he is reported to have fought twenty-six duels and was only wounded once, and that wound was caused by the breaking of his opponent's foil. He was full of wild escapades, for which he was often subjected to the ordinary punishments of the university.

To many Germans, their years at the university have been the turning-point of their life; but it was not so with Bismarck. To those who have been brought up in the narrow surroundings of civic life, student days form the single breath of freedom between the discipline of a school and the drudgery of an office. To a man who, like Bismarck, was accustomed to the truer freedom of the country, it was only a passing phase; as we shall see, it was not easy to tie him down to the drudgery of an office. He did not even form many friendships which he continued in later years; his associates in his corps must have been chiefly young Hanoverians; few of his comrades in Prussia were to be found at Göttingen; his knowledge of English enabled him to make the acquaintance of the Americans and English with whom Göttingen has always been a favourite university; among his fellow-students almost the only one with whom in after life he continued the intimacy of younger days was Motley. We hear little of his work; none of the professors seem to have left any marked influence on his mind or character; indeed they had little opportunity for doing so, for after the first term his attendance at lectures almost entirely ceased. Though never a student, he must have been at all times a considerable reader; he had a retentive memory and quick understanding; he read what interested him; absorbed, understood, and retained it. He left the university with his mind disciplined indeed but not drilled; he had a considerable knowledge of languages, law, literature, and history; he had not subjected his mind to the dominion of the dominant Hegelian philosophy, and to this we must attribute that freshness and energy which distinguishes him from so many of his ablest contemporaries; his brain was strong, and it worked as easily and as naturally as his body; his knowledge was more that of a man of the world than of a student, but in later life he was always able to understand the methods and to acquire the knowledge of the subjects he required in his official career. History was his favourite study; he never attempted, like some statesmen, to write; but if his knowledge of history was not as profound as that of a professed historian, he was afterwards to shew as a parliamentary debater that he had a truer perception of the importance of events than many great scholars who have devoted their lives to historical research, and he was never at a loss for an illustration to explain and justify the policy he had assumed. For natural science he shewed little interest, and indeed at that time it scarcely could be reckoned among the ordinary subjects of education; philosophy he pursued rather as a man than as a student, and we are not surprised to find that it was Spinoza rather than Kant or Fichte or Hegel to whom he devoted most attention, for he cared more for principles of belief and the conduct of life than the analysis of the intellect.

His university career does not seem to have left any mark on his political principles; during just those years, the agitation of which the universities had long been the scene had been forcibly repressed; it was the time of deep depression which followed the revolution of 1830, and the members of the aristocratic corps to which he belonged looked with something approaching contempt on this Burschenschaft, as the union was called, which propagated among the students the national enthusiasm.

After spending little more than a year at Göttingen, he left in September, 1833; in May of the following year he entered as a student at Berlin, where he completed his university course; we have no record as to the manner in which he spent the winter and early spring, but we find that when he applied to Göttingen for permission to enter at Berlin, it was accorded on condition that he sat out a term of imprisonment which he still owed to the university authorities. During part of his time in Berlin he shared a room with Motley. In order to prepare for the final examination he engaged the services of a crammer, and with his assistance, in 1835, took the degree of Doctor of Law and at once passed on to the public service.

He had, as we have seen, been destined for the Diplomatic Service from early life; he was well connected; his cousin Count Bismarck-Bohlen stood in high favour at Court. He was related to or acquainted with all the families who held the chief posts both in the military and civil service; with his great talents and social gifts he might therefore look forward to a brilliant career. Any hopes, however, that his mother might have had were destined to be disappointed; his early official life was varied but short. He began in the judicial department and was appointed to the office of Auscultator at Berlin, for in the German system the judicature is one department of the Civil Service. After a year he was at his own request transferred to the administrative side and to Aix-la-Chapelle; it is said that he had been extremely pained and shocked by the manner in which the officials transacted the duties of their office and especially by their management of the divorce matters which came before the court. The choice of Aix-la-Chapelle was probably owing to the fact that the president of that province was Count Arnim of Boytzenburg, the head of one of the most numerous and distinguished families of the Mark, with so many members of which Bismarck was in later years to be connected both for good and evil. Count Arnim was a man of considerable ability and moderate liberal opinions, who a few years later rose to be the first Minister-President in Prussia. Under him Bismarck was sure to receive every assistance. He had to pass a fresh examination, which he did with great success.

His certificate states that he shewed thoroughly good school studies, and was well grounded in law; he had thought over what he had learnt and already had acquired independent opinions. He had admirable judgment, quickness in understanding, and a readiness in giving verbal answers to the questions laid before him; we see all the qualities by which he was to be distinguished in after life. He entered on his duties at Aix-la-Chapelle at the beginning of June; at his own request Count Arnim wrote to the heads of the department that as young Bismarck was destined for a diplomatic career they were to afford him every opportunity of becoming acquainted with all the different sides of the administrative work and give him more work than they otherwise would have done; he was to be constantly occupied. His good resolutions did not, however, continue long; he found himself in a fashionable watering-place, his knowledge of languages enabled him to associate with the French and English visitors, he made excursions to Belgium and the Rhine, and hunting expeditions to the Ardennes, and gave up to society the time he ought to have spent in the office. The life at Aix was not strict and perhaps his amusements were not always edifying, but he acquired that complete ease in cosmopolitan society which he could not learn at Göttingen or Berlin, and his experiences during this year were not without use to him when he was afterwards placed in the somewhat similar society of Frankfort. This period in his career did not last long; in June, 1837, we find him applying for leave of absence on account of ill-health. He received leave for eight days, but he seems to have exceeded this, for four months afterwards he writes from Berne asking that his leave may be prolonged; he had apparently gone off for a long tour in Switzerland and the Rhine. His request was refused; he received a severe reprimand, and Count Arnim approved his resolution to return to one of the older Prussian provinces, "where he might shew an activity in the duties of his office which he had in vain attempted to attain in the social conditions of Aachen."

He was transferred to Potsdam, but he remained here only a few weeks; he had not as yet served in the army, and he now began the year as a private soldier which was required from him; he entered the Jaeger or Rifles in the Garde Corps which was stationed at Potsdam, but after a few weeks was transferred to the Jaeger at Stettin. The cause seems to have been partly the ill-health of his mother; she was dying, and he wished to be near her; in those days the journey from Berlin to Pomerania took more than a day; besides this there were pecuniary reasons. His father's administration of the family estates had not been successful; it is said that his mother had constantly pressed her husband to introduce innovations, but had not consistently carried them out; this was a not unnatural characteristic in the clever and ambitious woman who wished to introduce into agricultural affairs those habits which she had learnt from the bureaucrats in Berlin. However this may be, matters had now reached a crisis; it became necessary to sell the larger part of the land attached to the house at Schoenhausen, and in the next year, after the death of Frau von Bismarck, which took place on January 1, 1839, it was decided that Herr von Bismarck should in future live at Schoenhausen with his only daughter, now a girl of twelve years of age, while the two brothers should undertake the management of the Pomeranian estates.

So it came about that at the age of twenty-four all prospect of an official career had for the time to be abandoned, and Otto settled down with his brother to the life of a country squire. It is curious to notice that the greatest of his contemporaries, Cavour, went through a similar training. There was, however, a great difference between the two men: Cavour was in this as in all else a pioneer; when he retired to his estate he was opening out new forms of activity and enterprise for his countrymen; Bismarck after the few wild years away from home was to go back to the life which all his ancestors had lived for five hundred years, to become steeped in the traditions of his country and his caste. Cavour always points the way to what is new, Bismarck again brings into honour what men had hastily thought was antiquated. He had to some extent prepared himself for the work by attending lectures at a newly founded agricultural college in the outskirts of Greifswald. The management of the estate seems to have been successful; the two brothers started on their work with no capital and no experience, but after three or four years by constant attention and hard work they had put the affairs in a satisfactory state. In 1841, a division was made; Otto had wished this to be done before, as he found that he spent a good deal more money than his brother and was gaining an unfair advantage in the common household; from this time he took over Kniephof, and there he lived for the next four years, while his brother took up his abode four miles off at Kulz, where he lived till his death in 1895. Otto had not indeed given up the habits he had learnt at Göttingen; his wild freaks, his noisy entertainments, were the talk of the countryside; the beverage which he has made classical, a mixture of beer and champagne, was the common drink, and he was known far and wide as the mad Bismarck. These acts of wildness were, however, only a small part of his life; he entered as a lieutenant of Landwehr in the cavalry and thereby became acquainted with another form of military service. It was while he was at the annual training that he had an opportunity of shewing his physical strength and courage. A groom, who was watering horses in the river, was swept away by the current; Bismarck, who was standing on a bridge watching them, at once leaped into the river, in full uniform as he was, and with great danger to himself saved the drowning man. For this he received a medal for saving life. He astonished his friends by the amount and variety of his reading; it was at this time that he studied Spinoza. It is said that he had among his friends the reputation of being a liberal; it is probable enough that he said and did many things which they did not understand; and anything they did not understand would be attributed to liberalism by the country gentlemen of Pomerania; partly no doubt it was due to the fact that in 1843 he came back from Paris wearing a beard. We can see, however, that he was restless and discontented; he felt in himself the possession of powers which were not being used; there was in his nature also a morbid restlessness, a dissatisfaction with himself which he tried to still but only increased by his wild excesses. As his affairs became more settled he travelled; one year he went to London, another to Paris; of his visit to England we have an interesting account in a letter to his father. He landed in Hull [2] , thence he went to Scarborough and York, where he was hospitably received by the officers of the Hussars; "although I did not know any of them, they asked me to dinner and shewed me everything"; from York he went to Manchester, where he saw some of the factories.

"Generally speaking I cannot praise too highly the extraordinary courtesy and kindness of English people, which far surpass what I had expected; even the poor people are pleasant, very unassuming, and easy to get on with when one talks to them. Those who come much into intercourse with strangers--cab-drivers, porters, etc.--naturally have a tendency to extortion, but soon give in when they see that one understands the language and customs and is determined not to be put upon. Generally I find the life much cheaper than I expected."

In 1844, his sister, to whom he was passionately devoted, was married to an old friend, Oscar von Arnim. Never did an elder brother write to his young sister more delightful letters than those which she received from him; from them we get a pleasant picture of his life at this time. Directly after the wedding, when he was staying with his father at Schoenhausen, he writes:

"Just now I am living here with my father, reading, smoking, and walking; I help him to eat lamperns and sometimes play a comedy with him which it pleases him to call fox-hunting. We start out in heavy rain, or perhaps with 10 degrees of frost, with Ihle, Ellin, and Karl; then in perfect silence we surround a clump of firs with the most sportsmanlike precautions, carefully observing the wind, although we all, and probably father as well, are absolutely convinced that there is not a living creature in it except one or two old women gathering firewood. Then Ihle, Karl, and the two dogs make their way through the cover, emitting the most strange and horrible sounds, especially Ihle; father stands there motionless and on the alert with his gun cocked, just as though he really expected to see something. Ihle comes out just in front of him, shouting 'Hoo lala, hey heay, hold him, hie, hie,' in the strangest and most astonishing manner. Then father asks me if I have seen nothing, and I with the most natural tone of astonishment that I can command, answer 'No, nothing at all.' Then after abusing the weather we start off to another wood, while Ihle with a confidence that he assumes in the most natural manner praises its wealth in game, and there we play over the game again dal segno. So it goes on for three or four hours; father's, Ihle's, and Fingal's passion does not seem to cool for a moment. Besides that, we look at the orange house twice a day and the sheep once a day, observe the four thermometers in the room once every hour, set the weather-glass, and, since the weather has been fine, have set all the clocks by the sun and adjusted them so closely that the clock in the dining-room is the only one which ever gives a sound after the others have struck. Charles V. was a stupid fellow. You will understand that with so multifarious an occupation I have little time left to call on the clergymen; as they have no vote for the election it was quite impossible.

"The Elbe is full of ice, the wind E.S.E., the latest thermometer from Berlin shews 8 degrees, the barometer is rising and at 8.28. I tell you this as an example how in your letters you might write to father more the small events of your life; they amuse him immensely; tell him who has been to see you, whom you have been calling on, what you had for dinner, how the horses are, how the servants behave, if the doors creak and the windows are firm--in short, facts and events. Besides this, he does not like to be called papa, he dislikes the expression. Avis au lecteur."

On another occasion he says:

"Only with difficulty can I resist the temptation of filling a whole letter with agricultural lamentations over frosts, sick cattle, bad reap, bad roads, dead lambs, hungry sheep, want of straw, fodder, money, potatoes, and manure; outside Johann is persistently whistling a wretched schottische out of tune, and I have not the cruelty to interrupt it, for he seeks to still by music his violent love-sickness."

Then we have long letters from Nordeney, where he delighted in the sea, but space will not allow us to quote more. It is only in these letters, and in those which he wrote in later years to his wife, that we see the natural kindliness and simplicity of his disposition, his love of nature, and his great power of description. There have been few better letter-writers in Germany or any other country.

His ability and success as an agriculturist made a deep impression on his neighbours. As years went on he became much occupied in local business; he was appointed as the representative of his brother, who was Landrath for the district; in 1845 he was elected one of the members for the Provincial Diet of Pomerania. He also had a seat in the Diet for the Saxon province in which Schoenhausen was situated. These local Diets were the only form of representative government which existed in the rural districts; they had little power, but their opinion was asked on new projects of law, and they were officially regarded as an efficient substitute for a common Prussian Parliament. Many of his friends, including his brother, urged him again to enter the public service, for which they considered he was especially adapted; he might have had the post of Royal Commissioner for Improvements in East Prussia.

He did make one attempt to resume his official career. At the beginning of 1844 he returned to Potsdam and took up his duties as Referendar, but not for long; he seems to have quarrelled with his superior. The story is that he called one day to ask for leave of absence; his chief kept him waiting an hour in the anteroom, and when he was admitted asked him curtly, "What do you want?" Bismarck at once answered, "I came to ask for leave of absence, but now I wish for permission to send in my resignation." He was clearly deficient in that subservience and ready obedience to authority which was the best passport to promotion in the Civil Service; there was in his disposition already a certain truculence and impatience. From this time he nourished a bitter hatred of the Prussian bureaucracy.

This did not, however, prevent him carrying out his public duties as a landed proprietor. In 1846 we find him taking much interest in proposals for improving the management of the manorial courts; he wished to see them altered so as to give something of the advantages of the English system; he regrets the "want of corporate spirit and public feeling in our corn-growing aristocracy"; "it is unfortunately difficult among most of the gentlemen to awake any other idea under the words 'patrimonial power' but the calculation whether the fee will cover the expenses." We can easily understand that the man who wrote this would be called a liberal by many of his neighbours; what he wanted, however, was a reform which would give life, permanency, and independence to an institution which like everything else was gradually falling before the inroads of the dominant bureaucracy. The same year he was appointed to the position of Inspector of Dykes for Jerichow. The duties of this office were of considerable importance for Schoenhausen and the neighbouring estate; as he writes, "it depends on the managers of this office whether from time to time we come under water or not." He often refers to the great damages caused by the floods; he had lost many of his fruit-trees, and many of the finest elms in the park had been destroyed by the overflowing of the Elbe.

As Bismarck grew in age and experience he associated more with the neighbouring families. Pomerania was at this time the centre of a curious religious movement; the leader was Herr von Thadden, who lived at Triglaff, not many miles from Kniephof. He was associated with Herr von Semft and three brothers of the family of Below. They were all profoundly dissatisfied with the rationalistic religion preached by the clergy at that time, and aimed at greater inwardness and depth of religious feeling. Herr von Thadden started religious exercises in his own house, which were attended not only by the peasants from the village but by many of the country gentry; they desired the strictest enforcement of Lutheran doctrine, and wished the State directly to support the Church. This tendency of thought acquired greater importance when, in 1840, Frederick William IV succeeded to the throne; he was also a man of deep religious feeling, and under his reign the extreme Lutheran party became influential at Court. Among the ablest of these were the three brothers von Gerlach. One of them, Otto, was a theologian; another, Ludwig, was Over-President of the Saxon province, and with him Bismarck had much official correspondence; the third, Leopold, who had adopted a military career, was attached to the person of the King and was in later years to have more influence upon him than anyone except perhaps Bunsen. The real intellectual leader of the party was Stahl, a theologian.

From about the year 1844 Bismarck seems to have become very intimate with this religious coterie; his friend Moritz v. Blankenburg had married Thadden's daughter and Bismarck was constantly a visitor at Triglaff. It was at Blankenburg's wedding that he first met Hans v. Kleist, who was in later years to be one of his most intimate friends. He was, we are told, the most delightful and cheerful of companions; in his tact and refinement he shewed an agreeable contrast to the ordinary manners of Pomerania. He often rode over to take part in Shakespeare evenings, and amused them by accounts of his visit to England [3] . He was present occasionally at the religious meetings at Triglaff, and though he never quite adopted all the customs of the set the influence on him of these older men was for the next ten years to govern all his political action. That he was not altogether at one with them we can understand, when we are told that at Herr von Thadden's house it would never have occurred to anyone even to think of smoking. Bismarck was then, as in later life, a constant smoker.

The men who met in these family parties in distant Pomerania were in a few years to change the whole of European history. Here Bismarck for the first time saw Albrecht von Roon, a cousin of the Blankenburgs, then a rising young officer in the artillery; they often went out shooting together. The Belows, Blankenburgs, and Kleists were to be the founders and leaders of the Prussian Conservative party, which was Bismarck's only support in his great struggle with the Parliament; and here, too, came the men who were afterwards to be editors and writers of the Kreuz Zeitung.

The religious convictions which Bismarck learnt from them were to be lasting, and they profoundly influenced his character. He had probably received little religious training from his mother, who belonged to the rationalistic school of thought. It was by them that his monarchical feeling was strengthened. It is not at first apparent what necessary connection there is between monarchical government and Christian faith. For Bismarck they were ever inseparably bound together; nothing but religious belief would have reconciled him to a form of government so repugnant to natural human reason. "If I were not a Christian, I would be a Republican," he said many years later; in Christianity he found the only support against revolution and socialism. He was not the man to be beguiled by romantic sentiment; he was not a courtier to be blinded by the pomp and ceremony of royalty; he was too stubborn and independent to acquiesce in the arbitrary rule of a single man. He could only obey the king if the king himself held his authority as the representative of a higher power. Bismarck was accustomed to follow out his thought to its conclusions. To whom did the king owe his power? There was only one alternative: to the people or to God. If to the people, then it was a mere question of convenience whether the monarchy were continued in form; there was little to choose between a constitutional monarchy where the king was appointed by the people and controlled by Parliament, and an avowed republic. This was the principle held by nearly all his contemporaries. He deliberately rejected it. He did not hold that the voice of the people was the voice of God. This belief did not satisfy his moral sense; it seemed in public life to leave all to interest and ambition and nothing to duty. It did not satisfy his critical intellect; the word "people" was to him a vague idea. The service of the People or of the King by the Grace of God, this was the struggle which was soon to be fought out.

Bismarck's connection with his neighbours was cemented by his marriage. At the beginning of 1847, he was engaged to a Fräulein von Puttkammer, whom he had first met at the Blankenburgs' house; she belonged to a quiet and religious family, and it is said that her mother was at first filled with dismay when she heard that Johanna proposed to marry the mad Bismarck. He announced the engagement to his sister in a letter containing the two words, "All right," written in English. Before the wedding could take place, a new impulse in his life was to begin. As representative of the lower nobility he had to attend the meeting of the Estates General which had been summoned in Berlin. From this time the story of his life is interwoven with the history of his country.

CHAPTER III.

THE REVOLUTION.

1847-1852.

Bismarck was a subject of the King of Prussia, but Prussia was after all only one part of a larger unit; it was a part of Germany. At this time, however, Germany was little more than a geographical expression. The medieval emperors had never succeeded in establishing permanent authority over the whole nation; what unity there had been was completely broken down at the Reformation, and at the Revolution the Empire itself, the symbol of a union which no longer existed, had been swept away. At the restoration in 1815 the reorganisation of Germany was one of the chief tasks before the Congress of Vienna. It was a task in which the statesmen failed. All proposals to restore the Empire were rejected, chiefly because Francis, who had taken the style of Emperor of Austria, did not desire to resume his old title. Germany emerged from the Revolution divided into thirty-nine different States; Austria was one of the largest and most populous monarchies in Europe, but more than half the Austrian Empire consisted of Italian, Slavonic, and Hungarian provinces. The Emperor of Austria ruled over about 20,000,000 Germans. The next State in size and importance was Prussia. Then came four States, the Kingdoms of Saxony, Hanover, Bavaria, and Würtemberg, varying in size from five to two million inhabitants; below them were some thirty principalities of which the smallest contained only a few thousand inhabitants. By the principles adopted in the negotiations which preceded the Congress of Vienna, every one of these

States was recognised as a complete independent monarchy, with its own laws and constitutions. The recognition of this independence made any common government impossible. Neither Austria nor Prussia would submit to any external authority, or to one another; the Kings of Bavaria and Würtemberg were equally jealous of their independence. All that could be done was to establish a permanent offensive and defensive alliance between these States. For the management of common concerns, a Diet was appointed to meet at Frankfort; the Diet, however, was only a union of diplomatists; they had to act in accordance with instructions from their governments and they had no direct authority over the Germans; each German was officially regarded as a subject, as the case might be, of the King of Prussia, the Prince of Reuss, the Grand Duke of Weimar. There was no German army, no German law, no German church. No development of common institutions was possible, for no change could be introduced without the universal consent of every member of the Confederation.

This lamentable result of the Congress of Vienna caused much dissatisfaction among the thinking classes in Germany. A very strong national feeling had been aroused by the war against Napoleon. This found no satisfaction in the new political institutions. The discontent was increased when it was discovered that the Diet, so useless for all else, was active only against liberty. Prince Metternich, a very able diplomatist, knew that the Liberal and National ideas, which were so generally held at that time, would be fatal to the existence of the Austrian Empire; he therefore attempted to suppress them, not only in Austria, but also in Germany, as he did in Italy. Unfortunately the King of Prussia, Frederick William III., whose interests were really entirely opposed to those of Austria, was persuaded by

Metternich to adopt a repressive policy. The two great powers when combined could impose their will on Germany; they forced through the Diet a series of measures devoted to the restriction of the liberty of the press, the control of the universities, and the suppression of democratic opinion.

The result of this was great discontent in Germany, which was especially directed against Prussia; in 1830 the outbreak of revolution in Paris had been followed by disturbances in many German States; Austria and Prussia, however, were still strong enough to maintain the old system. The whole intellect of the country was diverted to a policy of opposition; in the smaller States of the south, Parliamentary government had been introduced; and the great aim of the Liberals was to establish a Parliament in Prussia also.

In 1840 the old King died; the son, Frederick William IV., was a man of great learning, noble character, high aspirations; he was, however, entirely without sympathy or understanding for the modern desires of his countrymen; he was a child of the Romantic movement; at the head of the youngest of European monarchies, he felt himself more at home in the Middle Ages than in his own time. There could be no sympathy between him and the men who took their politics from Rousseau and Louis Blanc, and their religion from Strauss. It had been hoped that he would at once introduce into Prussia representative institutions. He long delayed, and the delay took away any graciousness from the act when at last it was committed. By a royal decree published in 1822 it had been determined that no new loan could be made without the assent of an assembly of elected representatives; the introduction of railways made a loan necessary, and at the beginning of 1847 Frederick William summoned for the first time the States General.

The King of Prussia had thereby stirred up a power which he was unable to control; he had hoped that he would be able to gather round him the representatives of the nobles, the towns, and the peasants; that this new assembly, collecting about him in respectful homage, would add lustre to his throne; that they would vote the money which was required and then separate. How much was he mistaken! The nation had watched for years Parliamentary government in England and France; this was what they wished to have, and now they were offered a modern imitation of medieval estates. They felt themselves as grown men able and justified in governing their own country; the King treated them as children. The opening ceremony completed the bad impression which the previous acts of the King had made. While the majority of the nation desired a formal and written Constitution, the King in his opening speech with great emphasis declared that he would never allow a sheet of paper to come between him and God in heaven.

Bismarck was not present at the opening ceremony; it was, in fact, owing to an accident that he was able to take his seat at all; he was there as substitute for the member for the Ritterschaft of Jerichow, who had fallen ill. He entered on his Parliamentary duties as a young and almost unknown man; he did not belong to any party, but his political principles were strongly influenced by the friends he had found in Pomerania. They were soon to be hardened by conflict and confirmed by experience; during the first debates he sat silent, but his indignation rose as he listened to the speeches of the Liberal majority. Nothing pleased them; instead of actively co-operating with the Government in the consideration of financial measures, they began to discuss and criticise the proclamation by which they had been summoned. There was indeed ample scope for criticism; the Estates were so arranged that the representatives of the towns could always be outvoted by the landed proprietors; they had not even the right of periodical meetings; the King was not compelled to call them together again until he required more money. They not only petitioned for increased powers, they demanded them as a right; they maintained that an assembly summoned in this form did not meet the intentions of previous laws; when they were asked to allow a loan for a railway in East Prussia, they refused on the ground that they were not a properly qualified assembly.

This was too much for Bismarck: the action of the King might have been inconclusive; much that he said was indiscreet; but it remained true that he had taken the decisive step; no one really doubted that Prussia would never again be without a Parliament. It would be much wiser, as it would be more chivalrous, to adopt a friendly tone and not to attempt to force concessions from him. He was especially indignant at the statement made that the Prussian people had earned constitutional government by the part they took in the war of liberation; against this he protested:

"In my opinion it is a bad service to the national honour to assume that the ill-treatment and degradation that the Prussians suffered from a foreign ruler were not enough to make our blood boil, and to deaden all other feelings but that of hatred for the foreigners."

When told that he was not alive at the time, he answered:

"I cannot dispute that I was not living then, and I have been genuinely sorry that I was not born in time to take part in that movement; a regret which is diminished by what I have just heard. I had always believed that the slavery against which we fought lay abroad; I have just learned that it lay at home, and I am not grateful for the explanation."

The ablest of the Liberal leaders was George v. Vincke; a member of an old Westphalian family, the son of a high official, he was a man of honesty and independence, but both virtues were carried to excess; a born leader of opposition, domineering, quarrelsome, ill to please, his short, sturdy figure, his red face and red hair were rather those of a peasant than a nobleman, but his eloquence, his bitter invective, earned the respect and even fear of his opponents. Among these Bismarck was to be ranged; in these days began a rivalry which was not to cease till nearly twenty years later, when Vincke retired from the field and Bismarck stood triumphant, the recognised ruler of the State. At this time it required courage in the younger man to cross swords with the experienced and powerful leader.

Vincke was a strong Liberal, but in the English rather than the Prussian sense; his constant theme was the rule of law; he had studied English history, for at that time all Liberals prepared themselves for their part by reading Hallam or Guizot and Dahlmann; he knew all about Pym and Hampden, and wished to imitate them. The English Parliament had won its power by means of a Petition of Right and a Bill of Rights; he wished they should do the same in Prussia; it escaped him that the English could appeal to charters and ancient privileges, but that in Prussia the absolute power of the King was the undisputed basis on which the whole State had been built up, and that every law to which they owed their liberty or their property derived its validity from the simple proclamation of the King.

Bismarck, if he had read less, understood better the characteristics of England, probably because he knew better the conditions of his own country. He rose to protest against these parallels with England; Prussia had its own problems which must be settled in its own way.

"Parallels with foreign countries have always something disagreeable.... At the Revolution, the English people were in a very different condition from that of Prussia to-day; after a century of revolution and civil war, it was in a position to be able to give away a crown and add conditions which William of Orange accepted. On the other hand, we are in possession of a crown whose rights were actually unlimited, a crown held by the grace not of the people but of God, and which of its own free-will has given away to the people a portion of its rights--an example rare in history."

It shows how strong upon him was the influence of his friends in Pomerania that his longest and most important speech was in defence of the Christian monarchy. The occasion was a proposal to increase the privileges of the Jews. He said:

"I am no enemy of the Jews; if they become my enemies I will forgive them. Under certain circumstances I love them; I am ready to grant them all rights but that of holding the magisterial office in a Christian State. This they now claim; they demand to become Landrath, General, Minister, yes even, under circumstances, Minister of Religion and Education. I allow that I am full of prejudices, which, as I have said, I have sucked in with my mother's milk; I cannot argue them away; for if I think of a Jew face to face with me as a representative of the King's sacred Majesty, and I have to obey him, I must confess that I should feel myself deeply broken and depressed; the sincere self-respect with which I now attempt to fulfil my duties towards the State would leave me. I share these feelings with the mass of the lower strata of the people, and I am not ashamed of their society."

And then he spoke of the Christian State:

"It is as old as every European State; it is the ground in which they have taken root; no State has a secure existence unless it has a religious foundation. For me, the words, 'by the Grace of God,' which Christian rulers add to their name, are no empty phrase; I see in them a confession that the Princes desire to wield the sceptre which God has given them according to the will of God on earth. As the will of God I can only recognise that which has been revealed in the Christian Gospel--I believe that the realisation of Christian teaching is the end of the State; I do not believe that we shall more nearly approach this end by the help of the Jews.... If we withdraw this foundation, we retain in a State nothing but an accidental aggregate of rights, a kind of bulwark against the war of all against all, which ancient philosophy has assumed. Therefore, gentlemen, do not let us spoil the people of their Christianity; do not let us take from them the belief that our legislation is drawn from the well of Christianity, and that the State aims at the realisation of Christianity even if it does not attain its end."

We can well understand how delighted Herr von Thadden was with his pupil. "With Bismarck I naturally will not attempt to measure myself," he writes; "in the last debates he has again said many admirable things"; and in another letter, "I am quite enthusiastic for Otto Bismarck." It was more important that the King felt as if these words had been spoken out of his own heart.

Among his opponents, too, he had made his mark; they were never tired of repeating well-worn jests about the medieval opinions which he had sucked in with his mother's milk.

At the close of the session, he returned to Pomerania with fresh laurels; he was now looked upon as the rising hope of the stern and unbending Tories. His marriage took place in August, and the young Hans Kleist, a cousin of the bride, as he proposed the bridegroom's health, foretold that in their friend had arisen a new Otto of Saxony who would do for his country all that his namesake had done eight hundred years before. Careless words spoken half in jest, which thirty years later Kleist, then Over-President of the province, recalled when he proposed the bridegroom's health at the marriage of Bismarck's eldest daughter. The forecast had been more than fulfilled, but fulfilled at the cost of many an early friendship; and all the glory of later years could never quite repay the happy confidence and intimacy of those younger days.

Followed by the good wishes of all their friends, Bismarck and his young wife started on their wedding tour, which took them through Austria to Italy. At Venice he came across the King of Prussia, who took the opportunity to have more than one conversation with the man who had distinguished himself in the States General. At the beginning of the winter they returned to Schoenhausen to settle down to a quiet country life. Fate was to will it otherwise. The storm which had long been gathering burst over Europe. Bismarck was carried away by it; from henceforth his life was entirely devoted to public duties, and we can count by months the time he was able to spend with his wife at the old family house; more than forty years were to pass before he was able again to enjoy the leisure of his early years.

The revolution which at the end of February broke out in Paris quickly spread to Germany; the ground was prepared and the news quickly came to him, first of disorder in South Germany, then of the fall of the Ministry in Dresden and Munich; after a few days it was told that a revolution had taken place in Vienna itself. The rising in Austria was the signal for Berlin, and on the 18th of March the revolution broke out there also. The King had promised to grant a Constitution; a fierce fight had taken place in the streets of the city between the soldiers and the people; the King had surrendered to the mob, and had ordered the troops to withdraw from the city. He was himself almost a prisoner in his castle protected only by a civilian National Guard. He was exposed to the insults of the crowd; his brother had had to leave the city and the country. It is impossible to describe the enthusiasm and wild delight with which the people of Germany heard of these events. Now the press was free, now they also were going to be free and great and strong. All the resistance of authority was overthrown; nothing, it seemed, stood between them and the attainment of their ideal of a united and free Germany. They had achieved a revolution; they had become a political people; they had shewn themselves the equals of England and of France. They had liberty, and they would soon have a Constitution. Bismarck did not share this feeling; he saw only that the monarchy which he respected, and the King whom, with all his faults, he loved and honoured, were humiliated and disgraced. This was worse than Jena. A defeat on the field of battle can be avenged; here the enemies were his own countrymen; it was Prussian subjects who had made the King the laughing-stock of Europe. Only a few months ago he had pleaded that they should not lose that confidence between King and people which was the finest tradition of the Prussian State; could this confidence ever be restored when the blood of so many soldiers and citizens had been shed? He felt as though someone had struck him in the face, for his country's dishonour was to him as his own; he became ill with gall and anger. He had only two thoughts: first to restore to the King courage and confidence, and then—revenge on the men who had done this thing. He at least was not going to play with the revolution. He at once sat down and wrote to the King a letter full of ardent expressions of loyalty and affection, that he might know there still were men on whom he could rely. It is said that for months after, through all this terrible year, the King kept it open by him on his writing-table. Then he hurried to Berlin, if necessary to defend him with the sword. This was not necessary, but the situation was almost worse than he feared; the King was safe, but he was safe because he had surrendered to the revolution; he had proclaimed the fatal words that Prussia was to be dissolved in Germany.

At Potsdam Bismarck found his old friends of the Guard and the Court; they were all in silent despair. What could they do to save the monarchy when the King himself had deserted their cause? Some there were who even talked of seeking help from the Czar of Russia, who had offered to come to the help of the monarchy in Prussia and place himself at the head of the Prussian army, even if necessary against their own King. There was already a Liberal Ministry under Count Arnim, Bismarck's old chief at Aachen; the Prussian troops were being sent to support the people of Schleswig-Holstein in their rebellion against the

Danes; the Ministers favoured the aspirations of Poland for self-government; in Prussia there was to be a Constituent Assembly and a new Constitution drawn up by it. Bismarck did what he could; he went down to Schoenhausen and began to collect signatures for an address of loyalty to the King; he wished to instil into him confidence by appealing to the loyalty of the country against the radicalism of the town. Then he hurried back to Berlin for the meeting of the Estates General, which had been hastily summoned to prepare for the new elections. An address was proposed thanking the King for the concessions he had made; Bismarck opposed it, but he stood almost alone.

"I have not changed my opinion," he said, "in the last six months; the past is buried, and I regret more bitterly than any of you that no human power can reawaken it, now that the Crown itself has cast the earth on its coffin."

Two men alone voted against the address—Bismarck and Herr von Thadden. "It is easy to get fame nowadays," said the latter; "a little courage is all one requires."

Courage it did require; Berlin was terrorised; the new National Guard was unable to maintain order; men scarcely dared to appear in the streets in the ordinary dress of a gentleman. The city was full of Polish insurgents, many of whom had only just been released from prison. When the National Assembly came together, it became the organ of the extreme Republican party; all the more moderate men and more distinguished had preferred to be elected for that general German Assembly which at the same time was sitting at Frankfort to create a new Constitution for the whole Confederation. How quickly had the balance of parties altered: Vincke, until a few months ago the leader of the Liberals, found himself at Frankfort regarded as an extreme Conservative; and Frankfort was moderate compared to Berlin. At this time an ordinary English Radical would have been looked upon in Germany as almost reactionary. Bismarck did not seek election for either of the Assemblies; he felt that he could do no good by taking part in the deliberations of a Parliament, the very meeting of which seemed to him an offence against the laws and welfare of the State. He would indeed have had no logical position; both Parliaments were Constituent Assemblies; it was the duty of the one to build up a new Germany, of the other a new Prussia; their avowed object was the regeneration of their country. Bismarck did not believe that Prussia wanted regenerating; he held that the roots for the future greatness of the State must be found in the past. What happened to Germany he did not much care; all he saw was that every proposal for the regeneration of Germany implied either a dissolution of Prussia, or the subjection of the Prussian King to the orders of an alien Parliament.

During the summer he did what he could; he contributed articles to the newspapers attacking the Polish policy of the Government, and defending the landlords and country gentry against the attacks made on them. As the months went by, as the anarchy in Berlin increased, and the violence of the Assembly as well as the helplessness of the Government became more manifest, he and some of his friends determined to make their voices heard in a more organised way. It was at the house of his father-in-law at Rheinfeld that he, Hans Kleist, and Herr von Below determined to call together a meeting of well-known men in Berlin, who should discuss the situation and be a moral counterpoise to the meetings of the National Assembly; for in that the Conservative party and even the Moderate Liberals were scarcely represented; if they did speak they were threatened by the mob which encumbered the approaches to the House. Of more permanent importance was the foundation of a newspaper which should represent the principles of the Christian monarchy, and in July appeared the first number of the New Prussian Gazette, or, as it was to be more generally known, the Kreuz Zeitung, which was to give its name to the party of which it was the organ. Bismarck was among the founders, among whom were also numbered Stahl, the Gerlachs, and others of his older friends; he was a frequent contributor, and when he was at Berlin was almost daily at the office; when he was in the country he contributed articles on the rural affairs with which he was more specially qualified to deal.

These steps, of course, attracted the attention and the hostility of the dominant Liberal and Revolutionary parties; the Junker, as they were called, were accused of aiming at reaction and the restoration of the absolute monarchy. As a matter of fact, this is what many of them desired; they were, however, only doing their duty as members of society; it would have been mere cowardice and indolence had they remained inactive and seen all the institutions they valued overthrown without attempting to defend them. It required considerable courage in the middle of so violent a crisis to come forward and attempt to stop the revolution; it was a good example that they began to do so by constitutional and legal means. They shewed that Prussia had an aristocracy, and an aristocracy which was not frightened; deserted by the King they acted alone; in the hour of greatest danger they founded a Conservative party, and matters had come to this position that an organised Conservative party was the chief necessity of the time.

At first, however, their influence was small, for a monarchical party must depend for its success on the adhesion of the King, and the King had not yet resolved to separate himself from his Liberal advisers. Bismarck was often at Court and seems to have had much influence; both to his other companions and to the King himself he preached always courage and resolution; he spoke often to the King with great openness; he was supported by Leopold von Gerlach, with whom at this time he contracted a close intimacy. For long their advice was in vain, but in the autumn events occurred which shewed that some decision must be taken: the mob of Berlin stormed the Zeughaus where the arms were kept; the Constitution of the Assembly was being drawn up so as to leave the King scarcely any influence in the State; a resolution was passed calling on the Ministers to request all officers to leave the army who disliked the new order of things. The crisis was brought about by events in Vienna; in October the Austrian army under Jellachich and Windischgrätz stormed the city, proclaimed martial law, and forcibly overthrew the Revolutionary Government; the King of Prussia now summoned resolution to adopt a similar course. It is said that Bismarck suggested to him the names of the Ministers to whom the task should be entrusted. The most important were Count Brandenburg, an uncle of the King's, and Otto v. Manteuffel, a member of the Prussian aristocracy, who with Bismarck had distinguished himself in the Estates General. He seems to have been constantly going about among the more influential men, encouraging them as he encouraged the King, and helping behind the scenes to prepare for the momentous step. Gerlach had suggested Bismarck's name as one of the Ministers, but the King rejected it, writing on the side of the paper the characteristic words, "Red reactionary; smells of blood; will be useful later." Bismarck's language was of such a nature as to alarm even many of those who associated with him. Count Beust, the Saxon Minister, was at this time in

Berlin and met Bismarck for the first time; they were discussing the conduct of the Austrian Government in shooting Robert Blum, a leading demagogue who had been in Vienna during the siege. Beust condemned it as a political blunder. "No, you are wrong," said Bismarck; "when I have my enemy in my power I must destroy him."

The event fully justified Bismarck's forecast that nothing was required but courage and resolution. After Brandenburg had been appointed Minister, the Prussian troops under Wrangel again entered Berlin, a state of siege was proclaimed, the Assembly was ordered to adjourn to Brandenburg; they refused and were at once ejected from their meeting-place, and as a quorum was not found at Brandenburg, were dissolved. The Crown then of its own authority published a new Constitution and summoned a new Assembly to discuss and ratify it. Based on the discipline of the army the King had regained his authority without the loss of a single life.

Bismarck stood for election in this new Assembly, for he could accept the basis on which it had been summoned; he took his seat for the district of the West Havel in which the old city of Brandenburg, the original capital of the Mark, was situated. He had come forward as an opponent of the Revolution. "Everyone," he said in his election address, "must support the Government in the course they have taken of combating the Revolution which threatens us all." "No transaction with the Revolution," was the watchword proposed in the manifesto of his party. He appealed to the electors as one who would direct all his efforts to restore the old bond of confidence between Crown and people. He kept his promise. In this Assembly the Extreme Left was still the predominant party; in an address to the Crown they asked that the state of siege at Berlin should be raised, and that an amnesty to those who had fought on the 18th of March should be proclaimed. Bismarck did not yet think that the time for forgiveness had come; the struggle was indeed not yet over. He opposed the first demand because, as he said, there was more danger to liberty of debate from the armed mob than there was from the Prussian soldiers. In one of the most careful of his speeches he opposed the amnesty. "Amnesty," he said, "was a right of the Crown, not of the Assembly"; moreover the repeated amnesties were undermining in the people the feeling of law; the opinion was being spread about that the law of the State rested on the barricades, that everyone who disliked a law or considered it unjust had the right to consider it as non-existent. Who that has read the history of Europe during this year can doubt the justice of the remark? Then he continues:

"My third reason for voting against the amnesty is humanity. The strife of principles which during this year has shattered Europe to its foundations is one in which no compromise is possible. They rest on opposite bases. The one draws its law from what is called the will of the people, in truth, however, from the law of the strongest on the barricades. The other rests on authority created by God, an authority by the grace of God, and seeks its development in organic connection with the existing and constitutional legal status ... the decision on these principles will come not by Parliamentary debate, not by majorities of eleven votes; sooner or later the God who directs the battle will cast his iron dice."

These words were greeted with applause, not only by the men who sat on his side of the House, but by those opposite to him. The truth of them was to be shewn by the events which were taking place at that very time. They were spoken on the 22d of March. The next day was fought the battle of Novara and it seemed that the last hopes of the Italian patriots were shattered. Within a few months the Austrian army subdued with terrible vengeance the rising in Lombardy and Venetia; Hungary was prostrate before the troops whom the Czar sent to help the young Austrian Emperor, and the last despairing outbreak of rebellion in Saxony and in Baden was to be subdued by the Prussian army. The Revolution had failed and it had raised up, as will always happen, a military power, harder, crueller, and more resolute than that it had overthrown. The control over Europe had passed out of the hands of Metternich and Louis Philippe to fall into those of Nicholas, Schwarzenberg, and Napoleon III.

In Prussia the King used his power with moderation, the conflict of parties was continued within legal limits and under constitutional forms.

The Parliament which still claimed that control over the executive government which all Parliaments of the Revolution had exercised, was dissolved. A new Assembly met in August; the King had of his own authority altered the electoral law and the new Parliament showed a considerable majority belonging to the more moderate Liberal party. Bismarck retained his old seat. He still found much to do; his influence was increasing; he opposed the doctrines of the more moderate Liberalism with the same energy with which he had attacked the extreme Revolution. The most important debates were those concerning the Constitution; he took part in them, especially opposing the claim of the Parliament to refuse taxes. He saw that if the right was given to the Lower House of voting the taxes afresh every year they would be able to establish a complete control over the executive government; this he did not wish. He was willing that they should have the right of discussing and rejecting any new taxes and also, in agreement with the Crown and the Upper House, of determining the annual Budget. It was maintained by the Liberals that the right to reject supplies every year was an essential part of a constitutional system; they appealed to the practice in England and to the principles adopted in the French and Belgian Constitutions. Their argument was that this practice which had been introduced in other countries must be adopted also in Prussia. It was just one of those arguments which above all offended Bismarck's Prussian patriotism. Why should Prussia imitate other countries? Why should it not have its own Constitution in its own way? Constitution, as he said, was the mot d'ordre of the day, the word which men used when they were in want of an argument. "In Prussia that only is constitutional which arises from the Prussian Constitution; whatever be constitutional in Belgium, or in France, in Anhalt Dessau, or there where the morning red of Mecklenburg freedom shines, here that alone is constitutional which rests on the Prussian Constitution." If he defended the prerogative of the Crown he defended the Constitution of his country. A constitution is the collection of rules and laws by which the action of the king is governed; a state without a constitution is a mere Oriental despotism where each arbitrary whim of the king is transmuted into action; this was not what Bismarck desired or defended; there was no danger of this in Prussia. He did not even oppose changes in the law and practice of the Constitution; what he did oppose was the particular change which would transfer the sovereignty to an elected House of Parliament. "It has been maintained," he once said, "that a constitutional king cannot be a king by the Grace of God; on the contrary he is it above all others."

The references to foreign customs were indeed one of the most curious practices of the time; the matter was once being discussed whether the Crown had the power to declare a state of siege without the assent of the Chambers; most speakers attempted to interpret the text of the Prussian Constitution by precedents derived from the practice in France and England; we find the Minister of Justice defending his action on the ground of an event in the French Revolution, and Lothar Bucher, one of the ablest of the Opposition, complained that not enough attention had been paid to the procedure adopted in England for repealing the Habeas Corpus Act, entirely ignoring the fact that there was no Habeas Corpus Act in Prussia. We can easily understand how repulsive this was to a man who, like Bismarck, wished nothing more than that his countrymen should copy, not the details of the English Constitution, but the proud self-reliance which would regard as impertinent an application of foreign notions.

The chief cause for this peculiarity was the desire of the Liberal party to attain that degree of independence and personal liberty which was enjoyed in England or France; the easiest way to do this seemed to be to copy their institutions. There was, however, another reason: the study of Roman law in Germany in which they had been educated had accustomed them to look for absolute principles of jurisprudence which might be applied to the legislation of all countries; when, therefore, they turned their minds to questions of politics, they looked for absolute principles of constitutional government, on which, as on a law of nature, their own institutions might be built up. To find these they analysed the English Constitution, for England was the classical land of representative government; they read its rules as they would the institutions of a Roman Jurisconsult and used them to cast light on the dark places of their own law. Bismarck did not share this type of thought; his mind was rather of the English cast; he believed the old Prussian Constitution was as much a natural growth as that of England, and decided dark points by reference to older practice as an Englishman would search for precedents in the history of his own country.

At that time the absolute excellence of a democratic constitution was a dogma which few cared to dispute; it appeared to his hearers as a mere paradox when Bismarck pointed out how little evidence there was that a great country could prosper under the government of a Parliament elected by an extended franchise. Strictly speaking, there was no evidence from experience; France, as he said, was the parent of all these theories, but the example of France was certainly not seductive. "I see in the present circumstances of France nothing to encourage us to put the Nessus robe of French political teaching over our healthy body." (This was in September, 1849, when the struggle between the Prince President and the Assembly was already impending.) The Liberals appealed to Belgium; it had, at least, stood the storm of the last year, but so had Russia, and, after all, the Belgian Constitution was only eighteen years old, "an admirable age for ladies but not for constitutions." And then there was England.

"England governs itself, although the Lower House has the right of refusing taxes. The references to England are our misfortune; give us all that is English which we have not, give us English fear of God and English reverence before the law, the whole English Constitution, but above all the complete independence of English landed property, English wealth and English common-sense, especially an English Lower House, in short everything which we have not got, then I will say, you can govern us after the English fashion."

But this was not all. How could they appeal to England as a proof that a democratic Parliament was desirable? England had not grown great under a democratic but under an aristocratic constitution.

"English reform is younger than the Belgian Constitution; we have still to wait and see whether this reformed Constitution will maintain itself for centuries as did the earlier rule of the English aristocracy."

That, in Bismarck's opinion, it was not likely to do so, we see a few years later; with most Continental critics of English institutions, he believed that the Reform Bill had destroyed the backbone of the English Constitution. In 1857 he wrote:

"They have lost the 'inherited wisdom' since the Reform Bill; they maintain a coarse and violent selfishness and the ignorance of Continental relations."

It was not merely aristocratic prejudice; it was a wise caution to bid his countrymen pause before they adopted from foreign theorists a form of government so new and untried, and risked for the sake of an experiment the whole future of Prussia.

In later years Bismarck apologised for many of the speeches which he made at this period: "I was a terrible Junker in those days," he said; and biographers generally speak of them as though they required justification or apology. There seems no reason for this. It would have been impossible for him, had he at that time been entrusted with the government of the State, entirely to put into practice what he had said from his place in the Chamber. But he was not minister; he was only a party leader; his speeches were, as they were intended to be, party speeches; they had something of the exaggeration which conflict always produces. They were, moreover, opposition speeches, for he was addressing not so much the Government as the Chamber and the country, and in them the party to which he belonged was a very small minority. But why was there not to be a Conservative party in Prussia?

It was necessary for the proper development of constitutional life that the dominant Liberal doctrines should be opposed by this bold criticism. Bismarck was only doing what in England was done by the young Disraeli, by Carlyle, and by Ruskin; the world would not be saved by constitutional formulæ.

There were some of his party whose aims went indeed beyond what may be considered morally legitimate and politically practicable. The Gerlachs and many of their friends, and the purely military party which was headed by Prince Charles Frederick, the King's youngest brother, desired to do away with the Constitution, to dismiss the Parliament, and to restore the absolute monarchy in a form which would have been more extreme than that which it had had since 1815. The King himself sympathised with their wishes and he probably would have acted according to them were it not that he had sworn to maintain the Constitution. He was a religious man and he respected his oath. There does not appear any evidence that Bismarck wished for extreme action of this kind. Even in his private correspondence, at least in that part of it which has been published, one finds no desire to see Prussia entirely without a Parliament. It was a very different thing to wish as he did that the duties of the Parliament should be strictly limited and that they should not be allowed completely to govern the State. We must always remember how much he owed to representative assemblies. Had the Estates General never been summoned, had the Revolution never taken place, he would probably have passed his life as a country gentleman, often discontented with the Government of the country but entirely without influence. He owed to Parliament his personal reputation, but he owed to it something more than that. Up to 1847 the only public career open to a Prussian subject was the Civil Service; it was from them that not only the subordinate officials but the Ministers of the State were selected. Now we have seen that Bismarck had tried the Civil Service and deliberately retired from it. The hatred of bureaucracy he never overcame, even when he was at the head of the Prussian State. It arose partly from the natural opposition between the nobleman and the clerk. Bismarck felt in this like Stein, the greatest of his predecessors, who though he had taken service under the Prussian Crown never overcame his hatred of "the animal with a pen" as he called Prussian Civil Servants, and shed tears of indignation when he was first offered a salary. Bismarck was never a great nobleman like Stein and he did not dislike receiving a salary; but he felt that the Civil Servants were the enemies of the order to which he belonged. He speaks a few years later of "the biting acid of Prussian legislation which in a single generation can reduce a mediatised Prince to an ordinary voter." He is never tired of saying that it was the bureaucracy which was the real introducer of the Revolution into Prussia. In one of his speeches he defends himself and his friends against the charge of being enemies to freedom; "that they were not," he says;

"Absolutism with us is closely connected with the omnipotence of the Geheimrath and the conceited omniscience of the Professors who sit behind the green table, a product, and I venture to maintain a necessary product, of the Prussian method of education. This product, the bureaucracy, I have never loved."

When, as he often does, he maintains that the Prussian Parliament does not represent the people, he is thinking of the predominance among them of officials, for we must always remember that many of the extreme Liberal party and some of their most active leaders were men who were actually at that time in the service of the Crown.

It was the introduction of a Representative Assembly that for the first time in Prussian history made possible a Conservative opposition against the Liberalism of the Prussian Government. There are two kinds of Liberalism. In one sense of the word it means freedom of debate, freedom of the press, the power of the individual as against the Government, independence of character, and personal freedom. Of Liberalism in this sense of the word there was indeed little in the Prussian Government. But Liberalism also meant the overthrow of the old established institutions inherited from the Middle Ages, especially the destruction of all privileges held by the nobility; it meant on the Continent opposition to all form of dogmatic religious teaching; it meant the complete subjection of the Church to the State; it meant the abolition of all local distinctions and the introduction of a uniform system of government chiefly imitated from French institutions. It was in this sense of the word that, with the exception of the first few years of the reign of Frederick William IV., the Prussian Government had been Liberal, and it was this Liberalism which

Bismarck and his friends hated almost as much as they did the Liberalism of the Revolution.

The clearest instance of his attitude on such matters is to be found in his opposition to the Bill introduced for making civil marriage compulsory. He opposed it in a speech which was many years later to be quoted against him when he himself introduced a measure almost identical with that which he now opposed. Civil marriage, he said, was a foreign institution, an imitation of French legislation; it would simply serve to undermine the belief in Christianity among the people, "and" he said, "I have seen many friends of the illumination during the last year or two come to recognise that a certain degree of positive Christianity is necessary for the common man, if he is not to become dangerous to human society." The desire for introducing this custom was merely an instance of the constant wish to imitate what is foreign.

"It would be amusing," he said, "if it were not just our own country which was subjected to these experiments of French charlatanism. In the course of the discussion it has often been said by gentlemen standing in this place that Europe holds us for a people of thinkers. Gentlemen, that was in old days. The popular representation of the last two years has deprived us of this reputation. They have shown to a disappointed Europe only translators of French stucco but no original thinkers. It may be that when civil marriage also rejoices in its majority, the people will have their eyes opened to the swindle to which they have been sacrificed; when one after another the old Christian fundamental rights have been taken from them: the right to be governed by Christian magistrates; the right to know that they have secured to their children a Christian education in schools which Christian parents are compelled to maintain and to use; the right of being married in the Christian fashion which his faith requires from everyone, without being dependent on constitutional ceremonies. If we go on in this way I hope still to see the day when the fool's ship of the time will be wrecked on the rock of the Christian Church; for the belief in the revealed Word of God still stands firmer among the people than the belief in the saving power of any article of the Constitution."

In the same way he was able from his place in Parliament to criticise the proposals of the Government for freeing the peasants from those payments in kind, and personal service which in some of the provinces still adhered to their property; he attacked their financial proposals; he exposed the injustice of the land tax; he defended the manorial jurisdiction of the country gentlemen. Especially he defended the nobles of Prussia themselves, a class against whom so many attacks had been made. He pointed out that by them and by their blood the Prussian State had been built up; the Prussian nobles were, he maintained, not, as so often was said, unpopular; a third of the House belonged to them; they were not necessarily opposed to freedom; they were, at least, the truest defenders of the State. Let people not confuse patriotism and Liberalism. Who had done more for the true political independence of the State, that independence without which all freedom was impossible, than the Prussian nobles? At the end of the Seven Years' War boys had stood at the head of the army, the only survivors of their families. The privileges of the nobles had been taken from them, but they had not behaved like the democrats; their loyalty to the State had never wavered; they had not even formed a Fronde. He was not ashamed of the name of Junker: "We will bring the name to glory and honour," were almost the last words he spoke in Parliament.

Bismarck soon became completely at home in the House. Notwithstanding the strength of his opinions and the vigour with which he gave expression to them, he was not unpopular, even among his opponents. He was always a gentleman and a man of the world; he did not dislike mixing with men of all classes and all parties; he had none of that stiffness and hauteur which many of his friends had acquired from their military pursuits. His relations with his opponents are illustrated by an anecdote of which there are many versions. He found himself one day while in the refreshment room standing side by side with d'Ester, one of the most extreme of the Republican party. They fell into conversation, and d'Ester suggested that they should make a compact and, whichever party succeeded in the struggle for power, they should each agree to spare the other. If the Republicans won, Bismarck should not be guillotined; if the monarchists, d'Ester should not be hung. "No," answered Bismarck, "that is no use; if you come into power, life would not be worth living. There must be hanging, but courtesy to the foot of the gallows."

If he was in after years to become known as the great adversary of Parliamentary government, this did not arise from any incapacity to hold his own in Parliamentary debate. He did not indeed aim at oratory; then, as in later years, he always spoke with great contempt of men who depended for power on their rhetorical ability. He was himself deficient in the physical gifts of a great speaker; powerful as was his frame, his voice was thin and weak. He had nothing of the actor in him; he could not command the deep voice, the solemn tones, the imposing gestures, the Olympian mien by which men like Waldeck and Radowitz and Gagern dominated and controlled their audience. His own mind was essentially critical; he appealed more to the intellect than the emotions. His speeches were always controversial, but he was an admirable debater. It is curious to see how quickly he adopts the natural Parliamentary tone. His speeches are all subdued in tone and conversational in manner. Many of them were very carefully prepared, for though he did not generally write them out, he said them over and over again to himself or to Kleist, with whom he lived in Berlin. They are entirely unlike any other speeches—he has, in fact, in them, as in his letters, added a new chapter to the literature of his country, hitherto so poor in prose.

They shew a vivid imagination and an almost unequalled power of illustration. The thought is always concrete, and he is never satisfied with the vague ideas and abstract conceptions which so easily moved his contemporaries.

No speeches, either in English or in German, preserve so much of their freshness. He is almost the only Parliamentary orator whose speeches have become to some extent a popular book; no other orator has enriched the language as he has done with new phrases and images. The great characteristic of his speeches, as of his letters, is the complete absence of affectation and the very remarkable intellectual honesty. They are often deficient in order and arrangement; he did not excel in the logical exposition of a connected argument, but he never was satisfied till he had presented the idea which influenced him in words so forcible and original that it was impressed on the minds of his audience, and he was often able to find expressions which will not be forgotten so long as the German language is spoken.

We can easily imagine that under other circumstances, or in another country, he would have risen to power and held office as a Parliamentary Minister. He often appeals to the practice and traditions of the English Parliament, and there are few Continental statesmen who would have been so completely at home in the English House of Commons; he belonged to the class of men from whom so many of the great English statesmen had come and whom he himself describes:

"What with us is lacking is the whole class which in England carries on politics, the class of gentlemen who are well-to-do and therefore Conservative, who are independent of material interests and whose whole education is directed towards making them English statesmen, and the object of whose life is to take part in the Commonwealth of England."

They were the class to whom he belonged, and he would gladly have taken part in a Parliamentary government of this kind.

The weakness of his position arose from the fact that he was really acquainted with and represented the inhabitants of only one-half of the monarchy. So long as he is dealing with questions of landed property, or of the condition of the peasants, he has a minute and thorough knowledge. He did not always, however, avoid the danger of speaking as though Prussia consisted entirely of agriculturists. The great difficulty then as now of governing the State, was that it consisted of two parts: the older provinces, almost entirely agricultural, where the land was held chiefly by the great nobles, and the new provinces, the Rhine and Westphalia, where there was a large and growing industrial population. To the inhabitants of these provinces Bismarck's constant appeal to the old Prussian traditions and to the achievements of the Prussian nobility could have little meaning. What did the citizens of Cologne and

Aachen care about the Seven Years' War? If their ancestors took part in the war, it would be as enemies of the Kings of Prussia. When Bismarck said that they were Prussians, and would remain Prussian, he undoubtedly spoke the opinion of the Mark and of Pomerania. But the inhabitants of the Western Provinces still felt and thought rather as Germans than as Prussians; they had scarcely been united with the monarchy thirty years; they were not disloyal, but they were quite prepared—nay, they wished to see Prussia dissolved in Germany. No one can govern Prussia unless he is able to reconcile to his policy these two different classes in the State. It was this which the Prussian Conservatives, to which Bismarck at that time belonged, have always failed to do. The Liberals whom he opposed failed equally. In later years he was very nearly to succeed in a task which might appear almost impossible.

CHAPTER IV.

THE GERMAN PROBLEM.

1849-1852.

Bismarck, however, did not confine himself to questions of constitutional reform and internal government. He often spoke on the foreign policy of the Government, and it is in these speeches that he shews most originality.

The Revolution in Germany, as in Italy, had two sides; it was Liberal, but it was also National. The National element was the stronger and more deep-seated. The Germans felt deeply the humiliation to which they were exposed owing to the fact that they did not enjoy the protection of a powerful Government; they wished to belong to a national State, as Frenchmen, Englishmen, and Russians did. It was the general hope that the period of revolution might be used for establishing a government to which the whole of Germany would pay obedience. This was the task of the Constituent Assembly, which since the spring of 1848 had with the permission of the Governments been sitting at Frankfort. Would they be able to succeed where the diplomatists of Vienna had failed? They had at least good-will, but it was to be shewn that something more than honest endeavour was necessary. There were three great difficulties with which they had to contend. The first was the Republican party, the men who would accept no government but a Republic, and who wished to found the new state by insurrection. They were a small minority of the German people; several attempts at insurrection organised by them were suppressed, and they were outvoted in the Assembly. The second difficulty was Austria. A considerable portion of Germany was included in the Austrian Empire. If the whole of Germany were to be included in the new State which they hoped to found, then part of the Austrian Empire would have to be separated from the rest, subjected to different laws and a different government; nothing would remain but a personal union between the German and Slavonic provinces. The Government of Austria, after it had recovered its authority at the end of 1848, refused to accept this position, and published a new Constitution, binding all the provinces together in a closer union. The Assembly at Frankfort had no power to coerce the Emperor of Austria; they therefore adopted the other solution, viz.: that the rest of Germany was to be reconstituted, and the Austrian provinces left out. The question, however, then arose: Would Austria accept this—would she allow a new Germany to be created in which she had no part? Surely not, if she was able to prevent it. The third difficulty was the relation between the individual States and the new central authority. It is obvious that whatever powers were given to the new Government would be taken away from the Princes of the individual States, who hitherto had enjoyed complete sovereignty. Those people who in Germany were much influenced by attachment to the existing governments, and who wished to maintain the full authority of the Princes and the local Parliaments, were called Particularists. During the excitement of the Revolution they had been almost entirely silenced. With the restoration of order and authority they had regained their influence. It was probable that many of the States would refuse to accept the new Constitution unless they were compelled to do so. Where was the power to do this? There were many in the National Assembly who wished to appeal to the power of the people, and by insurrection and barricades compel all the Princes to accept the new Constitution. There was only one other power in Germany which could do the work, and that was the Prussian army. Would the King of Prussia accept this task?

The German Constitution was completed in March, 1849. By the exercise of much tact and great personal influence, Heinrich von Gagern, the President of the Assembly and the leader of the Moderate party in it, had procured a majority in favour of an hereditary monarchy, and the King of Prussia was elected to the post of first German Emperor. At the beginning of April there arrived in Berlin the deputation which was to offer to him the crown, and on his answer depended the future of Germany. Were he to accept, he would then have undertaken to put himself at the head of the revolutionary movement; it would be his duty to compel all the other States to accept the new Constitution, and, if necessary, to defend it on the field of battle against Austria. Besides this he would have to govern not only Prussia but Germany; to govern it under a Constitution which gave almost all the power to a Parliament elected by universal suffrage, and in which he had only a suspensive veto. Can we be surprised that he refused the offer? He refused it on the ground that he could not accept universal suffrage, and also because the title and power of German Emperor could not be conferred on him by a popular assembly; he could only accept it from his equals, the German Princes.

The decision of the King was discussed in the Prussian Assembly, and an address moved declaring that the Frankfort Constitution was in legal existence, and requesting the King to accept the offer. It was on this occasion that Bismarck for the first time came forward as the leader of a small party on the Extreme Right. He at once rose to move the previous question. He denied to the Assembly even the right of discussing this matter which belonged to the prerogative of the King.

He was still more strongly opposed to the acceptance of the offered crown. He saw only that the King of Prussia would be subjected to a Parliamentary Assembly, that his power of action would be limited. The motto of his speech was that Prussia must remain Prussia. "The crown of Frankfort," he said, "may be very bright, but the gold which gives truth to its brilliance has first to be won by melting down the Prussian crown." His speech caused great indignation; ten thousand copies of it were printed to be distributed among the electors so as to show them the real principles and objects of the reactionary party.

His opposition to any identification of Prussia and Germany was maintained when the Prussian Government itself took the initiative and proposed its own solution. During the summer of 1849, the Prussian programme was published. The Government invited the other States of Germany to enter into a fresh union; the basis of the new Constitution was to be that of Frankfort, but altered so far as might be found necessary, and the union was to be a voluntary one. The King in order to carry out this policy appointed as one of his Ministers Herr von Radowitz. He was a man of the highest character and extreme ability. An officer by profession, he was distinguished by the versatility of his interests and his great learning. The King found in him a man who shared his own enthusiasm for letters. He had been a member of the Parliament at Frankfort, and had taken a leading part among the extreme Conservatives; a Roman Catholic, he had come forward in defence of religion and order against the Liberals and Republicans; a very eloquent speaker, by his earnestness and eloquence he was able for a short time to give new life to the failing hopes of the German patriots.

Bismarck always looked on the new Minister with great dislike. Radowitz, indeed, hated the Revolution as much as he did; he was a zealous and patriotic Prussian; but there was a fundamental difference in the nature of the two men. Radowitz wished to reform Germany by moral influence. Bismarck did not believe in the possibility of this. To this perhaps we must add some personal feeling. The Ministry had hitherto consisted almost entirely of men who were either personal friends of Bismarck, or whom he had recommended to the King. With Radowitz there entered into it a man who was superior to all of them in ability, and over whom Bismarck could not hope to have any influence. Bismarck's distrust, which amounted almost to hatred, depended, however, on his fear that the new policy would bring about the ruin of Prussia. He took the extreme Particularist view; he had no interest in Germany outside Prussia; Würtemberg and Bavaria were to him foreign States. In all these proposals for a new Constitution he saw only that Prussia would be required to sacrifice its complete independence; that the King of Prussia would become executor for the decrees of a popular and alien Parliament. They were asked to cease to be Prussians in order that they might become Germans. This Bismarck refused to do. "Prussians we are," he said, "and Prussians we will remain." He had no sympathy with this idea of a United Germany which was so powerful at the time; there was only one way in which he was willing that Germany should be united, and that was according to the example which Frederick the Great had set. The ideals of the German nation were represented by Arndt's famous song, "Was ist des Deutschen Vaterland?" The fatherland of the Germans was not Suabia or Prussia, not Austria or Bavaria, it was the whole of Germany wherever the German tongue was spoken. From this Bismarck deliberately dissociated himself. "I have never heard," he said, "a Prussian soldier singing, 'Was ist des Deutschen Vaterland?'" The new flag of Germany was to be the German tricolour, black and white and gold.

"The Prussian soldiers," cried Bismarck, "have no tricoloured enthusiasm; among them you will find, as little as in the rest of the Prussian people, the desire for a national regeneration; they are contented with the name of Prussia, and proud of the name of Prussia. These troops follow the black and white flag, not the tricolour; under the black and white they die with joy for their country. The tricolour they have learnt since the 18th of March to look on as the colours of their foes."

These words aroused intense indignation. One of the speakers who followed referred to him as the Prodigal Son of the German Fatherland, who had deserted his father's house. Bismarck repudiated the epithet. "I am not a prodigal son," he said; "my father's house is Prussia and I have never left it." He could not more clearly repudiate the title German. The others were moved by enthusiasm for an idea, he by loyalty to an existing State.

Nothing was sound, he said, in Germany, except the old Prussian institutions.

"What has preserved us is that which is specifically Prussian. It was the remnant of the Stock-Preussenthum which has survived the Revolution, the Prussian army, the Prussian treasure, the fruits of many years of intelligent Prussian administration, and the living co-operation between King and people. It was the attachment of the

Prussian people to their hereditary dynasty, the old Prussian virtues of honour, loyalty, obedience, and the courage which, emanating from the officers who form its bone and marrow, permeates the army down to the youngest recruit."

He reminded the House how the Assembly at Frankfort had only been saved from the insurgent mob by a Prussian regiment, and now it was proposed to weaken and destroy all these Prussian institutions in order to change them into a democratic Germany. He was asked to assent to a Constitution in which the Prussian Government would sink to the level of a provincial council, under the guidance of an Imperial Ministry which itself would be dependent on a Parliament in which the Prussian interests would be in a minority. The most important and honourable duties of the Prussian Parliament would be transferred to a general Parliament; the King would lose his veto; he would be compelled against his will to assent to laws he disliked; even the Prussian army would be no longer under his sole command. What recompense were they to gain for this?

"The pleasant consciousness of having followed an unselfish and noble policy; of having satisfied the requirements of a national regeneration; of having carried out the historical task of Prussia, or some such vague expression."

With this he contrasted what would have been a true Prussian policy, a policy which Frederick the Great might have followed.

"He would have known that now as in the day of our fathers the sound of the trumpets which summoned them to their sovereign's flag has not lost its power for Prussian ears; he would have had the choice either of joining our old comrade Austria, and undertaking the brilliant part which the Emperor of Russia has played, and destroying the cause of the Revolution, or by the same right by which he took Silesia, he might, after refusing to accept the crown, have ordered the Germans what constitution they should have, and thrown the sword into the scale; then Prussia would have been in the position to win for Germany its place in the Council of Europe.

"We all wish the same. We all wish that the Prussian eagle should spread out his wings as guardian and ruler from the Memel to the Donnersberg, but free will we have him, not bound by a new Regensburg Diet. Prussians we are and Prussians will we remain; I know that in these words I speak the confession of the Prussian army and the majority of my fellow-countrymen, and I hope to God that we will still long remain Prussian when this sheet of paper is forgotten like a withered autumn leaf."

The policy of Radowitz was doomed to failure, not so much because of any inherent weakness in it, but because Prussia was not strong enough to defend herself against all the enemies she had called up. The other Courts of Germany were lukewarm, Austria was extremely hostile. The Kings of Hanover and Saxony retreated from the alliance on the ground that they would enter the union only if the whole of Germany joined; Bavaria had refused to do so; in fact the two other Kings had privately used all their influence to prevent Bavaria from joining, in order that they might always have an excuse for seceding. Prussia was, therefore, left surrounded by twenty-eight of the smaller States. A Parliament from them was summoned to meet at Erfurt in order to discuss the new Constitution. Bismarck was elected a member of it; he went there avowedly to protect the Prussian interests. He had demanded from the Government that at least the Constitution agreed on in Erfurt should again be submitted to the Prussian Chamber; he feared that many of the most important Prussian rights might be sacrificed. His request was refused, for it was obvious that if, after the Parliament of Erfurt had come to some conclusion, the new Constitution was to be referred back again to the twenty-eight Parliaments of the allied States, the new union would never come into effect at all. It is curious here to find Bismarck using the rights of the Prussian Parliament as a weapon to maintain the complete independence of Prussia. Sixteen years later, when he was doing the work in which Radowitz failed, one of his chief difficulties arose from the conduct of men who came forward with just the same demand which he now made, and he had to refuse their demands as Radowitz now refused his.

He did not take much part in the debates at Erfurt; as he was one of the youngest of the members, he held the position of Secretary; the President of the Assembly was Simpson, a very distinguished public man, but a converted Jew. "What would my father have said," observed Bismarck, "if he had lived to see me become clerk to a Jewish scholar?" On one occasion he became involved in what might have been a very serious dispute, when he used his power as Secretary to exclude from the reporters' gallery two journalists whose reports of the meeting were very partial and strongly opposed to Austria. His attitude towards the Assembly is shewn by the words:

"I know that what I have said to you will have no influence on your votes, but I am equally convinced that your votes will be as completely without influence on the course of events."

The whole union was, as a matter of fact, broken down by the opposition of Austria. Bismarck had, in one of his first speeches, warned against a policy which would bring Prussia into the position which Piedmont had held before the battle of Novara, when they embarked on a war in which victory would have brought about the overthrow of the monarchy, and defeat a disgraceful peace. It was his way of saying that he hoped the King would not eventually draw the sword in order to defend the new Liberal Constitution against the opposition of Austria. The day came when the King was placed in this position. Austria had summoned the old Diet to meet at Frankfort; Prussia denied that the Diet still legally existed; the two policies were clearly opposed to one another: Austria desiring the restoration of the old Constitution, Prussia, at the head of Liberal Germany, summoning the States round her in a new union. There were other disputes about Schleswig-Holstein and the affairs of Hesse, but this was the real point at issue. The Austrians were armed, and were supported by the Czar and many of the German States; shots were actually exchanged between the Prussian and Bavarian outposts in Hesse. The Austrian ambassador had orders to leave Berlin; had he done so, war could not have been avoided. He disobeyed his orders, remained in Berlin, asked for an interview with the King, and used all his influence to persuade him to surrender. The Ministry was divided; Radowitz stood almost alone; the other Ministers, Bismarck's friends, had always distrusted his policy. They wished to renew the old alliance with Austria; the Minister of War said they could not risk the struggle; it was rumoured that he had deliberately avoided making preparations in order to prevent the King putting himself at the head of the Liberal party. During the crisis, Bismarck was summoned to the King at Letzlingen; there can be no doubt what his advice was; eventually the party of peace prevailed, and Radowitz resigned. Bismarck on hearing the news danced three times round the table with delight. Brandenburg died almost immediately after; Manteuffel became Minister-President; he asked Schwarzenberg for an interview, travelled to Olmütz to meet him, and an agreement was come to by which practically Prussia surrendered every object of dispute between the two great Powers.

The convention of Olmütz was the most complete humiliation to which any European State has ever been subjected. Prussia had undertaken a policy, and with the strong approval of the great majority of the nation had consistently maintained it for over a year; Austria had required that this policy should be surrendered; the two States had armed; the ultimatum had been sent, everything was prepared for war, and then Prussia surrendered. The cause for this was a double one. It was partly that Prussia was really not strong enough to meet the coalition of Austria and Russia, but it was also that the King was really of two minds; he was constitutionally unable to maintain against danger a consistent course of policy.

Bismarck was one of the few men who defended the action of the Ministry. In the ablest of all his speeches he took up the gauntlet, and exposed all the weakness and the dangers of Radowitz's policy. This was not a cause in which Prussia should risk its existence. Why should they go to war in order to subject Prussia not to the Princes but to the Chambers of the smaller States? A war for the Union would, he said, remind him of the Englishman who had a fight with the sentry in order that he might hang himself in the sentry-box, a right which he claimed for himself and every free Briton. It was the duty of the councillors of the

King to warn him from a policy which would bring the State to destruction.

"Still I would not shrink, from the war; I would advise it, were anyone able to prove to me the necessity for it, or to point out a worthy end which could be attained by it and in no other way. Why do great States wage war nowadays? The only sound principle of action for a great State is political egoism and not Romanticism, and it is unworthy of a great State to fight for any matter which does not concern its own interests. Shew us, gentlemen, an object worthy of war and you have my vote. It is easy for a statesman in his office or his chamber to blow the trumpet with the breath of popularity and all the time to sit warming himself by his fireside, while he leaves it to the rifleman, who lies bleeding on the snow, whether his system attains victory and glory. Nothing is easier; but woe to the statesman who at such a time does not look about for a reason for the war which will be valid when the war is over. I am convinced you will see the questions which now occupy us in a different light a year hence, when you look back upon them through a long perspective of battle-fields and conflagrations, misery and wretchedness. Will you then have the courage to go to the peasant by the ashes of his cottage, to the cripple, to the childless father, and say: 'You have suffered much, but rejoice with us, the Union is saved. Rejoice with us, Hassenpflug is no longer Minister, Bayernhofer rules in Hesse.'"

Eloquent words; but what a strange comment on them his own acts were to afford. In 1850 Prussia had a clearer and juster cause of war than in 1866; every word of his speech might have been used with equal effect sixteen years later; the Constitution of 1850 was little different from that which Bismarck himself was to give to Germany. The policy of

Radowitz was the only true policy for Prussia; if he failed, it was because Prussia's army was not strong enough; war would have been followed by defeat and disaster. There was one man who saw the evils as they really were; the Prince of Prussia determined that if ever he became King the army of Prussia should be again made strong and efficient.

It was probably this speech which determined Bismarck's future career. He had defended the agreement with Austria and identified himself with the policy of the Government; what more natural than that they should use him to help to carry out the policy he had upheld. Prussia consented to recognise the restoration of the Diet; it would be necessary, therefore, to send an envoy. Now that she had submitted to Austria the only wise policy was to cultivate her friendship. Who could do this better than Bismarck? Who had more boldly supported and praised the new rulers of Austria? When the Gotha party, as they were called, had wished to exclude Austria from Germany, he it was who said that Austria was no more a foreign State than Würtemberg or Bavaria. The appointment of Bismarck would be the best proof of the loyal intentions of the Prussian Government.

A few years later he himself gave to Motley the following account of his appointment:

"In the summer of 1851," Motley writes, "he told me that the Minister, Manteuffel, asked him one day abruptly, if he would accept the post of Ambassador at Frankfort, to which (although the proposition was as unexpected a one to him as if I should hear by the next mail that I had been chosen Governor of Massachusetts) he answered, after a moment's deliberation, 'yes,' with out another word. The King, the same day, sent for him, and asked him if he would accept the place, to which he made the same brief answer, 'Ja.' His Majesty expressed a little surprise that he made no inquiries or conditions, when Bismarck replied that anything which the King felt strong enough to propose to him, he felt strong enough to accept. I only write these details, that you may have an idea of the man. Strict integrity and courage of character, a high sense of honour, a firm religious belief, united with remarkable talents, make up necessarily a combination which cannot be found any day in any Court; and I have no doubt that he is destined to be Prime Minister, unless his obstinate truthfulness, which is apt to be a stumbling-block for politicians, stands in his way."

CHAPTER V.

FRANKFORT.

1851-1857.

Bismarck when he went to Frankfort was thirty-six years of age; he had had no experience in diplomacy and had long been unaccustomed to the routine of official life. He had distinguished himself by qualities which might seem very undiplomatic; as a Parliamentary debater he had been outspoken in a degree remarkable even during a revolution; he had a habit of tearing away the veil from those facts which everyone knows and which all wish to ignore; a careless good-fellowship which promised little of that reserve and discretion so necessary in a confidential agent; a personal and wilful independence which might easily lead him into disagreement with the Ministers and the King. He had not even the advantage of learning his work by apprenticeship under a more experienced official; during the first two months at Frankfort he held the position of First Secretary, but his chief did not attempt to introduce him to the more important negotiations and when, at the end of July, he received his definite appointment as envoy, he knew as little of the work as when he arrived at Frankfort.

He had, however, occupied his time in becoming acquainted with the social conditions. His first impressions were very unfavourable. Frankfort held a peculiar position. Though the centre of the German political system it was less German than any other town in the country. The society was very cosmopolitan. There were the envoys of the German States and the foreign Powers, but the diplomatic circle was not graced by the dignity of a Court nor by the neighbourhood of any great administrative Power. Side by side with the diplomatists were the citizens of Frankfort; but here again we find indeed a great money-market, the centre of the finance of the Continent, dissociated from any great productive activity. In the neighbourhood were the watering-places and gambling-tables; Homburg and Wiesbaden, Soden and Baden-Baden, were within an easy ride or short railway journey, and Frankfort was constantly visited by all the idle Princes of Germany. It was a city in which intrigue took the place of statesmanship, and never has intrigue played so large a part in the history of Europe as during the years 1850-1870. Half the small States who were represented at Frankfort had ambitions beyond their powers; they liked to play their part in the politics of Europe. Too weak to stand alone, they were also too weak to be quite honest, and attempted to gain by cunning a position which they could not maintain by other means. This was the city in which Bismarck was to serve his diplomatic apprenticeship.

Two extracts from letters to his wife give the best picture of his personal character at this time:

"On Saturday I drove with Rochow to Rüdesheim; there I took a boat and rowed out on the Rhine, and bathed in the moonlight--only nose and eyes above the water, and floated down to the Rat Tower at Bingen, where the wicked Bishop met his end. It is something strangely dreamlike to lie in the water in the quiet, warm light, gently carried along by the stream; to look at the sky with the moon and stars above one, and, on either side, to see the wooded mountain-tops and castle parapets in the moonlight, and to hear nothing but the gentle rippling of one's own motion. I

should like a swim like this every evening. Then I drank some very good wine, and sat long talking with Lynar on the balcony, with the Rhine beneath us. My little Testament and the starry heavens brought us on Christian topics, and I long shook at the Rousseau-like virtue of his soul."
"Yesterday I was at Wiesbaden, and with a feeling of melancholy revisited the scenes of former folly. May it please God to fill with His clear and strong wine this vessel in which the champagne of twenty-one years foamed so uselessly.... I do not understand how a man who reflects on himself, and still knows, and will know, nothing of God, can endure his life for contempt and weariness. I do not know how I endured this in old days; if, as then, I were to live without God, thee, and the children, I do not know why I should not put life aside like a dirty shirt; and yet most of my acquaintances live thus."

Now let us see what he thinks of his new duties:

"Our intercourse here is at best nothing but a mutual suspicion and espionage; if only there was anything to spy out and to hide! It is pure trifles with which they worry themselves, and I find these diplomatists with their airs of confidence and their petty fussiness much more absurd than the member of the Second Chamber in his conscious dignity. Unless some external events take place, and we clever men of the Diet can neither direct nor foresee them, I know already what we shall bring about in one or two or three years, and will do it in twenty-four hours if the others will only be reasonable and truthful for a single day. I am making tremendous progress in the art of saying nothing in many words; I write reports many pages long, which are smooth and finished like leading articles, and if Manteuffel after reading them can say what they contain, he can do more than I. We all do as though we believed of each other that we are full of thoughts and plans, if only we would express them, and all the time we none of us know a hair's breadth more what will become of Germany."

Of the Austrian Envoy who was President of the Diet he writes:

"Thun in his outward appearance has something of a hearty good fellow mixed with a touch of the Vienna roué. Underneath this he hides, I will not say great political power and intellectual gifts, but an uncommon cleverness and cunning, which with great presence of mind appears from underneath the mask of harmless good-humour as soon as politics are concerned. I consider him as an opponent who is dangerous to anyone who honestly trusts him, instead of paying back in his own coin."

His judgment on his other colleagues is equally decisive; of the Austrian diplomatists he writes:

"one must never expect that they will make what is right the foundation of their policy for the simple reason that it is the right. Cautious dishonesty is the characteristic of their association with us. They have nothing which awakens confidence. They intrigue under the mask of good-fellowship."

It was impossible to look for open co-operation from them;

"their mouths are full of the necessity for common action, but when it is a question of furthering our wishes, then officially it is, 'We will not oppose,' and a secret pleasure in preparing obstacles."

It was just the same with the envoys of the other countries: with few exceptions there is none for whom right has any value in itself.

"They are caricatures of diplomatists who put on their official physiognomy if I ask them for a light, and select gestures and words with a truly Regensburg caution, if they ask for the key of the water-closet." Writing to Gerlach he speaks of "the lying, double-tongued policy of the Austrians. Of all the lies and intrigues that go on up and down the Rhine an honest man from the old Mark has no conception. These South German children of nature are very corrupt."

His opinion of the diplomatists does not seem to have improved as he knew them better. Years later he wrote:

"There are few diplomatists who in the long run do not prefer to capitulate with their conscience and their patriotism, and to guard the interests of their country and their sovereign with somewhat less decision, rather than, incessantly and with danger to their personal position, to contend with the difficulties which are prepared for them by a powerful and unscrupulous enemy."

He does not think much better of his own Prussian colleagues; he often complains of the want of support which he received. "With us the official diplomacy," he writes, "is capable of playing under the same roof with strangers against their own countrymen."

These letters are chiefly interesting because of the light they throw on his own character at the beginning of his diplomatic career; we must not take them all too seriously. He was too good a raconteur not to make a good story better, and too good a letter-writer not to add something to the effect of his descriptions; besides, as he says elsewhere, he did not easily see the good side of people; his eyes were sharper for their faults than their good qualities. [4] After the first few passages of arms he got on well enough with Thun; when he was recalled two years later Bismarck spoke of him with much warmth. "I like him personally, and should be glad to have him for a neighbour at Schönhausen."

It is however important to notice that the first impression made on him by diplomatic work was that of wanton and ineffective deceit. Those who accuse him, as is so often done, of lowering the standard of political morality which prevails in Europe, know little of politics as they were at the time when Schwarzenberg was the leading statesman.

It was his fate at once to be brought in close contact with the most disagreeable side of political life. In all diplomatic work there must be a good deal of espionage and underhand dealing. This was a part of his duties which Bismarck had soon to learn. He was entrusted with the management of the Press. This consisted of two parts: first of all, he had to procure the insertion of articles in influential papers in a sense agreeable to the plans of the Prussian Government; secondly, when hostile articles appeared, or inconvenient information was published, he had to trace the authors of it,—find out by whom the obnoxious paper had been inspired, or who had conveyed the secret information. This is a form of activity of which it is of course not possible to give any full account; it seems, however, clear that in a remarkably short time Bismarck shewed great aptitude for his new duties. His letters to Manteuffel are full of curious information as to the intrigues of those who are hostile to Prussia. He soon learns to distrust the information supplied by the police; all through his life he had little respect for this department of the Prussian State. He soon had agents of his own. We find him gaining secret information as to the plans of the Ultramontane party in Baden from a compositor at Freiburg who was in his pay. On other occasions, when a Court official at Berlin had conveyed to the newspapers private information, Bismarck was soon able to trace him out. We get the impression, both from his letters and from what other information we possess, that all the diplomatists of Germany were constantly occupied in calumniating one another through anonymous contributions to a venal Press.

It is characteristic of the customs of the time that he had to warn his wife that all her letters to him would be read in the post-office before he received them. It was not only the Austrians who used these methods; each of the Prussian Ministers would have his own organ which he would use for his own purposes, and only too probably to attack his own colleagues. It was at this time that a curious fact came to light with regard to Herr von Prokesch-Osten, the Austrian Ambassador at Berlin. He had been transferred from Berlin to Frankfort, and on leaving his house sold some of his furniture. In a chest of drawers was found a large bundle of papers consisting of newspaper articles in his handwriting, which had been communicated to different papers, attacking the Prussian Government, to which he at the time was accredited. Of Prokesch it is that Bismarck once writes: "As to his statements I do not know how much you will find to be Prokesch, and how much to be true." On another occasion, before many witnesses, Bismarck had disputed some statement he made. "If it is not true," cried Prokesch, "then I should have lied in the name of the Royal and Imperial Government." "Certainly," answered Bismarck. There was a dead pause in the conversation.

Prokesch afterwards officially admitted that the statement had been incorrect.

This association with the Press formed in him a habit of mind which he never lost: the proper use of newspapers seemed to him, as to most German statesmen, to be not the expression of public opinion but the support of the Government; if a paper is opposed to the Government, the assumption seems to be that it is bribed by some other State.

"The whole country would rejoice if some of the papers which are supported by foreign sources were suppressed, with the express recognition of their unpatriotic attitude. There may be opposition in the internal affairs, but a paper which in Prussia takes part against the policy of the King on behalf of foreign countries, must be regarded as dishonoured and treated as such."

Politically his position was very difficult; the Diet had been restored by Austria against the will of Prussia; the very presence of a Prussian Envoy in Frankfort was a sign of her humiliation. He had indeed gone there full of friendly dispositions towards Austria; he was instructed to take up again the policy which had been pursued before 1848, when all questions of importance had been discussed by the two great Powers before they were laid before the Diet. Bismarck, however, quickly found that this was no longer the intention of Austria; the Austria which he had so chivalrously defended at Berlin did not exist; he had expected to find a warm and faithful friend—he found a cunning and arrogant enemy. Schwarzenberg had spared Prussia but he intended to humble her; he wished to use the Diet as a means of permanently asserting the supremacy of Austria, and he would not be content until Prussia had been forced like Saxony or Bavaria to acquiesce in the position of a vassal State. The task might not seem impossible, for Prussia appeared to be on the downward path.

Of course the Diet of Frankfort was the place where the plan had to be carried out; it seemed an admirable opportunity that Prussia was represented there by a young and untried man. Count Thun and his successors used every means to make it appear as though Prussia was a State not of equal rank with Austria. They carried the war into society and, as diplomatists always will, used the outward forms of social intercourse as a means for obtaining political ends. On this field, Bismarck was quite capable of meeting them. He has told many stories of their conflicts.

As President of the Diet, Thun claimed privileges for himself which others did not dare to dispute.

"In the sittings of the military commission when Rochow was Prussian envoy, Austria alone smoked. Rochow, who was a passionate smoker, would also have gladly done so, but did not venture. When I came I did not see any reason against it; and asked for a light from the Presiding State; this seemed to be noticed with astonishment and displeasure by him and the other gentlemen; it was obviously an event for them. This time only Austria and Prussia smoked. But the others obviously held it so important that they sent home a report on it. Someone must have written about it to Berlin, as a question from the late King arrived; he did not smoke himself and probably did not find the affair to his taste. It required much consideration at the smaller Courts, and for quite half a year only the two great Powers smoked. Then Schrenk, the Bavarian envoy, began to maintain the dignity of his position by smoking. The Saxon Nostitz would doubtless have liked to begin too, but I suppose he had not yet received permission from his Minister. But when next time he saw that Bothmer, the Hanoverian, allowed himself a cigar, he must have come to an understanding with his neighbour (he was a good Austrian, and had sons in the Austrian army), for he brought out his pouch and lit up. There remained only the Würtemberger and the Darmstadter, and they did not smoke at all, but the honour and the importance of their States required it, and so on the following day the Würtemberger really brought out his cigar. I can see him with it now, a long, thin, yellow thing, the colour of rye-straw,--and with sulky determination, as a sacrifice for his Swabian fatherland, he smoked at least half of it. Hesse-Darmstadt alone refrained."

On another occasion Thun received Bismarck in his shirt sleeves: "You are quite right," said Bismarck, "it is very hot," and took off his own coat.

In the transaction of business he found the same thing. The plan seemed to be deliberately to adopt a policy disadvantageous to Prussia, to procure the votes of a majority of the States, thereby to cause Prussia to be outvoted, and to leave her in the dilemma of accepting a decision which was harmful to herself or of openly breaking with the Federation. On every matter which came up the same scenes repeated themselves; now it was the disposal of the fleet, which had to a great extent been provided for and maintained by Prussian money; Austria demanded that it should be regarded as the property of the Confederation even though most of the States had never paid their contribution. Then it was the question of the Customs' Union; a strong effort was made by the anti-Prussian party to overthrow the union which Prussia had established and thereby ruin the one great work which she had achieved. Against these and similar attempts Bismarck had constantly to be on the defensive. Another time it was the publication of the proceedings of the Diet which the Austrians tried to make a weapon against Prussia. The whole intercourse became nothing but a series of disputes, sometimes serious, sometimes trivial.

Bismarck was soon able to hold his own; poor Count Thun, whose nerves were not strong, after a serious discussion with him used to go to bed at five o'clock in the afternoon; he complained that his health would not allow him to hold his post if there were to be continuous quarrels. When his successor, Herr v. Prokesch, left Frankfort for Constantinople, he said that "it would be like an Eastern dream of the blessed to converse with the wise Ali instead of Bismarck."

As soon as the first strangeness had passed off Bismarck became reconciled to his position. His wife and children joined him, he made himself a comfortable home, and his house soon became one of the most popular in the town; he and his wife were genial and hospitable and he used his position to extend his own influence and that of his country. His old friend, Motley, visited him there in 1855 and wrote to his wife:

"FRANKFORT,

"Monday, July 30, 1855.

" ... The Bismarcks are as kind as ever--nothing can be more frank and cordial than her manners. I am there all day long. It is one of those houses where everyone does what he likes. The show apartments where they receive formal company are on the front of the house. Their living rooms, however, are a salon and dining-room at the back, opening upon the garden. Here there are young and old, grandparents and children and dogs all at once, eating, drinking, smoking, piano-playing, and pistol-firing (in the garden), all going on at the same time. It is one of those establishments where every earthly thing that can be eaten or drunk is offered you; porter, soda water, small beer, champagne, burgundy, or claret are about all the time, and everybody is smoking the best Havana cigars every minute."

He had plenty of society, much of it congenial to him. He had given up playing since his marriage, and was one of the few diplomatists who was not found at the Homburg gaming-tables, but he had a sufficiency of sport and joined with the British envoy, Sir Alexander Malet, in taking some shooting. A couple of years later in contradicting one of the frequent newspaper reports, that he aimed at supplanting the Minister, he says:

"My castle in the air is to spend three to five years longer at Frankfort, then perhaps the same time in Vienna or Paris, then ten years with glory as Minister, then die as a country gentleman."

A prospect which has been more nearly fulfilled than such wishes generally are.

He was for the first year still a member of the Second Chamber and occasionally appeared in it; his interest in his diplomatic work had, however, begun to overshadow his pleasure in Parliamentary debate.

"I am thoroughly tired of my life here," he writes in May, 1853, to his wife from Berlin, "and long for the day of my departure. I find the intrigues of the House immeasurably shallow and undignified; if one always lives among them, one deceives oneself and considers them something wonderful. When I come here from Frankfort and see them as they really are, I feel like a sober man who has fallen among drunkards. There is something very demoralising in the air of the Chambers; it makes the best people vain without their knowing it."

So quickly has he outgrown his feelings of a year ago: then it was the intrigues of diplomatists that had seemed to him useless and demoralising. Now it was Parliamentary debates; in the opinion he formed at this time he never wavered.

His distaste for Parliamentary life was probably increased by an event which took place about this time. As so often before in the course of debate he had a sharp passage of words with Vincke; the latter referred contemptuously to Bismarck's diplomatic achievements. "All I know of them is the famous lighted cigar."

Bismarck answered with some angry words and at the close of the sitting sent a challenge. Four days later a duel with pistols took place—the only one he ever fought. Neither was injured. It seems that Vincke, who had the first shot, seeing that Bismarck (who had received the sacrament the night before) was praying, missed on purpose; Bismarck then shot into the air.

For these reasons he did not stand for re-election when the Chamber was dissolved in 1852, although the King was very much displeased with his determination. He was shortly afterwards appointed member of the newly constituted House of Lords, but though he occasionally voted, as in duty bound, for Government measures, he never spoke; he was not to be heard again in the Parliament until he appeared there as President of the Ministry. He was glad to be freed from a tie which had interfered with his duties at Frankfort; to these he devoted himself with an extraordinary energy; all his old repugnance to official life had disappeared; he did not confine himself to the mere routine of his duties, or to carrying out the instructions sent to him from Berlin.

His power of work was marvellous: there passed through his hands a constant series of most important and complicated negotiations; up to this time he had no experience or practice in sedentary literary work, now he seems to go out of the way to make fresh labours for himself. He writes long and careful despatches to his Minister on matters of general policy; some of them so carefully thought out and so clearly expressed that they may still be looked on as models. He is entirely free from that circumlocution and involved style which makes so much diplomatic correspondence almost worthless. His arguments are always clear, complete, concise. He used to work long into the night, and then, when in the early morning the post to Berlin had gone, he would mount his horse and ride out into the country. It was in these years that he formed those habits to which the breakdown of his health in later years was due; but now his physical and intellectual vigour seemed inexhaustible.

He never feared to press his own views as to the policy which should be pursued. He also kept up a constant correspondence with Gerlach, and many of these letters were laid before the King, so that even when absent he continued as before to influence both the official and unofficial advisers. He soon became the chief adviser on German affairs and was often summoned to Berlin that his advice might be taken; within two years after his appointment he was sent on a special mission to Vienna to try and bring about an agreement as to the rivalry concerning the Customs' Union. He failed, but he had gained a knowledge of persons and opinions at the Austrian Court which was to be of much use to him.

During these years, indeed, he acquired a most remarkable knowledge of Germany; before, he had lived entirely in Prussia, now he was at the centre of the German political system, continually engaged in important negotiations with the other Courts; after a few years there was not a man of importance in German public life whose character and opinions he had not gauged.

Further experience only confirmed in him the observations he had made at the beginning, that it was impossible to maintain a good understanding with Austria. The tone of his letters soon changes from doubt and disappointment to settled and determined hostility. In other matters also he found that the world was not the same place it had seemed to him; he had been accustomed to regard the Revolution as the chief danger to be met; at Frankfort he was in the home of it; here for nearly a year the German Assembly had held its meetings; in the neighbouring States of Baden, Hesse, and in the Palatinate, the Republican element was strong; he found them as revolutionary as ever, but he soon learnt to despise rather than fear them:

"The population here would be a political volcano if revolutions were made with the mouth; so long as it requires blood and strength they will obey anyone who has courage to command and, if necessary, to draw the sword; they would be dangerous only under cowardly governments. "I have never seen two men fighting in all the two years I have been here. This cowardice does not prevent the people, who are completely devoid of all inner Christianity and all respect for authority, from sympathising with the Revolution."

His observations on the character of the South Germans only increased his admiration for the Prussian people and his confidence in the Prussian State.

He had not been at Frankfort a year before he had learnt to look on this hostility of Austria as unsurmountable. As soon as he had convinced himself of this, he did not bewail and bemoan the desertion of their ally; he at once accustomed himself to the new position and considered in what way the Government ought to act. His argument was simple. Austria is now our enemy; we must be prepared to meet this enmity either by diplomacy or war; we are not strong enough to do so alone; therefore we must have allies. There was no sure alliance to be had in Germany; he despised the other German States. If there were to be a war he would rather have them against him than on his side. He must find help abroad; Austria had overcome Prussia by the alliance with Russia. Surely the only thing to be done was to seek support where it could be got, either with Russia or with France, if possible with both. In this he was only reverting to the old policy of Prussia; the alliance with Austria had only begun in 1813. From now until 1866 his whole policy was ceaselessly devoted to bringing about such a disposition of the forces of Europe that Austria might be left without allies and Prussia be able to regain the upper hand in German affairs.

The change was in his circumstances, not in his character; as before he was moved by a consuming passion of patriotism; something there was too of personal feeling,—his own pride, his own ambitions were engaged, though this was as nothing compared to love of his country and loyalty to the King. He was a soldier of the Prussian Crown: at Berlin he had to defend it against internal enemies; now the danger had shifted, the power of the Government was established, why waste time in fighting with Liberalism? Other enemies were pressing on. When Jellachich and Windischgätz had stood victorious by the blood-stained altar of St. Stephen's, the Austrian army had destroyed the common foe; now it was the same Austrian army and Austrian statesmen who desired to put a limit to Prussian ambition. Bismarck threw himself into the conflict of diplomacy with the same courage and relentless persistence that he had shewn in Parliamentary debates. He had already begun to divine that the time might come when the Prussian Crown would find an ally in Italian patriots and Hungarian rebels.

It was the Eastern complications which first enabled him to shew his diplomatic abilities in the larger field of European politics. The plans for the dismemberment of the Turkish Empire which were entertained by the Czar were opposed by England, France, and Austria; Prussia, though not immediately concerned, also at first gave her assent to the various notes and protests of the Powers; so that the ambition of the Czar was confronted by the unanimous voice of Europe.

Bismarck from the beginning regarded the situation with apprehension; he saw that Prussia was being entangled in a struggle in which she had much to lose and nothing to gain. If she continued to support the Western Powers she would incur the hatred of Russia; then, perhaps, by a sudden change of policy on the part of Napoleon, she would be left helpless and exposed to Russian vengeance. If war were to break out, and Prussia took part in the war, then the struggle between France and Russia would be fought out on German soil, and, whoever was victorious, Germany would be the loser. What interests of theirs were at stake that they should incur this danger? why should Prussia sacrifice herself to preserve English influence in the Mediterranean, or the interests of Austria on the Danube? He wished for exactly the opposite policy; the embarrassment of Austria must be the opportunity of Prussia; now was the time to recover the lost position in Germany. The dangerous friendship of Austria and Russia was dissolved; if Prussia came to an understanding with the Czar, it was now Austria that would be isolated. The other German States would not desire to be dragged into a war to support Austrian dominion in the East. Let Prussia be firm and they would turn to her for support, and she would once more be able to command a majority of the Diet.

For these reasons he recommended his Government to preserve an armed neutrality, in union, if possible, with the other German States. If they were to take sides, he preferred it should not be with the Western Powers, for, as he said,—

"We must look abroad for allies, and among the European Powers Russia is to be had on the cheapest terms; it wishes only to grow in the East, the two others at our expense."

It shews the advance he had made in diplomacy that throughout his correspondence he never refers to the actual cause of dispute; others might discuss the condition of the Christians in Turkey or the Holy Places of Jerusalem; he thinks only of the strength and weakness of his own State. The opening of the Black Sea, the dismemberment of Turkey, the control of the Mediterranean, the fate of the Danubian Principalities—for all this he cared nothing, for in them Prussia had no interests; they only existed for him so far as the new combinations among the Powers might for good or evil affect Prussia.

The crisis came in 1854: a Russian army occupied Moldavia and Wallachia; England and France sent their fleets to the Black Sea; they determined on war and they wished for the alliance of Austria. Austria was inclined to join, for the presence of Russian troops on the Danube was a menace to her; she did not dare to move unless supported by Prussia and Germany; she appealed to the Confederacy and urged that her demands might be supported by the armies of her allies; but the German States were little inclined to send the levies of their men for the Eastern interests of the Emperor. If they were encouraged by Prussia, they would refuse; the result in Germany, as in Europe, depended on the action of Prussia, and the decision lay with the King.

Was Prussia to take part with Russia or the Western Powers? That was the question which for many months was debated at Berlin.

The public opinion of the nation was strong for the Western Powers; they feared the influence of Russia on the internal affairs of Germany; they had not forgotten or forgiven the part which the Czar had taken in 1849; the choice seemed to lie between Russia and England, between liberty and despotism, between civilisation and barbarism. On this side also were those who wished to maintain the alliance with Austria. Russia had few friends except at the Court and in the army, but the party of the Kreuz Zeitung, the Court Camarilla, the princes and nobles who commanded the Garde Corps, wished for nothing better than a close alliance with the great Emperor who had saved Europe from the Revolution. "Let us draw our sword openly in defence of Russia," they said, "then we may bring Austria with us; the old alliance of the three monarchies will be restored, and then will be the time for a new crusade against France, the natural enemy of Germany, and the upstart Emperor."

The conflict of parties was keenest in the precincts of the Court; society in Berlin was divided between the Russian and the English; the Queen was hot for Russia, but the English party rallied round the Prince of Prussia and met in the salons of his wife. Between the two the King wavered; he was, as always, more influenced by feeling than by calculation, but his feelings were divided. How could he decide between Austria and Russia, the two ancient allies of his house? He loved and reverenced the Czar; he feared and distrusted Napoleon; alliance with infidels against Christians was to him a horrible thought, but he knew how violent were the actions and lawless the desires of Nicholas. He could not ignore the opinions of Western Europe and he wished to stand well with England. The men by whose advice he was guided stood on opposite sides: Bunsen was for England, Gerlach for Russia; the Ministry also was divided. No efforts were spared to influence him; the Czar and Napoleon each sent special envoys to his Court; the Queen of England and her husband warned him not to forget his duty to Europe and humanity; if he would join the allies there would be no war. Still he wavered; "he goes to bed an Englishman and gets up a Russian," said the Czar, who despised his brother-in-law as much as he was honoured by him.

While the struggle was at its height, Bismarck was summoned to Berlin, that his opinion might also be heard. At Berlin and at Letzlingen he had frequent interviews with the King. In later years he described the situation he found there:

"It was nothing strange, according to the custom of those days, that half a dozen ambassadors should be living in hotels intriguing against the policy of the Minister."

He found Berlin divided into two parties: the one looked to the Czar as their patron and protector, the other wished to win the approval of England; he missed a reasonable conviction as to what was the interest of Prussia. His own advice was against alliance with the Western Powers or Austria; better join Russia than England; better still, preserve neutrality and hold the balance of Europe. He had the reputation of being very Russian, but he protested against the term. "I am not Russian," he said, "but Prussian." He spoke with great decision against the personal adherents of the King, men who looked to the Czar rather than to their own sovereign, and carried their subservience even to treason. As in former days, courage he preached and resolution. Some talked of the danger of isolation; "With 400,000 men we cannot be isolated," he said. The French envoy warned him that his policy might lead to another Jena; "Why not to Waterloo?" he answered. Others talked of the danger of an English blockade of their coasts; he pointed out that this would injure England more than Prussia.

"Let us be bold and depend on our own strength; let us frighten Austria by threatening an alliance with Russia, frighten Russia by letting her think we may join the Western Powers; if it were true that we could never side with Russia, at least we must retain the possibility of threatening to do so."

The result was what we might expect from the character of the King; unable to decide for either of the contending factors, he alternated between the two, and gave his support now to one, now to the other. In March, when Bismarck was still in Berlin, sudden disgrace fell upon the English party; Bunsen was recalled from London, Bonin, their chief advocate in the Ministry, was dismissed; when the Prince of Prussia, the chief patron of the Western alliance, protested, he was included in the act of disfavour, and had to leave Berlin, threatened with the loss of his offices and even with arrest. All danger of war with Russia seemed to have passed; Bismarck returned content to Frankfort. Scarcely had he gone when the old affection for Austria gained the upper hand, and by a separate treaty Prussia bound herself to support the Austrian demands, if necessary by arms. Bismarck heard nothing of the treaty till it was completed; the Ministers had purposely refrained from asking his advice on a policy which they knew he would disapprove. He overcame his feelings of disgust so far as to send a cold letter of congratulation to Manteuffel; to Gerlach he wrote:

"His Majesty should really see to it that his Ministers should drink more champagne; none of the gentry ought to enter his Council without half a bottle under his belt. Our policy would soon get a respectable colour."

The real weakness lay, as he well knew, in the character of the King. "If here I say to one of my colleagues, 'We remain firm even if Austria drives matters to a breach,' he laughs in my face and says, 'As long as the King lives it will not come to a war between Austria and Prussia.'" And again, "The King has as much leniency for the sins of Austria as I hope to have from the Lord in Heaven."

It was a severe strain on his loyalty, but he withstood it; he has, I believe, never expressed his opinion about the King; we can guess what it must have been. It was a melancholy picture: a King violent and timid, obstinate and irresolute; his will dragged now this way, now that, by his favourites, his wife and his brother; his own Ministers intriguing against each other; ambassadors recommending a policy instead of carrying out their instructions; and the Minister-President standing calmly by, as best he could, patching up the appearance of a Consistent policy.

It was probably the experience which he gained at this time which in later years, when he himself had become Minister, made Bismarck so jealous of outside and irresponsible advisers; he did not choose to occupy the position of Manteuffel, he laid down the rule that none of his own subordinates should communicate with the King except through himself; a Bismarck as Foreign Minister would not allow a Gerlach at Court, nor a Bismarck among his envoys. He had indeed been careful not to intrigue against his chief, but it was impossible to observe that complete appearance of acquiescence which a strong and efficient Minister must demand. Bismarck was often asked his opinion by the King directly; he was obliged to say what he believed to be the truth, and he often disapproved of that which Manteuffel advised. In order to avoid the appearance of disloyalty, he asked Gerlach that his letters should be shewn to Manteuffel; not all of them could be shewn, still less would it be possible to repeat all he said. If they were in conflict, his duty to the King must override his loyalty to the Minister, and the two could not always be reconciled. To Englishmen indeed it appears most improper that the

King should continually call for the advice of other politicians without the intervention or the knowledge of his Ministers, but this is just one of those points on which it is impossible to apply to Prussian practice English constitutional theory. In England it is a maxim of the Constitution that the sovereign should never consult anyone on political matters except the responsible Ministry; this is possible only because the final decision rests with Parliament and the Cabinet and not with the sovereign. It was, however, always the contention of Bismarck that the effective decision in Prussia was with the King. This was undoubtedly the true interpretation of the Prussian Constitution; but it followed from this that the King must have absolute freedom to ask the advice of everyone whose opinions would be of help to him; he must be able to command the envoys to foreign countries to communicate with him directly, and if occasion required it, to consult with the political opponents of his own Ministers. To forbid this and to require that all requests should come to him by the hands of the Ministers would be in truth to substitute ministerial autocracy for monarchical government.

Something of this kind did happen in later years when the German Emperor had grown old, and when Bismarck, supported by his immense experience and success, guided the policy of the country alone, independent of Parliament, and scarcely allowing any independent adviser to approach the Emperor. This was exceptional; normally a Prussian Minister had to meet his opponents and critics not so much in public debate as in private discussion. Under a weak sovereign the policy of the country must always be distracted by palace intrigue, just as in England under a weak Cabinet it will be distracted by party faction. The Ministers must always be prepared to find their best-laid schemes overthrown by the influence exerted upon the royal mind by his private friends or even by his family. It may be said that tenure of office under these conditions would be impossible to a man of spirit; it was certainly very difficult; an able and determined Minister was as much hampered by this private opposition as by Parliamentary discussion. It is often the fashion to say that Parliamentary government is difficult to reconcile with a strong foreign policy; the experiences of Prussia from the year 1815 to 1863 seem to shew that under monarchical government it is equally difficult.

Meanwhile he had been maturing in his mind a bolder plan: Why should not Prussia gain the support she required by alliance with Napoleon?

The Germans had watched the rise of Napoleon with suspicion and alarm; they had long been taught that France was their natural enemy. When Napoleon seized the power and assumed the name of Emperor, the old distrust was revived; his very name recalled memories of hostility; they feared he would pursue an ambitious and warlike policy; that he would withdraw the agreements on which the peace of Europe and the security of the weaker States depended, and that he would extend to the Rhine the borders of France. He was the first ruler of France whose internal policy awoke no sympathy in Germany; his natural allies, the Liberals, he had alienated by the overthrow of the Republic, and he gained no credit for it in the eyes of the Conservatives. The monarchical party in Prussia could only have admiration for the man who had imprisoned a Parliament and restored absolute government; they could not repudiate an act which they would gladly imitate, but they could not forgive him that he was an usurper.

According to their creed the suppression of liberty was the privilege of the legitimate King.

It was the last remnant of the doctrine of legitimacy, the belief that it was the duty of the European monarchs that no State should change its form of government or the dynasty by which it was ruled; the doctrine of the Holy Alliance that kings must make common cause against the Revolution. How changed were the times from the days when Metternich had used this as a strong support for the ascendancy of the House of Austria! Austria herself was no longer sound; the old faith lingered only in St. Petersburg and Berlin; but how weak and ineffective it had become! There was no talk now of interference, there would not be another campaign of Waterloo or of Valmy; there was only a prudish reserve; they could not, they did not dare, refuse diplomatic dealings with the new Emperor, but they were determined there should be no cordiality: the virgin purity of the Prussian Court should not be deflowered by intimacy with the man of sin. [5] If there could not be a fresh crusade against Buonapartism, at least, there should be no alliance with it.

From the beginning Bismarck had little sympathy with this point of view; he regarded the coup d'état as necessary in a nation which had left the firm ground of legitimacy; France could not be governed except by an iron hand. As a Prussian, however, he could not be pleased, for he saw an enemy who had been weak strengthened, but he did not believe in Napoleon's warlike desires. In one way it was an advantage,—the overthrow of the Republic had broken the bond which joined the German revolutionists to France. He did not much mind what happened in other countries so long as Prussia was safe.

There is no ground for surprise that he soon began to go farther; he warned his friends not to irritate the Emperor; on the occasion of the Emperor's marriage the Kreuz Zeitung published a violent article, speaking of it as an insult and threat to Prussia. Bismarck's feelings as a gentleman were offended by this useless scolding; it seemed, moreover, dangerous. If Prussia were to quarrel with France, they would be obliged to seek the support of the Eastern Powers: if Russia and Austria should know this, Prussia would be in their hands. The only effect of this attitude would be to cut off the possibility of a useful move in the game of diplomacy:

"There is no good in giving our opposition to France the stamp of irrevocability; it would be no doubt a great misfortune if we were to unite ourselves with France, but why proclaim this to all the world? We should do wiser to act so that Austria and Russia would have to court our friendship against France than treat us as an ally who is presented to them."

It is a topic to which he often refers:

"We cannot make an alliance with France without a certain degree of meanness, but very admirable people, even German princes, in the Middle Ages have used a sewer to make their escape, rather than be beaten or throttled."

An alliance with Napoleon was, however, according to the code of honour professed, if not followed, in every German State, the sin for which there was no forgiveness. It was but a generation ago that half the German princes had hurried to the Court of the first Napoleon to receive at his hands the estates of their neighbours and the liberties of their subjects. No one doubted that the new Napoleon would be willing to use similar means to ensure the power of France; would he meet with willing confederates? The Germans, at least, do not seem to have trusted one another; no prince dared show ordinary courtesy to the ruling family of France, no statesman could visit Paris but voices would be heard crying that he had sold himself and his country. An accusation of this kind was the stock-in-trade which the Nationalist press was always ready to bring against every ruler who was obnoxious to them. It required moral courage, if it also shewed political astuteness, when Bismarck proposed deliberately to encourage a suspicion from which most men were anxious that their country should be free. He had already plenty of enemies, and reports were soon heard that he was in favour of a French alliance; they did not cease for ten years; he often protests in his private letters against these unworthy accusations; the protests seem rather absurd, for if he did not really wish for an alliance between Prussia and France, he at least wished that people should dread such an alliance. A man cannot frighten his friends by the fear he will rob them, and at the same time enjoy the reputation for strict probity.

He explains with absolute clearness the benefits which will come from a French alliance:

"The German States are attentive and attracted to us in the same degree in which they believe we are befriended by France. Confidence in us they will never have, every glance at the map prevents that; and they know that their separate interests and the misuse of their sovereignty always stand in the way of the whole tendency of Prussian policy. They clearly recognise the danger which lies in this; it is one against which the unselfishness of our Most Gracious Master alone gives them a temporary security. The opinions of the King, which ought at least for a time to weaken their mistrust, will gain his Majesty no thanks; they will only be used and exploited. In the hour of necessity gratitude and confidence will not bring a single man into the field. Fear, if it is used with foresight and clearness, can place the whole Confederacy at our feet, and in order to instil fear into them we must give clear signs of our good relations with France."

He objected to Prussia following what was called a German policy, for, as he said, by a national and patriotic policy is meant that Prussia should do what was for the interest, not of herself, but of the smaller States.

It was not till after the Crimean War that he was able to press this policy. Napoleon had now won his position in Europe; Gerlach had seen with pain and disgust that the Queen of England had visited his Court. The Emperor himself desired a union with Prussia. In this, sympathy and interest combined: he had much affection for Germany; his mind, as his education, was more German than French; he was a man of ideas; he was the only ruler of France who has sincerely desired and deliberately furthered the interests of other countries; he believed that the nation should be the basis of the State; his revolutionary antecedents made him naturally opposed to the House of Austria; and he was ready to help Prussia in resuming her old ambitious policy.

The affair of Neuchâtel gave him an opportunity of earning the personal gratitude of the King, and he did not neglect it, for he knew that in the royal prejudice was the strongest impediment to an alliance. In 1857 Bismarck was sent to Paris to discuss this and other matters. Two years before he had been presented to the Emperor, but it had been at the time when he was opposed to the French policy. Now for the first time the two men who were for ten years to be the leaders, now friends, then rivals, in the realm of diplomacy, were brought into close connection. Bismarck was not impressed by the Emperor's ability. He wrote:

"People exaggerate his intellect, but underrate his heart." Napoleon was very friendly; his wish to help the King went farther than his duty to follow French policy. He said: "Why should we not be friends; let us forget the past; if everyone were to attach himself to a policy of memories, two nations that have once been at war must be at war to all eternity; statesmen must occupy themselves with the future."

This was just Bismarck's opinion; he wrote home suggesting that he might prepare the way for a visit of the Emperor to Prussia; he would like to come and it would have a good effect. This was going farther than the King, grateful though he was, would allow; he told Gerlach not to answer this part of the letter at all while Bismarck was in Paris. Bismarck, however, continued in his official reports and private letters to urge again and again the political advantages of an understanding with France; it is Austria that is the natural enemy, for it is Austria whose interests are opposed to Prussia. If they repel the advance of Napoleon, they will oblige him to seek an alliance with Russia, and this was a danger which even in those days Bismarck never ceased to fear. Prince Napoleon, cousin of the Emperor, was at that time on a visit to Berlin; on his way through Frankfort he had singled out Bismarck, and (no doubt under instructions) had shown great friendliness to him; the Kreuz Zeitung again took the opportunity of insulting the ruler of France; Bismarck again remonstrated against the danger of provoking hostility by these acts of petty rancour, disguised though they might be under the name of principle. He did not succeed in persuading the King or his confidant; he was always met by the same answer: "France is the natural enemy of Germany; Napoleon is the representative of the Revolution; there can be no union between the King of Prussia and the Revolution." "How can a man of your intelligence sacrifice your principles to a single individual?" asks Gerlach, who aimed not at shewing that an alliance with France would be foolish, but that it would be wrong. Five years before, Bismarck would have spoken as Gerlach did; but in these years he had seen and learnt much; he had freed himself from the influence of his early friends; he had outgrown their theoretic formalism; he had learned to look at the world with his own eyes, and to him, defending his country against the intrigues of weaker and the pressure of more powerful States, the world was a different place from what it was to those who passed their time in the shadow of the Court. He remembered that it was not by strict obedience to general principles that Prussia had grown great. Frederick the Second had not allowed himself to be stopped by these narrow searchings of heart; his successor had not scrupled to ally himself with revolutionary France. This rigid insistence on a rule of right, this nice determining of questions of conscience, seemed better suited to the confessor's chair than to the advisers of a great monarch. And the principle to which he was asked to sacrifice the future of his country,—was it after all a true principle? Why should Prussia trouble herself about the internal constitution of other States, what did it concern her whether France was ruled by a Bourbon or an Orleans or a Bonaparte? How could Prussia continue the policy of the Holy Alliance when the close union of the three Eastern monarchies no longer existed? If France were to attack Germany, Prussia could not expect the support of Russia, she could not even be sure of that of Austria. An understanding with France was required, not by ambition, but by the simplest grounds of self-preservation.

These and other considerations he advanced in a long and elaborate memorandum addressed to Manteuffel, which was supplemented by letters to the Minister and Gerlach. For closeness of reasoning, for clearness of expression, for the wealth of knowledge and cogency of argument these are the most remarkable of his political writings. In them he sums up the results of his apprenticeship to political life, he lays down the principles on which the policy of the State ought to be conducted, the principles on which in future years he was himself to act.

"What," he asks, "are the reasons against an alliance with France? The chief ground is the belief that the Emperor is the chief representative of the Revolution and identical with it, and that a compromise with the Revolution is as inadmissible in internal as in external policy." Both statements he triumphantly overthrows. "Why should we look at Napoleon as the representative of the Revolution? there is scarcely a government in Europe which has not a revolutionary origin."

"What is there now existing in the world of politics which has a complete legal basis? Spain, Portugal, Brazil, all the American Republics, Belgium, Holland, Switzerland, Greece, Sweden, England, which State with full consciousness is based on the Revolution of 1688, are all unable to trace back their legal systems to a legitimate origin. Even as to the German princes we cannot find any completely legitimate title for the ground which they have won partly from the Emperor and the Empire, partly from their fellow-princes, partly from the Estates."

He goes farther: the Revolution is not peculiar to France; it did not even originate there:

"It is much older than the historical appearance of Napoleon's family and far wider in its extent than France, If we are to assign it an origin in this world, we must look for it, not in France, but in England, or go back even earlier, even to Germany or Rome, according as we regard the exaggerations of the Reformation or of the Roman Church as responsible."

But if Napoleon is not the sole representative of revolutions, why make opposition to him a matter of principle? He shews no desire of propagandism.

"To threaten other States by means of the Revolution has been for years the trade of England, and this principle of not associating with a revolutionary power is itself quite modern: it is not to be found in the last century. Cromwell was addressed as Brother by European potentates and they sought his friendship when it appeared useful. The most honourable Princes joined in alliance with the States-General before they were recognised by Spain. Why should Prussia now alone, to its own injury, adopt this excessive caution?"

He goes farther: not only does he reject the principle of legitimacy,—he refuses to be bound by any principles; he did not free himself from one party to bind himself to another; his profession was diplomacy and in diplomacy there was no place for feelings of affection and antipathy.

What is the proper use of principles in diplomacy? It is to persuade others to adopt a policy which is convenient to oneself.

"My attitude towards Foreign Governments springs not from any antipathy, but from the good or evil they may do to Prussia." "A policy of sentiment is dangerous, for it is one-sided; it is an exclusively Prussian peculiarity." "Every other Government makes its own interests the sole criterion of its actions, however much it may drape them in phrases about justice and sympathy." "My ideal for foreign policy is freedom from prejudice; that our decisions should be independent of all impressions of dislike or affection for Foreign States and their governments."

This was the canon by which he directed his own actions, and he expected obedience to it from others.

"So far as foreigners go I have never in my life had sympathy for anyone but England and its inhabitants, and I am even now not free from it; but they will not let us love them, and as soon as it was proved to me that it was in the interest of a sound and well-matured Prussian policy, I would let our troops fire on French, English, Russian, or Austrian, with the same satisfaction."

"I cannot justify sympathies and antipathies as regards Foreign Powers and persons before my feeling of duty in the foreign service of my country, either in myself or another; therein lies the embryo of disloyalty against my master or my country. In my opinion not even the King himself has the right to subordinate the interests of his country to his own feelings of love or hatred towards strangers; he is, however, responsible towards God and not to me if he does so, and therefore on this point I am silent."

This reference to the King is very characteristic. Holding, as he did, so high an ideal of public duty himself, he naturally regarded with great dislike the influence which, too often, family ties and domestic affection exercised over the mind of the sovereign. The German Princes had so long pursued a purely domestic policy that they forgot to distinguish between the interests of their families and their land. They were, moreover, naturally much influenced in their public decisions, not only by their personal sympathies, but also by the sympathies and opinions of their nearest relations. To a man like Bismarck, who regarded duty to the State as above everything, nothing could be more disagreeable than to see the plans of professional statesmen criticised by irresponsible people and perhaps overthrown through some woman's whim. He was a confirmed monarchist but he was no courtier. In his letters at this period he sometimes refers to the strong influence which the Princess of Prussia exercised over her husband, who was heir to the throne. He regarded with apprehension the possible effects which the proposed marriage of the Prince of Prussia's son to the Princess Royal of England might have on Prussian policy. He feared it would introduced English influence and Anglomania without their gaining any similar influence in England. "If our future Queen remains in any degree English, I see our Court surrounded by English influence." He was not influenced in this by any hostility to England; almost at the same time he had written that England was the only foreign country for which he had any sympathy. He was only (as so often) contending for that independence and self-reliance which he so admired in the English. For two hundred years English traditions had absolutely forbidden the sovereign to allow his personal and family sympathies to interfere with the interests of the country. If the House of Hohenzollern were to aspire to the position of a national monarch it must act in the same way. At this very time the Emperor Napoleon was discussing the Prussian marriage with Lord Clarendon. "It will much influence the policy of the Queen in favour of Prussia," he said. "No, your Majesty," answered the English Ambassador. "The private feelings of the Queen can never have any influence on that which she believes to be for the honour and welfare of England." This was the feeling by which Bismarck was influenced; he was trying to educate his King, and this was the task to which for many years he was devoted. What he thought of the duties of princes we see from an expression he uses in a letter to Manteuffel: "Only Christianity can make princes what they ought to be, and free them from that conception of life which causes many of them to seek in the position given them by God nothing but the means to a life of pleasure and irresponsibility." All his attempts to win over the King and Gerlach to his point of view failed; the only result was that his old friends began to look on him askance; his new opinions were regarded with suspicion. He was no longer sure of his position in Court; his outspokenness had caused offence; after reading his last letter, Gerlach answered: "Your explanation only shews me that we are now far asunder"; the correspondence, which had continued for almost seven years, stopped. Bismarck felt that he was growing lonely; he had to accustom himself to the thought that the men who had formerly been both politically and personally his close friends, and who had once welcomed him whenever he returned to Berlin, now desired to see him kept at a distance. In one of his last letters to Gerlach, he writes: "I used to be a favourite; now all that is changed. His Majesty has less often the wish to see me; the ladies of the Court have a cooler smile than formerly; the gentlemen press my hand less warmly. The high opinion of my usefulness is sunk, only the Minister [Manteuffel] is warmer and more friendly." Something of this was perhaps exaggerated, but there was no doubt that a breach had begun which was to widen and widen: Bismarck was no longer a member of the party of the Kreuz

Zeitung. It was fortunate that a change was imminent in the direction of the Prussian Government; the old figures who had played their part were to pass away and a new era was to begin.

CHAPTER VI.

ST. PETERSBURG AND PARIS.

1858-1862.

In the autumn of 1857 the health of the King of Prussia broke down; he was unable to conduct the affairs of State and in the month of September was obliged to appoint his brother as his representative to carry on the Government. There was from the first no hope for his recovery; the commission was three times renewed and, after a long delay, in October of the following year, the King signed a decree appointing his brother Regent. At one time, in the spring of 1858, the Prince had, it is said, thought of calling on Bismarck to form a Ministry. This, however, was not done. It was, however, one of the first actions of the Prince Regent to request Manteuffel's resignation; he formed a Ministry of moderate Liberals, choosing as President the Prince of Hohenzollern, head of the Catholic branch of his own family.

The new era, as it was called, was welcomed with delight by all parties except the most extreme Conservatives. No Ministry had been so unpopular as that of Manteuffel. At the elections which took place immediately, the Government secured a large majority. The Prince and his Ministers were able to begin their work with the full support of Parliament and country.

Bismarck did not altogether regret the change; his differences with the dominant faction at Court had extended to the management of home as well as of foreign affairs; for the last two years he had been falling out of favour. He desired, moreover, to see fresh blood in the Chamber.

"The disease to which our Parliamentary life has succumbed, is, besides the incapacity of the individual, the servility of the Lower House. The majority has no independent convictions, it is the tool of ministerial omnipotence. If our Chambers do not succeed in binding the public interest to themselves and drawing the attention of the country, they will sooner or later go to their grave without sympathy."

Curious it is to see how his opinion as to the duties and relations of the House towards the Government were to alter when he himself became Minister. He regarded it as an advantage that the Ministry would have the power which comes from popularity; his only fear was that they might draw the Regent too much to the left; but he hoped that in German and foreign affairs they would act with more decision, that the Prince would be free from the scruples which had so much influenced his brother, and that he would not fear to rely on the military strength of Prussia.

One of their first acts was to recall Bismarck from Frankfort; the change was inevitable, and he had foreseen it. The new Government naturally wished to be able to start clear in their relations to Austria; the Prince Regent did not wish to commit himself from the beginning to a policy of hostility. It was, however, impossible for a cordial co-operation between the two States to be established in German affairs so long as Bismarck remained at Frankfort; the opinions which he had formed during the last eight years were too well known. It was, moreover, evident that a crisis in the relations with Austria was approaching; war between France and Austria was imminent; a new factor and a new man had appeared in Europe,—Piedmont and Cavour.

In August, 1858, Cavour had had a secret and decisive interview with Napoleon at Plombières; the two statesmen had come to an agreement by which France engaged to help the Piedmontese to expel the Austrians from Italy. Bismarck would have desired to seize this opportunity, and use the embarrassment of Austria as the occasion for taking a stronger position in Germany; if it were necessary he was prepared to go as far as an alliance with France. He was influenced not so much by sympathy with Piedmont, for, as we have seen, he held that those who were responsible for foreign policy should never give way to sympathy, but by the simple calculation that Austria was the common enemy of Prussia and Piedmont, and where there were common interests an alliance might be formed. The Government were, however, not prepared to adopt this policy. It might have been supposed that a Liberal Ministry would have shewn more sympathy with the Italian aspirations than the Conservatives whom they had succeeded. This was not the case, as Cavour himself soon found out.

After his visit to Plombières, Cavour had hurried across the frontier and spent two days at Baden-Baden, where he met the Prince of Prussia, Manteuffel, who was still Minister, and other German statesmen. Bismarck had been at Baden-Baden in the previous week and returned a few days later; he happened, however, on the two days when Cavour was there, to be occupied with his duties at Frankfort; the two great statesmen therefore never met. Cavour after his visit wrote to La Marmora saying that he had been extremely pleased with the sympathy which had been displayed to him, both by the Prince and the other Prussians. So far as he could foresee, the attitude of Prussia would not be hostile to Italian aspirations. In December, however, after the change of Ministry, he writes to the Italian Envoy at Frankfort that the language of Schleinitz, the new Foreign Minister, is less favourable than that of his predecessor. The Cabinet do not feel the same antipathy to Austria as that of Manteuffel did; German ideas have brought about a rapprochement.

"I do not trust their apparently Liberal tendencies. It is possible that your colleague, Herr von Bismarck, will support us more closely, but I fear that even if he is kept at Frankfort he will not exercise so much influence as under the former Ministry."

Cavour's insight did not deceive him. The Italian question had for the moment re-awakened the old sympathy for Austria; Austria, it seemed, was now the champion of German nationality against the unscrupulous aggression of France. There were few men who, like Bismarck, were willing to disregard this national feeling and support the Italians. To have deliberately joined Napoleon in what after all was an unprovoked attack on a friendly prince of the same nation, was an act which could have been undertaken only by a man of the calibre of Frederick the Great. After all, Austria was German; the Austrian provinces in Italy had been assigned to the Emperor by the same authority as the Polish provinces to Prussia. We can imagine how great would have been the outcry had Austria joined with the French to set up a united Poland, taking Posen and West Prussia for the purpose; and yet this act would have been just of the same kind as that which would have been committed had Prussia at this time joined or even lent diplomatic support to the French-Italian alliance. It is very improbable that even if Bismarck had been Minister at this period he would have been able to carry out this policy.

The Prussian Government acted on the whole correctly. As the war became more imminent the Prince Regent prepared the Prussian army and eventually the whole was placed on a war footing. He offered to the Emperor of Austria his armed neutrality and a guarantee of the Austrian possessions in Italy, In return he required that he himself should have the command of all the forces of the German Diet. Had Austria accepted these terms, either the war would have been stopped or the whole force of Germany under the King of Prussia would have attacked France on the Rhine. The Emperor however refused to accept them; he required a guarantee not only of his possessions in Italy but also of his treaties with the other Italian princes. Moreover, he would accept the assistance of Prussia only on condition that the Prussian army was placed under the orders of the general appointed by the Diet. It was absurd to suppose that any Prussian statesman would allow this. The action of Austria shewed in fact a distrust and hatred of Prussia which more than justified all that Bismarck had written during his tenure of office at Frankfort. In the end, rather than accept Prussian assistance on the terms on which it was offered, the Emperor of Austria made peace with France; he preferred to surrender Lombardy rather than save it by Prussian help. "Thank God," said Cavour, "Austria by her arrogance has succeeded in uniting all the world against her."

The spring of the year was spent by Bismarck at St. Petersburg. He had been appointed Prussian Minister to that capital—put out in the cold, as he expressed it. From the point of dignity and position it was an advance, but at St. Petersburg he was away from the centre of political affairs. Russia had not yet recovered from the effects of the Crimean War; the Czar was chiefly occupied with internal reforms and the emancipation of the serfs. The Eastern Question was dormant, and Russia did not aim at keeping a leading part in the settlement of Italian affairs. Bismarck's immediate duties were not therefore important and he no longer had the opportunity of giving his advice to the Government upon the general practice. It is improbable that Herr von Schleinitz would have welcomed advice. He was one of the weakest of the Ministry; an amiable man of no very marked ability, who owed his position to the personal friendship of the Prince Regent and his wife. The position which Bismarck had occupied during the last few years could not but be embarrassing to any Minister; this man still young, so full of self-confidence, so unremitting in his labours, who, while other diplomatists thought only of getting through their routine work, spent the long hours of the night in writing despatches, discussing the whole foreign policy of the country, might well cause apprehension even to the strongest Minister.

From the time of Bismarck's departure from Frankfort our knowledge of his official despatches ceases; we lose the invaluable assistance of his letters to Manteuffel and Gerlach. For some time he stood so much alone that there was no one to whom he could write unreservedly on political matters.

He watched with great anxiety the progress of affairs with regard to Italy. At the beginning of May he wrote a long letter to Schleinitz, as he had done to Manteuffel, urging him to bold action; he recounted his experiences at the Diet, he reiterated his conviction that no good would come to Prussia from the federal tie—the sooner it was broken the better; nothing was so much to be desired as that the Diet should overstep its powers, and pass some resolution which Prussia could not accept, so that Prussia could take up the glove and force a breach. The opportunity was favourable for a revision of the Constitution. "I see," he wrote "in our Federal connection only a weakness of Prussia which sooner or later must be cured, ferro et igni." Probably Schleinitz's answer was not of such a kind as to tempt him to write again. In his private letters he harps on the same string; he spent June in a visit to Moscow but he hurried back at the end of the month to St. Petersburg to receive news of the war. Before news had come of the peace of Villafranca he was constantly in dread that Prussia would go to war on behalf of Austria:

"We have prepared too soon and too thoroughly, the weight of the burden we have taken on ourselves is drawing us down the incline. We shall not be even an Austrian reserve; we shall simply sacrifice ourselves for Austria and take away the war from her."

How disturbed he was, we can see by the tone of religious resignation which he assumes—no doubt a sign that he fears his advice has not yet been acted upon.

"As God will. Everything here is only a question of time; peoples and men, wisdom and folly, war and peace, they come and go like rain and water, and the sea alone remains. There is nothing on earth but hypocrisy and deceit."

The language of this and other letters was partly due to the state of his health; the continual anxiety and work of his life at Frankfort, joined to irregular hours and careless habits, had told upon his constitution. He fell seriously ill in St. Petersburg with a gastric and rheumatic affection; an injury to the leg received while shooting in Sweden, became painful; the treatment adopted by the doctor, bleeding and iodine, seems to have made him worse. At the beginning of July, 1860, he returned on leave to Berlin; there he was laid up for ten days; his wife was summoned and under her care he began to improve. August he spent at Wiesbaden and Nauheim, taking the waters, the greater part of the autumn in Berlin; in October he had to go Warsaw officially to receive and accompany the Czar, who came to Breslau for an interview with the Prince Regent. From Breslau he hurried back to Berlin, from Berlin down to Pomerania, where his wife was staying with her father; then the same week back to Berlin, and started for St. Petersburg. The result of these long journeys when his health was not completely reestablished was very serious. He was to spend a night on the journey to St. Petersburg with his old friend, Herr von Below, at Hohendorf, in East Prussia; he had scarcely reached the house when he fell dangerously ill of inflammation of the lungs and rheumatic fever. He remained here all the winter, and it was not until the beginning of March, 1860, that he was well enough to return to Berlin. Leopold von Gerlach, who met him shortly afterwards, speaks of him as still looking wretchedly ill. This prolonged illness forms an epoch in his life. He never recovered the freshness and strength of his youth. It left a nervous irritation and restlessness which often greatly interfered with his political work and made the immense labour which came upon him doubly distasteful. He loses the good humour which had been characteristic of him in early life; he became irritable and more exacting. He spent the next three months in Berlin attending the meetings of the Herrenhaus, and giving a silent vote in favour of the Government measures; he considered it was his duty as a servant of the State to support the Government, though he did not agree with the Liberal policy which in internal affairs they adopted. At this time he stood almost completely alone. His opinions on the Italian question had brought about a complete breach with his old friends. Since the conclusion of the war, public opinion in Germany, as in England, had veered round. The success of Cavour had raised a desire to imitate him; a strong impulse had been given to the national feeling, and a society, the National Verein, had been founded to further the cause of United Germany under Prussian leadership. The question of the recognition of the new Kingdom of Italy was becoming prominent; all the Liberal party laid much stress on this. The Prince Regent, however, was averse to an act by which he might seem to express his approval of the forcible expulsion of princes from their thrones. As the national and liberal feeling in the country grew, his monarchical principles seemed to be strengthened. The opinions which Bismarck was known to hold on the French alliance had got into the papers and were much exaggerated; he had plenty of enemies to take care that it should be said that he wished Prussia to join with France; to do as Piedmont had done, and by the cession of the left bank of the Rhine to France to receive the assistance of Napoleon in annexing the smaller states. In his letters of this period Bismarck constantly protests against the truth of these accusations. "If I am to go to the devil," he writes, "it will at least not be a French one. Do not take me for a Bonapartist, only for a very ambitious Prussian." It is at this time that his last letter to Gerlach was written. They had met at the end of April, and Gerlach wrote to protest against the opinion to which Bismarck had given expression:

"After the conversation which I have had with you I was particularly distressed that, by your bitterness against Austria, you had allowed yourself to be diverted from the simple attitude towards law and the Revolution. For you an alliance with France and Piedmont is a possibility, a thought which is far from me and, dear Bismarck, ought to be far from you. For me Louis Napoleon is even more than his uncle the incarnation of the Revolution, and Cavour is a Rheinbund Minister like Montgellas. You cannot and ought not to deny the principles of the Holy Alliance; they are no other than that authority comes from God, and that the Princes must govern as servants appointed by God."

Bismarck answers the letter the next day:

"I am a child of other times than you. No one loses the mark impressed on him in the period of his youth. In you the victorious hatred of Bonaparte is indelible; you call him the incarnation of the Revolution and if you knew of any worse name you would bestow it upon him. I have lived in the country from my twenty-third to my thirty-second year and will never be rid of the longing to be back again; I am in politics with only half my heart; what dislike I have of France is based rather on the Orleans than the Bonapartist régime. It is opposed to bureaucratic corruption under the mask of constitutional government. I should be glad to fight against Bonaparte till the dogs lick up the blood but with no more malice than against Croats, Bohemians, and Bamberger fellow-countrymen."

The two friends were never to meet again. The old King of Prussia died at the beginning of the next year, and Gerlach, who had served him so faithfully, though perhaps not always wisely, survived his master scarcely a week.

In the summer of 1860 Bismarck returned to his duties in Russia; and this time, with the exception of a fortnight in October, he spent a whole year in St. Petersburg. He had still not recovered from the effects of his illness and could not, therefore, go out much in society, but he was much liked at Court and succeeded in winning the confidence both of the Emperor and his family. His wife and children were now with him, and after the uncertainty of his last two years he settled down with pleasure to a quieter mode of life. He enjoyed the sport which he had in the Russian forests; he studied Russian and made himself completely at home. Political work he had little to do, except what arose from the charge of "some 200,000 vagabond Prussians" who lived in Russia. Of home affairs he had little knowledge:

"I am quite separated from home politics, as besides the newspapers I receive scarcely anything but official news which does not expose the foundation of affairs."

For the time the reports of his entering the Ministry had ceased; he professed to be, and perhaps was, quite satisfied.

"I am quite contented with my existence here; I ask for no change in my position until it be God's will I settle down quietly at Schönhausen or Reinfeld and can leisurely set about having my coffin made."

In October he had to attend the Czar on a journey to Warsaw where he had an interview with the Prince Regent.

The Prince was accompanied by his Minister-President, the Prince of Hohenzollern, who took the opportunity of having long conversations with the Ambassador to St. Petersburg. It is said that as a result of this the Minister, who wished to be relieved from a post which was daily becoming more burdensome, advised the Prince Regent to appoint Bismarck Minister-President. The advice, however, was not taken.

Meanwhile events were taking place in Prussia which were to bring about important constitutional changes. The success of the Ministry of the new era had not answered the expectations of the country. Their foreign policy had been correct, but they had shewn no more spirit than their predecessors, and the country was in that excited state in which people wanted to see some brilliant and exciting stroke of policy, though they were not at all clear what it was they desired. Then a rift had begun to grow between the Regent and his Ministers. The Liberalism of the Prince had never been very deep; it owed its origin in fact chiefly to his opposition to the reactionary government of his brother. As an honest man he intended to govern strictly in accordance with the Constitution. He had, however, from the beginning no intention of allowing the Chambers to encroach upon the prerogatives of the Crown. The Ministers on the other hand regarded themselves to some extent as a Parliamentary Ministry; they had a majority in the House and they were inclined to defer to it. The latent causes of difference were brought into activity by the question of army reform.

The Prince Regent was chiefly and primarily a soldier. As a second son it had been doubtful whether he would ever succeed to the throne. He had an intimate acquaintance with the whole condition of the army, and he had long known that in many points reform was necessary. His first action on succeeding his brother was to appoint a Commission of the War Office to prepare a scheme of reorganisation. A memorandum had been drawn up for him by Albert von Roon, and with some alterations it was accepted by the Commission. The Minister of War, Bonin (the same who had been dismissed in 1854 at the crisis of the Eastern complications), seems to have been indifferent in the matter; he did not feel in himself the energy for carrying through an important reform which he had not himself originated, and of which perhaps he did not altogether approve. The Prince Regent had set his mind upon the matter; the experience gained during the mobilisation of 1859 had shewn how serious the defects were; the army was still on a war footing and it was a good opportunity for at once carrying through the proposed changes. Bonin therefore resigned his office and Roon, in December, 1859, was appointed in his place.

This appointment was to have far-reaching results; it at once destroyed all harmony in the Ministry itself. The rest of the Ministers were Liberals. Roon was a strong Conservative. He was appointed professedly merely as a departmental Minister, but he soon won more confidence with the Regent than all the others. He was a man of great energy of character and decision in action. The best type of Prussian officer, to considerable learning he joined a high sense of duty founded on deep-rooted and simple religious faith. The President of the Ministry had practically retired from political life and the Government had no longer a leader. Roon's introduction was in fact the beginning of all the momentous events which were to follow. But for him there would have been no conflict in the Parliament and Bismarck would never have become Minister.

At the beginning of 1860 the project of law embodying the proposals for army reform was laid before the Lower House. It was ordered by them in accordance with the practice to be referred to a small Committee.

The proposals consisted of (a) an increase in the number of recruits to be raised each year, (b) a lengthening of the term of service with the colours, (c) an alteration in the relations of the Landwehr to the rest of the army.

The Committee appointed to consider these reforms accepted the first, but rejected the second and third. They asserted that the three years' service with the colours was not necessary, and they strongly disliked any proposal for interfering with the Landwehr. The report of the Committee was accepted by the House. It was in vain that the more far-seeing members of the Liberal party tried to persuade their leaders to support the Government; it was in vain that the Ministers pointed out that the Liberal majority had been elected as a Government majority, and it was their duty to support Ministers taken from their own party. The law had to be withdrawn and the Government, instead, asked for a vote of nine million thalers, provisionally, for that year only, as a means of maintaining the army in the state to which it had been raised. In asking for this vote it was expressly stated that the principles of the organisation should be in no wise prejudiced.

"The question whether in future a two or three years' service shall be required; whether the period with the Reserve shall be extended; in what position the Landwehr shall be placed--all this is not touched by the present proposal."

On this condition the House voted the money required, but for one year only. The Government, however, did not keep this pledge; the Minister of War simply continued to carry out the reorganisation in accordance with the plan which had been rejected; new regiments were formed, and by the end of the year the whole army had been reorganised. This action was one for which the Prince and Roon were personally responsible; it was done while the other Ministers were away from Berlin, and without their knowledge.

When the House met at the beginning of the next year they felt that they had been deceived; they were still more indignant when Roon informed them that he had discovered that the whole of the reorganisation could be legally carried through in virtue of the prerogative of the Crown, and that a fresh law was not required; that therefore the consideration of the changes was not before the House, and that all they would have to do would be to vote the money to pay for them. Of course the House refused to vote the money; after long debates the final settlement of the question was postponed for another year; the House, though this time by a majority of only eleven votes, granting with a few modifications the required money, but again for one year only.

All this time Bismarck was living quietly at St. Petersburg; he had no influence on affairs, for the military law had nothing to do with him, and the Regent did not consult him on foreign policy. No one, however, profited by Roon's appointment so much as he; he had once more a friend and supporter at Court, who replaced the loss of Gerlach. Roon and he had known one another in the old Pomeranian days. There was a link in Moritz Blankenburg, who was a "Dutz" friend of Bismarck's and Roon's cousin. We can understand how untenable Roon's position was when we find the Minister of War choosing as his political confidants two of the leaders of the party opposed to the Ministry to which he belonged.

Ever since Roon had entered the Government there had been indeed a perpetual crisis.

The Liberal Ministers were lukewarm in their support of the military bill; they only consented to adopt it on condition that the King would give his assent to those measures which they proposed to introduce, in order to maintain their positions as leaders of the party; they proposed to bring in bills for the reform of the House of Lords, for the responsibility of Ministers, for local government. These were opposed to the personal opinions of the King; he was supported in his opposition by Roon and refused his assent, but he neither dismissed the Ministers nor did they resign. So long as they were willing to hold office on the terms he required, there was indeed no reason why he should dismiss them; to do so would be to give up the last hope of getting the military Bill passed. All through 1861 the same uncertainty continued; Roon indeed again and again wrote to his master, pointing out the necessity for getting rid of his colleagues; he wished for a Conservative Ministry with Bismarck as President. Here, he thought, was the only man who had the courage to carry through the army reform. Others thought as he did. Who so fitted to come to the help of the Crown as this man who, ten years before, had shewn such ability in Parliamentary debate? And whenever the crisis became more acute, all the Quidnuncs of Berlin shook their heads and said, "Now we shall have a Bismarck Ministry, and that will be a coup d'état and the overthrow of the Constitution."

Bismarck meanwhile was living quietly at St. Petersburg, awaiting events. At last the summons came; on June 28, 1861, Roon telegraphed to him that the pear was ripe; he must come at once; there was danger in delay. His telegram was followed by a letter, in which he more fully explained the situation. The immediate cause of the crisis was that the King desired to celebrate his accession, as his brother had done, by receiving the solemn homage of all his people; the Ministry refused their assent to an act which would appear to the country as "feudal" and reactionary. A solemn pledge of obedience to the King was the last thing the Liberals wanted to give, just for the same reasons that the King made a point of receiving it; his feelings were deeply engaged, and Roon doubtless hoped that his colleagues would at last be compelled to resign; he wished, therefore, to have Bismarck on the spot.

Bismarck could not leave St. Petersburg for some days; he, however, answered by a telegram and a long letter; he begins in a manner characteristic of all his letters at this period:

"Your letter disturbed me in my comfortable meditations on the quiet time which I was going to enjoy at Reinfeld. Your cry 'to horse' came with a shrill discord. I have grown ill in mind, tired out, and spiritless since I lost the foundation of my health."

And at the end:

"Moving, quarrelling, annoyance, the whole slavery day and night form a perspective, which already makes me homesick for Reinfeld or St. Petersburg. I cannot enter the swindle in better company than yours; but both of us were happier on the Sadower Heath behind the partridges."

So he wrote late at night, but the next morning in a postscript he added: "If the King will to some extent meet my views, then I will set to the work with pleasure." In the letter he discusses at length the programme; he does not attach much importance to the homage; it would be much better to come to terms on the military question, break with the Chamber, and dissolve. The real difficulty he sees, however, is foreign policy; only by a change in the management of foreign affairs can the Crown be relieved from a pressure to which it must ultimately give way; he would not himself be inclined to accept the Ministry of the Interior, because no good could be done unless the foreign policy was changed, and that the King himself would probably not wish that.

"The chief fault of our policy is that we have been Liberal at home and Conservative abroad; we hold the rights of our own King too cheap, and those of foreign princes too high; a natural consequence of the difference between the constitutional tendency of the Ministers and the legitimist direction which the will of his Majesty gives to our foreign policy. Of the princely houses from Naples to Hanover none will be grateful for our love, and we practise towards them a truly evangelical love of our enemies at the cost of the safety of our own throne. I am true to the sole of my foot to my own princes, but towards all others I do not feel in a single drop of blood the slightest obligation to raise up a little finger to help them. In this attitude I fear that I am so far removed from our Most Gracious Master, that he will scarcely find me fitted to be a Councillor of his Crown. For this reason he will anyhow prefer to use me at the Home-Office. In my opinion, however, that makes no difference, for I promise myself no useful results from the whole Government unless our attitude abroad is more vigorous and less dependent on dynastic sympathies."

Bismarck arrived in Berlin on July 9th. When he got there the crisis was over; Berlin was nearly empty; Roon was away in Pomerania, the King in Baden-Baden; a compromise had been arranged; there was not to be an act of homage but a coronation. There was, therefore, no more talk of his entering the Ministry; Schleinitz, however, told him that he was to be transferred from Russia, but did not say what post he was to have. The next day, in obedience to a command, he hurried off to Baden-Baden; the King wished to have his advice on many matters of policy, and instructed him to draw up a memorandum on the German question. He used the opportunity of trying to influence the King to adopt a bolder policy. At the same time he attempted to win over the leaders of the Conservative party. A general election was about to take place; the manifesto of the Conservative party was so worded that we can hardly believe it was not an express and intentional repudiation of the language which Bismarck was in the habit of using; they desired

"the unity of our German fatherland, though not like the Kingdom of Italy through 'blood and fire' [Blut und Brand; almost the words which Bismarck had used to describe the policy which must be followed], but in the unity of its princes and peoples holding firm to authority and law."

Bismarck, on hearing this, sent to his old friend Herr von Below, one of the leaders of the party, a memorandum on German affairs, and accompanied it by a letter. He repeated his old point that Prussia was sacrificing the authority of the Crown at home to support that of other princes in whose safety she had not the slightest interest. The solidarity of Conservative interests was a dangerous fiction, unless it was carried out with the fullest reciprocity; carried out by Prussia alone it was Quixotry; it prevented King and

Government from executing their true task, the protection of Prussia from all injustice, whether it came from home or abroad; this was the task given to the King by God.

"We make the unhistorical, the jealous, and lawless mania for sovereignty of the German Princes the bosom child of the Conservative party in Prussia, we are enthusiastic for the petty sovereignties which were created by Napoleon and protected by Metternich, and are blind to the dangers which threaten Prussia and the independence of Germany."

He wishes for a clear statement of their policy; a stricter concentration of the German military forces, reform of the Customs' Unions, and a number of common institutions to protect material interests against the disadvantages which arise from the unnatural configuration of the different states.

"Besides all this I do not see why we should shrink back so bashfully from the idea of a representation of the people. We cannot fight as revolutionary an institution which we Conservatives cannot do without even in Prussia, and is recognised as legitimate in every German State." [6]

This letter is interesting as shewing how nearly his wishes on German affairs coincided with those of the Liberal party and of the National Verein: he was asking the Conservatives to adopt the chief points in their opponents' programme. Of course they would not do so, and the King himself was more likely to be alarmed than attracted by the bold and adventurous policy that was recommended to him. Bismarck's anticipation was justified; the King was not prepared to appoint him Foreign Minister. Herr von Schleinitz indeed resigned, but his place was taken by Bernstorff, Minister at London; he had so little confidence in the success of his office that he did not even give up his old post, and occupied the two positions, one of which Bismarck much desired to have.

After attending the coronation at Königsberg, Bismarck, therefore, returned to his old post at St. Petersburg; his future was still quite uncertain; he was troubled by his own health and that of his children; for the first time he begins to complain of the cold.

"Since my illness I am so exhausted that I have lost all my energy for excitement. Three years ago I would have made a serviceable Minister; when I think of such a thing now I feel like a broken-down acrobat. I would gladly go to London, Paris, or remain here, as it pleases God and his Majesty. I shudder at the prospect of the Ministry as at a cold bath."

In March he is still in ignorance; his household is in a bad state.

"Johanna has a cough, which quite exhausts her; Bill is in bed with fever, the doctor does not yet know what is the matter with him; the governess has no hope of ever seeing Germany again."

He does not feel up to taking the Ministry; even Paris would be too noisy for him.

"London is quieter; but for the climate and the children's health, I would prefer to stay here. Berne is an old idea of mine; dull places with pretty neighbourhoods suit old people; only there is no sport there, as I do not like climbing after chamois."

The decision depended on the events at home; the position of the Government was becoming untenable. The elections had been most unfavourable; the Radicals had ceased to efface themselves, the old leaders of 1848 had appeared again; they had formed a new party of "Progressives," and had won over a hundred seats at the expense of the Conservatives and the moderate Liberals; they were pledged not to carry out the military reforms and to insist on the two years' service. They intended to make the difference of opinion on this point the occasion of a decisive struggle to secure and extend the control of the House over the administration, and for this purpose to bring into prominence constitutional questions which both Crown and Parliament had hitherto avoided. From the day the session opened it was clear that there was now no chance of the money being voted for the army. Before the decisive debate came on, the majority had taken the offensive and passed what was a direct vote of want of confidence in the Ministry. On this the Ministry handed in their resignations to the King; their place was taken by members of the Conservative party and Parliament again dissolved after sitting only six weeks. It was the end of the new era.

It was doubtful whether the new Ministers would have the skill and resolution to meet the crisis; they still were without a leader; Prince von Hohenlohe, a member of the Protestant branch of the family to which the present Chancellor of the Empire belongs, was appointed provisional President. The opinions of the country was clear enough; the elections resulted in the complete defeat not only of the Conservatives but of the moderate Liberals; not a single one of the Ministers was returned. There was, therefore, no doubt that the King would either have to give in on the question of the army or to govern against the will of the majority of the Chamber. The struggle was no longer confined to the question of the army; it was a formal conflict for power between the House and the Crown. The attempt to introduce a Parliamentary government which had been thwarted ten years before was now revived. Who could say what the end would be? All precedent seemed to shew that in a struggle between Crown and Parliament sooner or later the King must be beaten, unless, indeed, he was prepared to adopt the means which Napoleon used. The King would not give in; he believed that the army reform was necessary to the safety of his country; on the other hand, he was a man of too loyal a character to have recourse to violence and a breach of the Constitution. If, however, the Constitution proved to be of such a kind that it made it impossible for him to govern the country, he was prepared to retire from his post; the position would indeed be untenable if on his shoulders lay the responsibility of guiding the policy and defending the interests of Prussia, and at the same time the country refused to grant him the means of doing so.

The elections had taken place on May 6th; four days later Bismarck arrived in Berlin; he had at last received his recall. As soon as he was seen in Berlin his appointment as Minister-President was expected; all those who wished to maintain the authority of the Crown, looked on him as the only man who could face the danger. Roon was active, as usual, on his side and was now supported by some of his colleagues, but Schleinitz, who had the support of the Queen, wished to be President himself; there were long meetings of the Council and audiences of the King; but the old influences were still at work; Bismarck did not wish to enter the Ministry except as Foreign Minister, and the King still feared and distrusted him. An incident which occurred during these critical days will explain to some extent the apprehensions which Bismarck so easily awoke. The chronic difficulties with the Elector of Hesse had culminated in an act of great discourtesy; the King of Prussia had sent an autograph letter to the Elector by General Willisen; the Elector on receiving it threw it unopened on the table; as the letter contained the final demands of Prussia, the only answer was to put some of the neighbouring regiments on a war footing. Bernstorff took the opportunity of Bismarck's presence in Berlin to ask his advice; the answer was: "The circumstance that the Elector has thrown a royal letter on the table is not a clever casus belli; if you want war, make me your Under Secretary; I will engage to provide you a German civil war of the best quality in a few weeks." The King might naturally fear that if he appointed Bismarck, not Under Secretary, but Minister, he would in a few weeks, whether he liked it or not, find himself involved in a German civil war of the best quality. He wanted a man who would defend the Government before the Chambers with courage and ability; Bismarck, who had gained his reputation as a debater, was the only man for the post. He could have had the post of Minister of the Interior; he was offered that of Minister-President without a Portfolio; but if he did not actually refuse, he strongly disapproved of the plan; he would not be able to get on with Bernstorff, and Schleinitz would probably interfere. "I have no confidence in Bernstorff's eye for political matters; he probably has none in mine." Bernstorff was "too stiff," "his collars were too high." During these long discussions he wrote to his wife:

"Our future is obscure as in Petersburg. Berlin is now to the front; I do nothing one way or another; as soon as I have my credentials for Paris in my pocket I will dance and sing. At present there is no talk of London, but all may change again. I scarcely get free of the discussions all day long; I do not find the Ministers more united than their predecessors were."

Disgusted with the long waiting and uncertainty he pressed for a decision; after a fortnight's delay he was appointed Minister at Paris, but this was in reality only a fresh postponement; nothing had really been decided; the King expressly told him not to establish himself there. To his wife he wrote from Berlin:

"I am very much pleased, but the shadow remains in the background. I was already as good as caught for the Ministry. Perhaps when I am out of their sight they will discover another Minister-President. I expect to start for Paris to-morrow; whether for long, God knows; perhaps only for a few months or even weeks. They are all conspired together that I should stay here. I have had to be very firm to get away from this hotel life even for a time."

He did not really expect to be away more than ten days or a fortnight. At a farewell audience just before he started, the King seems to have led him to expect that he would in a very few days be appointed as he wished, Foreign Minister.

He arrived in Paris on the 30th, to take up his quarters in the empty Embassy. He did not wait even to see his wife before starting and he wrote to her that she was not to take any steps towards joining him.

"It is not decided that I am to stay here; I am in the middle of Paris lonelier than you are in Reinfeld and sit here like a rat in a deserted house. How long it will last God knows. Probably in eight or ten days I shall receive a telegraphic summons to Berlin and then game and dance is over. If my enemies knew what a benefit they would confer on me by their victory and how sincerely I wish it for them, Schleinitz out of pure malice would probably do his best to bring me to Berlin."

Day after day, however, went by and the summons did not come; on the contrary Bernstorff wrote as though he were proposing to stay on; he did not however, suggest giving up his post in London, Roon wrote that he had raised the question in conversation with the King; that he had found the old leaning towards Bismarck, and the old irresolution. The Chamber had met, but the first few weeks of the session passed off with unexpected quiet and it was not till the autumn that the question of the Budget would come up. Bismarck wrote to Bernstorff to try and find out what was to happen to him, but the King, before whom the letter was laid, was quite unable to come to any decision.

Bismarck therefore determined to use his enforced leisure in order to go across to London for a few days. He had only visited England once as a young man, and, expecting as he did soon to be responsible for the conduct of foreign affairs, it was desirable that he should make the personal acquaintance of the leading English statesmen. Undoubtedly, one of the reasons why he had been sent to Paris was that he might renew his acquaintance with the Emperor. There was also a second International Exhibition and everyone was going to London. We have, unfortunately, no letters written from England; after his return he writes to Roon:

"I have just come back from London; people there are much better informed about China and Turkey than about Prussia. Loftus must write more nonsense to his Ministers than I thought."

The only event of which we have any information was his meeting with Mr. Disraeli, who at that time was leader of the Opposition in the House of Commons; it took place at a dinner given by the Russian Ambassador to the Grand Duchess of Saxe-Weimar. Among the guests was Count Vitzthum, Saxon Envoy; he saw Bismarck and Disraeli engaged in a long conversation after dinner; afterwards the English statesman told him the substance of it. Bismarck had spoken as follows:

"I shall soon be compelled to undertake the leadership of the Prussian Government. My first care will be, with or without the help of Parliament, to reorganise the army. The King has rightly set himself this task; he cannot however carry it through with his present councillors. When the army has been brought to such a state as to command respect, then I will take the first opportunity to declare war with Austria, burst asunder the German Confederation, bring the middle and smaller States into subjection, and give Germany a national union under the leadership of Prussia. I have come here to tell this to the Queen's Ministers."

Disraeli added to Vitzthum, who, of course, as Saxon Envoy was much interested: "Take care of that man; he means what he says." It does not appear that Bismarck had an opportunity of explaining his project either to Lord Palmerston or to Lord Russell.

All through July he remained in Paris, to which he was called back in order to receive some despatches which after all never arrived; the same uncertainty continued; there was no work to be done there, Emperor and Ministers were going away; he was still all alone in the Embassy without servants, or furniture. As he wrote to his wife, he did not know what to have for dinner or what to eat it on. He therefore applied for leave; he was himself of opinion that as the King would not immediately give him the Foreign Office it was not yet time for him to enter the Ministry. Writing to Roon he advised that the Government should prolong the conflict, draw the Chamber into disputes on small matters which would weary the country; then when they were getting worn out and hoped that the Government would meet them half-way so as to end the conflict, then would be the time to summon him,

"as a sign that we are far from giving up the battle. The appearance of a new battalion in the Ministerial array would then perhaps make an impression that would be wanting now, especially if beforehand a commotion was created by expressions about a coup d'état and a new Constitution; then my own reputation for careless violence would help me and people would think, 'now it is coming!' Then, all the half-hearted would be inclined to negotiation. I am astonished at the political incapacity of our Chambers and yet we are an educated country. Undoubtedly too much so; others are not cleverer but they have not the childish self-confidence with which our political leaders publish their incapacity in its complete nakedness as a model and pattern. How have we Germans got the reputation of retiring modesty? There is not a single one of us who does not think that he understands everything, from strategy to picking the fleas off a dog, better than professionals who have devoted their lives to it."

It was only with difficulty he could even get leave of absence, for the King was as irresolute as ever; as to the cause of the difficulty we get some hint in Roon's letters. There was a party which was pushing Schleinitz, the only member of the Liberal Ministry who remained in office; he had very influential support.

"Her Majesty the Queen returns to Babelsburg on Sunday; she is much agitated, there will be scenes; the temperature towards the Ministry will fall to zero or below."

He eventually got away at the end of July with six weeks' leave of absence; he travelled down to Bordeaux and Bayonne and across the Pyrenees to San Sebastian; he was away from all news of the world; for weeks he scarcely saw even a German paper.

On the 14th of September he was at Toulouse; the sea-bathing, the mountain air, the freedom from work and anxiety, and the warmth had completely restored his health; for the first time since he went to St. Petersburg he had recovered his old spirit, his decision, and directness of action. He wrote that he must have some definite decision; otherwise he would send in his resignation. "My furniture is at St. Petersburg and will be frozen up, my carriages are at Stettin, my horses at Berlin, my family in Pomerania, and I on the highroad." He was prepared to be his Majesty's Envoy at Paris but he was also ready at once to enter the Ministry. "Only get me certainty, one way or another," he writes to Roon, "and I will paint angels' wings on your photograph." Two days later, just as a year before, he received a telegram from Roon telling him to come at once. On the 17th he was in Paris and on the morning of the 20th he arrived in Berlin.

The long-delayed crisis had at last come; the debates on the Budget and the vote for the army reform began on September 11th; it was continued for five days, and at the end the House, by a majority of 273 to 62, refused the money required for the increased establishment. The result of this vote would be that if the wishes of the House were carried out, the whole of the expenditure which had already been made for eight months of the current year was illegal; moreover, the regiments which had already existed for two years must be disbanded. It was a vote which could not possibly be carried into effect, as the money had already been spent. At a meeting of the Ministry which was held the next morning, the majority, including this time even Roon, seemed to have been inclined to attempt a compromise. The King alone remained firm. When he had heard the opinion of all the Ministers, he rose and said that in that case it would be impossible for him to carry on the Government any longer; it would only remain for him to summon the Crown Prince. As he said this he put his hand on the bell to call a messenger. The Ministers all sprang from their chairs and assured him that he might depend upon them, and they would support him to the end. Such were the circumstances in which Roon summoned Bismarck. None the less the influence of the Queen and the Crown Prince were so strong that the King still doubted whether he ought to continue the struggle; on one thing he was determined, that if he had to give way he would abdicate. Two days later he again asked Roon his advice. "Appoint Bismarck Minister-President," was the answer. "But he is not here, he will not accept," objected the King, referring doubtless to the difficulties which Bismarck had raised formerly. "He is in Berlin at this moment," said Roon. The King ordered him to come to Potsdam. When Bismarck arrived there he found the King sitting at his table, and in front of him the act of abdication, already signed. The King asked him whether he was willing to undertake the Government, even against the majority of the Parliament and without a Budget. Bismarck said he would do so. It was one last chance, and the King tore up the act of abdication. Two days later Bismarck was appointed provisional Minister-President, and, at the beginning of October, received his definite appointment as President and Foreign Minister.

CHAPTER VII.

THE CONFLICT.

1862-1863.

The circumstances under which Bismarck accepted office were such as to try the nerves of the strongest man. The King had not appealed to him so long as there was anyone else who would carry on the Government; he was the last resource, and had taken up a burden from which all others shrunk. He had pledged himself to support the King in a conflict against the whole nation; with the exception of the Upper House he had no friends or supporters. The opinion in Europe was as decisively against him as that in Prussia; he was scarcely looked on as a serious politician; everyone believed that in a few weeks he would have to retire, and the King to give up the useless conflict on which he was staking his throne.

Bismarck was under no illusion as to his position; he had been summoned by the King, he depended for his office entirely on the King, but would the King have the strength of will and courage to resist? Only a few days after his appointment, the King had gone to Baden-Baden for a week, where he met the Queen. When he came back, he was completely disheartened. Bismarck, who had travelled part of the way to meet him, got into the train at a small roadside station. He found that the King, who was sitting alone in an ordinary first-class carriage, was prepared to surrender. "What will come of it?" he said. "Already I see the place before my castle on which your head will fall, and then mine will fall too." "Well, as far as I am concerned," answered Bismarck, "I cannot think of a finer death than one on the field of battle or the scaffold. I would fall like Lord Strafford; and your Majesty, not as Louis XVI., but as Charles I. That is a quite respectable historical figure."

For the moment the centre of interest lay in the House. The new Minister began by what he intended as an attempt at reconciliation: he announced that the Budget for 1863 would be withdrawn; the object of this was to limit as much as possible the immediate scope of difference; a fresh Budget for the next year would be laid before them as soon as possible. There would remain only the settlement of the Budget for the current year. This announcement was badly received; the House was distrustful, and they interpreted it as an attempt to return to the old practice of deferring consideration of the Budget until the beginning of the year to which it applied. The first discussion in which Bismarck took part was not in the House itself, but in the Budget Committee. The Committee proposed a resolution requiring the Government at once to lay before the House the Budget for 1863, and declaring that it was unconstitutional to spend any money which had been expressly and definitely refused by the House of Representatives. On this there took place a long discussion, in which Bismarck spoke repeatedly; for the discussions in Committee, which consisted only of about thirty members, were conversational in their nature. There was no verbatim report, but the room was crowded with members who had come to hear the new Minister. They were not disappointed. He spoke with a wit, incisiveness, and versatility to which, as one observer remarked, they were not accustomed from Prussian Ministers. He warned them not to exaggerate their powers. The Prussian Constitution did not give the House of Representatives the sole power of settling the Budget; it must be settled by arrangement with the other House and the Crown. There was a difference of opinion in the interpretation of the Constitution; all constitutional government required compromise; a constitution was not something dead, it must be enlivened; it was interpreted by custom and practice; it would be wiser not to hasten this practice too quickly; then the question of law might easily become one of power. It was not the fault of the Government that they had got into this position; people took the situation too tragically, especially in the press; they spoke as though the end of all things was come; "but," he added, "a constitutional struggle is not a disgrace, it is rather an honour; after all we are all children of the same country." A true note, but one which he was not always able to maintain in the struggle of the coming years. Then he expounded the view of the German character which we have learnt from his letters: it was customary to speak of the sobriety of the Prussian people; yes, but the great independence of the individual made it difficult in Prussia to govern with the Constitution; in France it was different; there this individual independence was wanting; "we are perhaps too educated to endure a constitution; we are too critical"; the capacity for judging measures of the

Government and acts of the Representatives was too universal; there were in the country too many Catilinarian existences, which had an interest in revolutions. He reminded them that Germany did not care for the Liberalism of Prussia, but for its power; Bavaria, Wurtemberg, Baden, might indulge in Liberalism; Prussia must concentrate its power and hold itself ready for the favourable moment which had already been passed over more than once; Prussia's boundaries, as fixed by the Congress of Vienna, were not favourable to a sound political life; "not by speeches and majority votes are the great questions of the time decided—that was the great blunder of 1848 and 1849—but by blood and iron." He appealed for confidence: "Do not force a quarrel; we are honest people and you can trust us."

The effect of these speeches was very unfavourable; the very quickness of thought and originality of expression produced a bad impression; even the free indulgence in long foreign words offended patriotic journalists. They seemed to his audience reckless; what was this reference to the Treaties of Vienna but an imitation of Napoleonic statesmanship? They had the consciousness that they were making history, that they were involved in a great and tragic conflict, and they expected the Minister to play his part seriously and solemnly; instead of that they had listened to a series of epigrams with no apparent logical connection. We know how dangerous it is, even in England, for a responsible statesman to allow himself to be epigrammatic in dealing with serious affairs. Much more was it in Germany, where the Ministers were nearly always officials by training. Bismarck had the dangerous gift of framing pregnant and pithy sentences which would give a ready handle to his opponents: Macht geht vor Recht; he had not said these words, but he had said something very much like them, and they undoubtedly represented what seemed to his audience the pith of his speeches. And then these words, blood and iron. He has told us in later years what he really meant:

"Put the strongest possible military power, in other words, as much blood and iron as you can, into the hands of the King of Prussia, then he will be able to carry out the policy you wish; it cannot be done with speeches and celebrations and songs, it can only be done by blood and iron." [7]

What everyone thought he meant was that blood must be shed and iron used; and perhaps they were not so far wrong.

The attempt at conciliation failed; the report of the Committee was adopted, and an amendment proposed by Vincke, which Bismarck was prepared to accept, was rejected. Bismarck warned the House not to push the conflict too far; the time would come when the prospect of a peaceful solution would have disappeared; then the Government too would be prepared to oppose theory to theory and interpretation to interpretation.

He showed to the President of the House a twig of olive. "I gathered this in Avignon to bring it to the House; it does not seem to be time yet."

The Budget was sent up to the House of Lords in the amended form in which the House of Representatives had passed it; the Lords unanimously threw it out, as they were legally justified in doing; not content with that, they altered it to the original form in which it had been proposed by the Government and sent it down again to the Lower House. This was clearly illegal. Their action, however, was most useful to the Government. A conflict had now arisen between the two Houses, and technically the responsibility for the failure to bring the conciliation about was taken away from the Government; they could entrench themselves behind the impregnable position that the law required the Budget to be passed by both Houses; until this was done they could do nothing. The Houses would not agree; the Government was helpless. The House of Representatives at once passed a motion declaring the vote of the Upper House for altering the Budget null and void, as indeed it was; in the middle of the discussion a message was brought down by the President announcing that the House was to be prorogued that afternoon; they had just time to pass the resolution and to send it in a cab which was waiting at the door to the Upper House, where it was read out amidst the boisterous laughter of the Peers; then both Chambers were summoned to the Palace, and the session closed. The first round in the conflict was over.

The recess was short; the next session was by the Constitution obliged to begin not later than January 15th; there were many who expected that the Constitution would be ignored and the Parliament not summoned. This was not Bismarck's plan; he fulfilled all the technical requirements in the strictest way; he carefully abstained from any action which he could not justify by an appeal to the letter of the Constitution; the government of the country was carried on with vigour and success; he allowed no loophole by which his opponents might injure his influence with the King. It is true that they were spending money which had not been voted, but then, as he explained, that was not his fault; the provisions of the law were quite clear.

It was the duty of the Government to submit the Budget to the Lower House, who could amend it; it had then to be passed in the form of a law, and for this the assent of both Houses of Parliament and of the Crown was required. The Upper House had not the right of proposing amendments, but they had the right of rejecting them. In this case they had made use of their right; no law had been passed the two Houses had not agreed. What was to happen? The Constitution gave no help; there was a gap in it. The Government therefore had to act as best they could. They could not be expected to close the Government offices, cease to pay the troops, and let the government of the country come to an end; they must go on as best they could, taking all the responsibility until they could come to some agreement.

As soon as the House met it began to vote an address to the King. They adopted the obvious fiction, which, in fact, they could not well avoid, that he was being misled by his Ministers, and the attitude of the country misrepresented to him; even had they known as well as we do that the Ministers were only carrying out the orders of the King, they could not well have said so. Bismarck, however, did not attempt to conceal the truth; the address, he said, touched the King; the acts complained of were done in the name of the King; they were setting themselves against him. The contest was, who was to rule in Prussia, the House of Hohenzollern or the House of Parliament. He was at once accused of disloyalty; he was, they said, protecting himself behind the person of the sovereign, but, of course, it was impossible for him not to do so. The whole justification for his action was that he was carrying out the King's orders. What was at the root of the conflict but the question, whether in the last resort the will of the King or the majority of the House should prevail? To have adopted the English practice, to have refrained from mentioning the King's name, would have been to adopt the very theory of the Constitution for which the House was contending, the English theory that the sovereign has neither the right of deciding nor responsibility; it would have been to undermine the monarchical side of the Constitution which Bismarck was expressly defending. The King himself never attempted to avoid the responsibility; in a public speech he had already said that the army organisation was his own work: "It is my own and I am proud of it; I will hold firmly to it and carry it through with all my energy." In his answer to the address from the House, both on this and on later occasions, he expressly withdrew the assumption that he was not well informed or that he did not approve of his Ministers' action.

The address was carried by a majority of 255 to 68; the King refused to receive it in person. The House then proceeded to throw out a Bill for military reorganisation which was laid before them; they adopted a resolution that they reserved for later discussion the question, for what part of the money illegally spent in 1862 they would hold the Ministry personally responsible. They then proceeded to the Budget of 1863, and again rejected the army estimates; they refused the money asked for raising the salaries of the ambassadors (Bismarck himself, while at St. Petersburg, had suffered much owing to the insufficiency of his salary, and he wished to spare his successors a similar inconvenience); and they brought in Bills for the responsibility of Ministers. The public attention, however was soon directed from these internal matters to even more serious questions of foreign policy.

At the beginning of February the Poles had once more risen in revolt against the Russian Government. Much sympathy was felt for them in Western Europe. England, France, and

Austria joined in representations and remonstrances to the Czar; they expected that Prussia would join them.

Nothing could have been more inconvenient to Bismarck; he was at the time fully occupied in negotiations about German affairs, and he was probably anxious to bring to a speedy issue the questions between Prussia and Austria; it was therefore most important to him to be on good terms with France and England, for he would not challenge Austria unless he was sure that Austria would have no allies; now he must quarrel with either Russia or with France. An insurrection in Poland was, however, a danger to which everything else must be postponed; on this his opinion never varied, here there could be no compromise. He was perfectly open: "The Polish question is to us a question of life and death," he said to Sir Andrew Buchanan. There were two parties among the Poles; the one, the extreme Republican, wished for the institution of an independent republic; the other would be content with self-government and national institutions under the Russian Crown; they were supported by a considerable party in Russia itself. Either party if successful would not be content with Russian Poland; they would demand Posen, they would never rest until they had gained again the coast of the Baltic and deprived Prussia of her eastern provinces. The danger to Prussia would be greatest, as Bismarck well knew, if the Poles became reconciled to the Russians; an independent republic on their eastern frontier would have been dangerous, but Polish aspirations supported by the Panslavonic party and the Russian army would have been fatal. Russia and Poland might be reconciled, Prussia and Poland never can be. Prussia therefore was obliged to separate itself from the other Powers; instead of sending remonstrances to the Czar, the King wrote an autograph letter proposing that the two Governments should take common steps to meet the common danger; General von Alvensleben, who took the letter, at once concluded a convention in which it was agreed that Prussian and Russian troops should be allowed to cross the frontier in pursuit of the insurgents; at the same time two of the Prussian army corps were mobilised and drawn up along the Polish frontier.

The convention soon became known and it is easy to imagine the indignation with which the Prussian people and the House of Representatives heard of what their Government had done. The feeling was akin to that which would have prevailed in America had the President offered his help to the Spanish Government to suppress the insurrection in Cuba. The answers to questions were unsatisfactory, and on February 26th Heinrich von Sybel rose to move that the interests of Prussia required absolute neutrality. It was indeed evident that Bismarck's action had completely isolated Prussia; except the Czar, she had now not a single friend in Europe and scarcely a friend in Germany. Bismarck began his answer by the taunt that the tendency to enthusiasm for foreign nationalities, even when their objects could only be realised at the cost of one's own country, was a political disease unfortunately limited to Germany. It was, however, an unjust taunt, for no one had done more than Sybel himself in his historical work to point out the necessity, though he recognised the injustice, of the part Prussia had taken in the partition of Poland; nobody had painted so convincingly as he had, the political and social demoralisation of Poland. Bismarck then dwelt on the want of patriotism in the House, which in the middle of complicated negotiations did not scruple to embarrass their own Government. "No English House of Commons," he said, "would have acted as they did," a statement to which we cannot assent; an English Opposition would have acted exactly as the majority of the Prussian Parliament did. When a Minister is in agreement with the House on the general principles of policy, then indeed there rests on them the obligation not to embarrass the Government by constant interpolation with regard to each diplomatic step; self-restraint must be exercised, confidence shewn. This was not the case here; the House had every reason to believe that the objects of Bismarck were completely opposed to what they wished; they could not be expected to repose confidence in him. They used this, as every other opportunity, to attempt to get rid of him.

The question of Poland is one on which Bismarck never altered his attitude. His first public expression of opinion on foreign affairs was an attack on the Polish policy of the Prussian Government in 1848.

"No one then," he wrote, "could doubt that an independent Poland would be the irreconcilable enemy of Prussia and would remain so till they had conquered the mouth of the Vistula and every Polish-speaking village in West and East Prussia, Pomerania, and Silesia."

Forty years later one of the last of his great speeches in the Reichstag was devoted to attacking the Polish sympathies of the Catholic party in Prussia. He was never tired of laughing at the characteristic German romanticism which was so enthusiastic for the welfare of other nations. He recalled the memories of his boyhood when, after the rebellion of 1831, Polish refugees were received in every German town with honours and enthusiasm greater than those paid to the men who had fought for Germany, when German children would sing Polish national airs as though they were their own.

Nothing shews the change which he has been able to bring about in German thought better than the attitude of the nation towards Poland. In the old days the Germans recollected only that the partition of Poland had been a great crime; it was their hope and determination that they might be able to make amends for it. In those days the Poles were to be found in every country in Europe, foremost in fighting on the barricades; they helped the Germans to fight for their liberty, and the Germans were to help them to recover independence. In 1848, Mieroslawski had been carried like a triumphant hero through the streets of Berlin; the Baden rebels put themselves under the leadership of a Pole, and it was a Pole who commanded the Viennese in their resistance to the Austrian army; a Pole led the Italians to disaster on the field of Novara. At a time when poets still were political leaders, and the memory and influence of Byron had not been effaced, there was scarcely a German poet, Platen, Uhland, Heine, who had not stirred up the enthusiasm for Poland. It was against this attitude of mind that Bismarck had to struggle and he has done so successfully. He has taught that it is the duty of Germany to use all the power of the State for crushing and destroying the Polish language and nationality; the Poles in Prussia are to become Prussian, as those in Russia have to become Russian. A hundred years ago the Polish State was destroyed; now the language and the nation must cease to exist.

It is a natural result of the predominance of Prussia in Germany. The enthusiasm for Poland was not unnatural when the centre of gravity of Germany was still far towards the West. Germany could be great, prosperous, and happy, even if a revived Poland spread to the shores of the Baltic, but Prussia would then cease to exist and Bismarck has taught the Germans to feel as Prussians.

The danger during these weeks was real; Napoleon proposed that Austria, England, and France should present identical notes to Prussia remonstrating with and threatening her. Lord Russell refused; it was, as Bismarck said in later years, only the friendly disposition of Lord Russell to Germany which saved Prussia from this danger. Bismarck's own position was very insecure; but he withstood this attack as he did all others, though few knew at what expense to his nerves and health; he used to attribute the frequent illnesses of his later years to the constant anxiety of these months; he had a very nervous temperament, self-control was difficult to him, and we must remember that all the time when he was defending the King's Government against this public criticism he had to maintain himself against those who at Court were attempting to undermine his influence with the King.

He had, however, secured the firm friendship of Russia. When he was in St. Petersburg he had gained the regard of the Czar; now to this personal feeling was added a great debt of gratitude. What a contrast between the action of Austria and Prussia! The late Czar had saved Austria from dissolution, and what had been the reward? Opposition in the East, and now Austria in the Polish affair was again supporting the Western Powers. On the other hand Prussia, and Prussia alone, it was which had saved Russia from the active intervention of France and England. Napoleon had proposed that a landing should he made in Lithuania in order to effect a junction with the Poles; Bismarck had immediately declared that if this were done he should regard it as a declaration of war against Prussia. So deep was the indignation of Alexander that he wrote himself to the King of Prussia, proposing an alliance and a joint attack on France and Austria. It must have been a great temptation to Bismarck, but he now shewed the prudence which was his great characteristic as a diplomatist; he feared that in a war of this kind the brunt would fall upon Prussia, and that when peace was made the control of negotiations would be with the Czar. He wished for war with Austria, but he was determined that when war came he should have the arrangement of the terms of peace. On his advice the King refused the offer.

The bitterness of the feeling created by these debates on Poland threatened to make it impossible for Ministers any longer to attend in the House; Bismarck did his part in increasing it.

"You ask me," he said, "why, if we disagree with you, we do not dissolve; it is that we wish the country to have an opportunity of becoming thoroughly acquainted with you."

He was tired and angry when during one of these sittings he writes to Motley:

"I am obliged to listen to particularly tasteless speeches out of the mouths of uncommonly childish and excited politicians, and I have therefore a moment of unwilling leisure which I cannot use better than in giving you news of my welfare. I never thought that in my riper years I should be obliged to carry on such an unworthy trade as that of a Parliamentary Minister. As envoy, although an official, I still had the feeling of being a gentleman; as [Parliamentary] Minister one is a helot. I have come down in the world, and hardly know how.

"April 18th. I wrote as far as this yesterday, then the sitting came to an end; five hours' Chamber until three o'clock; one hour's report to his Majesty; three hours at an incredibly dull dinner, old important Whigs; then two hours' work; finally, a supper with a colleague, who would have been hurt if I had slighted his fish. This morning, I had hardly breakfasted, before Karolyi was sitting opposite to me; he was followed without interruption by Denmark, England, Portugal, Russia, France, whose Ambassador I was obliged to remind at one o'clock that it was time for me to go to the House of phrases. I am sitting again in the latter; hear people talk nonsense, and end my letter. All these people have agreed to approve our treaties with Belgium, in spite of which twenty speakers scold each other with the greatest vehemence, as if each wished to make an end of the other; they are not agreed about the motives which make them unanimous, hence, alas! a regular German squabble about the Emperor's beard; querelle d'Allemand. You Anglo-Saxon Yankees have something of the same kind also.... Your battles are bloody; ours wordy; these chatterers really cannot govern Prussia. I must bring some opposition to bear against them; they have too little wit and too much self-complacency--stupid and audacious. Stupid, in all its meanings, is not the right word; considered individually, these people are sometimes very clever, generally educated--the regulation German university culture; but of politics, beyond the interests of their own church tower, they know as little as we knew as students, and even less; as far as external politics go, they are also, taken separately, like children. In all other questions they become childish as soon as they stand together in corpore. In the mass stupid, individually intelligent."

Recalling these days, Bismarck said in later years:

"I shall never forget how I had every morning to receive the visit of Sir Andrew Buchanan, the English Ambassador, and Talleyrand, the representative of France, who made hell hot for me over the inexcusable leanings of Prussian policy towards Russia, and held threatening language towards us, and then at midday I had the pleasure of hearing in the Prussian Parliament pretty much the same arguments and attacks which in the morning the foreign Ambassadors had made against me."

Of course the language used in the House weakened his influence abroad, and the foreign Governments shewed more insistence when they found out that the Prussian Parliament supported their demands. It was noticed with satisfaction in the English Parliament that the nation had dissociated itself from the mean and disgraceful policy of the Government.

At last personal friction reached such a point that the session had to be closed. In order to understand the cause of this we must remember that in Prussia the Ministers are not necessarily members of either House; they enjoy, however, by the Constitution, the right of attending the debates and may at any time demand to be heard; they do not sit in the House among the other members, but on a raised bench to the right of the President, facing the members. They have not, therefore, any feeling of esprit de corps as members of the assembly; Bismarck and his colleagues when they addressed the House spoke not as members, not as the representatives of even a small minority, but as strangers, as the representatives of a rival and hostile authority; it is this which alone explains the almost unanimous opposition to him; he was the opponent not of one party in the House but of the Parliament itself and of every other Parliament. In the course of a debate he came into conflict with the Chair; the President pointed out that some of his remarks had nothing to do with the subject; Bismarck at once protested: "I cannot allow the President the right to a disciplinary interruption in my speech. I have not the honour of being a member of this assembly; I have not helped to vote your standing orders; I have not joined in electing the President; I am not subject to the disciplinary power of the Chamber. The authority of the President ends at this barrier. I have one superior only, his Majesty the King." This led to a sharp passage with the President, who maintained that his power extended as far as the four walls; he could not indeed withdraw the right of speech from a Minister, but could interrupt him. Bismarck at once repeated word for word the obnoxious passage of his speech. The President threatened, if he did so again, to close the sitting; Bismarck practically gave way; "I cannot," he said, "prevent the President adjourning the House; what I have said twice I need not repeat a third time"; and the debate continued without further interruption. A few weeks later a similar scene occurred, but this time it was not Bismarck but Roon, and Roon had not the same quick feeling for Parliamentary form; Bismarck had defied the President up to the extreme point where his legal powers went, Roon passed beyond them. The President wished to interrupt the Minister; Roon refused to stop speaking; the President rang his bell. "When I interrupt the Minister," he said, "he must be silent. For that purpose I use my bell, and, if the Minister does not obey, I must have my hat brought me." When the Chairman put on his hat the House would be adjourned. Roon answered, "I do not mind if the President has his hat brought; according to the Constitution I can speak if I wish, and no one has the right to interrupt me." After a few more angry words on either side, as Roon continued to dispute the right of the President, the latter rose from his seat and asked for his hat, which he placed on his head. All the members rose and the House was adjourned. Unfortunately the hat handed to him was not his own; it was much too large and completely covered his head and face, so that the strain of the situation was relieved by loud laughter. After this the Ministers refused to attend the House unless they received an assurance that the President no longer claimed disciplinary authority over them; a series of memoranda were exchanged between the House and the Ministry; the actual point in dispute was really a very small one; it is not even clear that there was any difference of opinion; everyone acknowledged that the Ministers might make as many speeches as they liked, and that the Chairman could not require them to stop speaking. The only question was whether he might interrupt them in order to make any remarks himself; but neither side was prepared to come to an understanding. The King, to whom the House appealed, supported the Ministry, and a few days later the House was prorogued. The second session was over.

Three days later, by Royal proclamation, a series of ordinances was published creating very stringent regulations for the control of the Press; they gave the police the right of forbidding a newspaper to appear for no other reason except disapproval of its general tendency. It was a power more extreme than in the worst days of the Carlsbad decrees had ever been claimed by any German Government. The ordinances were based on a clause in the Constitution which gave the Government at times of crisis, if Parliament were not sitting, the power of making special regulations for the government of the Press. The reference to the Constitution seemed almost an insult; the kind of crisis which was meant was obviously a period of civil war or invasion; it seemed as though the Government had taken the first pretext for proroguing Parliament to be able to avail themselves of this clause. The ordinances reminded men of those of Charles X.; surely, they said, this was the beginning of a reign of violence.

The struggle was now no longer confined to Parliament. Parliament indeed was clearly impotent; all that could be done by speeches and votes and addresses had been done and had failed; the King still supported the Ministry. It was now the time for the people at large; the natural leaders were the corporations of the large towns; the Liberal policy of the Prussian Government had given them considerable independence; they were elected by the people, and in nearly every town there was a large majority opposed to the Government. Headed by the capital, they began a series of addresses to the King; public meetings were organised; at Cologne a great festival was arranged to welcome Sybel and the other representatives from the Rhine. It was more serious that in so monarchical a country the discontent with the personal action of the King found public expression. The Crown Prince was at this time on a tour of military inspection in East Prussia; town after town refused the ordinary loyal addresses; they would not welcome him or take part in the usual ceremonies; the ordinary loyal addresses to the King and other members of the Royal Family were refused. It was no longer a conflict between the Ministry and the Parliament, but between the King and the country.

Suddenly the country learned that the Crown Prince himself, the Heir Apparent to the throne, was on their side. He had always disliked Bismarck; he was offended by the brusqueness of his manner. He disliked the genial and careless bonhommie with which Bismarck, who hated affectation, discussed the most serious subjects; he had opposed his appointment, and he now held a position towards his father's Government similar to that which ten years before his father had held towards his own brother. He was much influenced by his English relations, and the opinion of the English Court was strongly unfavourable to

Bismarck. Hitherto the Crown Prince had refrained from any public active opposition; he had, however, not been asked his opinion concerning the Press ordinances, nor had he even received an invitation to the council at which they were passed. Bitterly offended at this slight upon himself, seriously alarmed lest the action of the Government might even endanger the dynasty, on his entry into Danzig he took occasion to dissociate himself from the action of the Government. He had not, he said, been asked; he had known nothing about it; he was not responsible. The words were few and they were moderate, but they served to shew the whole of Germany what hitherto only those about the Court had known, that the Crown Prince was to be counted among the opponents of the Government.

An incident followed a few days later which could only serve to increase the breach. After his speech at Danzig, the Crown Prince had offered to surrender all his official positions; the King had not required this of him, but had strictly ordered him not again to come into opposition to his Government. The Crown Prince had promised obedience, but continued his private protests against "these rude and insolent Ministers." The letters on both sides had been affectionate and dignified. A few days later, however, the Berlin correspondent of the Times was enabled to publish the contents of them. It is not known who was to blame for this very serious breach of confidence; but the publication must have been brought about by someone very closely connected with the Crown Prince; suspicion was naturally directed towards the Court of Coburg. It was not the last time that the confidence of the Crown Prince was to be abused in a similar manner.

The event naturally much increased Bismarck's dislike to the entourage of the Prince. There was indeed a considerable number of men, half men of letters, half politicians, who were glad to play a part by attaching themselves to a Liberal Prince; they did not scruple to call in the help of the Press of the foreign countries, especially of England, and use its influence for the decision of Prussian affairs. Unfortunately their connections were largely with England; they had a great admiration for English liberty, and they were often known as the English party. This want of discretion, which afterwards caused a strong prejudice against them in Germany, was used to create a prejudice also against England. People in Germany confused with the English nation, which was supremely indifferent to Continental affairs, the opinions of a few writers who were nearly always German. For many years after this, the relations between Bismarck and the Crown Prince were very distant, and the breach was to be increased by the very decided line which the Crown Prince afterwards took with regard to the Schleswig-Holstein affair.

The event shewed that Bismarck knew well the country with which he was dealing; the Press ordinances were not actually illegal, they were strictly enforced; many papers were warned, others were suppressed; the majority at once changed their tone and moderated their expression of hostility to the Government. In England, under similar circumstances, a host of scurrilous pamphlets have always appeared; the Prussian police were too prompt for this to be possible. The King refused to receive the addresses; an order from the Home Office forbade town councils to discuss political matters; a Bürgermeister who disregarded the order was suspended from his office; public meetings were suppressed. These measures were successful; the discontent remained and increased, but there was no disorder and there were no riots. Great courage was required to defy public opinion, but with courage it could be defied with as much impunity as that of the Parliament. Englishmen at the time asked why the people did not refuse to pay the taxes; the answer is easy: there would have been no legal justification for this, for though, until the estimates had been passed, the Ministers were not legally enabled to spend a farthing of public money, the taxes could still be levied; they were not voted annually; once imposed, they continued until a law was passed withdrawing them. The situation, in fact, was this, that the Ministry were obliged to collect the money though they were not authorised in spending it. To this we must add that the country was very prosperous; the revenue was constantly increasing; there was no distress. The socialist agitation which was just beginning was directed not against the Government but against society; Lassalle found more sympathy in Bismarck than he did with the Liberal leaders. He publicly exhorted his followers to support the Monarchy against these miserable Bourgeois, as he called the Liberals. Except on the one ground of the constitutional conflict, the country was well governed; there was no other interference with liberty of thought or action.

Moreover, there was a general feeling that things could not last long; the Liberals believed that the future was with them; time itself would bring revenge. At the worst they would wait till the death of the King; he was already nearly seventy years of age; the political difficulties had much injured his health. When he was gone, then with the Crown Prince the constitutional cause would triumph.

How different was the future to be! Year after year the conflict continued. Each year the House was summoned and the Budget laid before it; each year the House rejected the Budget; they threw out Government measures, they refused the loans, and they addressed the King to dismiss his Ministers. The sessions, however, were very short; that of 1864 lasted only a few weeks.

Each year Bismarck's open contempt for the Parliament and their unqualified hatred of him increased. The people still continued to support their representatives. The cities still continued to withhold their loyal addresses to the King. With each year, however, the Government gained confidence. It was easy to see that the final result would depend on the success of the Government in external affairs. To these we must now turn.

English opinion at that time was unanimously opposed to the King; it is difficult even now to judge the issue. It was natural for Englishmen to sympathise with those who wished to imitate them. Their pride was pleased when they found the ablest Parliamentary leaders, the most learned historians and keenest jurists desirous to assimilate the institutions of Prussia to those which existed in England. It is just this which ought to make us pause. What do we think of politicians who try to introduce among us the institutions and the faults of foreign countries? "Why will not the King of Prussia be content with the position which the Queen of England holds, or the King of the Belgians,—then all his unpopularity would be gone?" was a question asked at the time by an English writer. We may ask, on the other hand, why should the King of Prussia sacrifice his power and prerogative? The question is really as absurd as it would be to ask, why is not an English Parliament content with the power enjoyed by the Prussian Parliament? It was a commonplace of the time, that the continued conflict shewed a want of statesmanship; so it did, if it is statesmanship always to court popularity and always to surrender one's cause when one believes it to be right, even at the risk of ruining one's country. It must be remembered that through all these years the existence of Prussia was at stake. If the Prussian Government insisted on the necessity for a large and efficient army, they were accused of reckless militarism. People forgot that the Prussian Monarchy could no more maintain itself without a large army than the British Empire could without a large navy. In all the secret diplomatic negotiations of the time, the dismemberment of Prussia was a policy to be considered. France wished to acquire part of the left bank of the Rhine, Austria had never quite given up hope of regaining part of Silesia; it was not fifty years since Prussia had acquired half the kingdom of Saxony; might not a hostile coalition restore this territory? And then the philanthropy of England and the intrigues of France were still considering the possibility of a revived Poland, but in Poland would have to be included part of the territory which Prussia had acquired.

It is often said that from this conflict must be dated the great growth of militarism in Europe; it is to the victory of the King and Bismarck that we are to attribute the wars which followed and the immense armaments which since then have been built up in Europe. To a certain extent, of course, this is true, though it is not clear that the presence of these immense armies is an unmixed evil. It is, however, only half the truth; the Prussian Government was not solely responsible. It was not they who began arming, it was not they who first broke the peace which had been maintained in Europe since 1815. Their fault seems to have been, not that they armed first, but that when they put their hand to the work, they did it better than other nations. If they are exposed to any criticism in the matter, it must rather be this, that the Government of the late King had unduly neglected the army; they began to prepare not too soon but almost too late. It was in Austria in 1848 that the new military dominion began; Austria was supported by Russia and imitated by France; Prussia, surrounded by these empires, each at least double herself in population, was compelled to arm in self-defence. By not doing so sooner she had incurred the disgrace of Olmütz; her whole policy had been weak and vacillating, because the Government was frightened at stirring up a conflict in which they would almost certainly be defeated.

There is one other matter with regard to the conflict so far as regards Bismarck personally. We must always remember that he was not responsible for it. It had originated at a time when he was absent from Germany, and had very little influence on the conduct of affairs. Had he been Minister two years before, there probably would have been no conflict at all. The responsibility for it lies partly with the leaders of the Liberal party, who, as we know from memoirs that have since been published, were acting against their own convictions, in opposing the military demands of the Government, for they feared that otherwise the party would not follow them. Much of the responsibility also rests with the Ministry of the new era; they had mismanaged affairs; the mismanagement arose from the want of union among them, for the Liberal majority were in many matters opposed to the King and the throne. It was this want of cordial co-operation in the Ministry which led to the great blunder by which the Minister of War acted in a way which seemed to be, and in fact was, a breach of an engagement made by the Minister of Finance. Had Bismarck been in authority at the time, we can hardly doubt that he would have found some way of effecting a compromise between the Government and the leaders of the Moderate Liberal party. At least no blame attached to him for what had happened. Still less can we afford him anything but the highest commendation, that, when the King had got into an absolutely untenable position, he came forward, and at the risk of his reputation, his future, perhaps his life, stood by his side.

CHAPTER VIII.

SCHLESWIG-HOLSTEIN.

1863-1864.

We have seen that the result of the conflict would eventually depend upon the management of foreign affairs. Bismarck before his appointment had always said that the Government could only gain freedom at home by a more vigorous policy abroad. He was now in a position to follow the policy he desired. The conflict made him indispensable to the King; if he retired, the King would have to surrender to the House. This was always present to his mind and enabled him to keep his influence against all his enemies, who throughout the spring had used every effort to undermine his authority with the King.

There were many who thought that he deliberately maintained the friction in order to make himself indispensable, and in truth his relations to the Parliament had this advantage, that there was no use in attempting to take into consideration their wishes. Had he been supported by a friendly House he would have had to justify his policy, perhaps to modify it; as it was, since they were sure to refuse supplies whatever he did, one or two more votes of censure were a matter of indifference to him, and he went on his own way directing the diplomacy of the country with as sure and firm a hand as though no Parliament existed.

In the autumn he had the first opportunity for shewing how great his influence already was. During the summer holidays, he was in almost constant attendance on the King, who as usual had gone to Gastein for a cure. Perhaps he did not venture to leave the King, but he often complained of the new conditions in which his life was passed; he wished to be back with his wife and children in Pomerania. He writes to his wife from Baden: "I wish that some intrigue would necessitate another Ministry, so that I might honourably turn my back on this basin of ink and live quietly in the country. The restlessness of this life is unbearable; for ten weeks I have been doing clerk's work at an inn—it is no life for an honest country gentleman."

At the end of July, a proposal came from the Emperor of Austria which, but for Bismarck's firmness, might have had very far-reaching results. The Emperor had visited the King and discussed with him proposals for the reform of the Confederation. He explained an Austrian plan for the reform which was so much needed, and asked the King if he would join in an assembly of all the German Princes to discuss the plan. The King for many reasons refused; nevertheless two days afterwards formal invitations were sent out to all the Princes and to the Burgomasters of the free cities, inviting them to a Congress which was to meet at Frankfort. All the other Princes accepted, and the Congress met on the 15th of August. The Emperor presided in person, and he hoped to be able to persuade them to adopt his proposals, which would be very favourable for Austria. It was, however, apparent that without the presence of the King of Prussia the Congress would come to no result; it was therefore determined to send a special deputation to invite him to reconsider his refusal. The King had the day before moved from Karlsbad to Baden and was therefore in the immediate neighbourhood of Frankfort. It was very difficult for him not to accept this special invitation. "How can I refuse," he said, "when thirty Princes invite me and they send the message by a King!"

Personally he wished to go, though he agreed with Bismarck that it would be wiser to stay away; all his relations pressed him to go. It would have been pleasant for once to meet in friendly conclave all his fellow Princes. Bismarck, however, was determined that it should not be. He also had gone to Baden-Baden; the King consulted him before sending the answer. After a long and exhausting struggle, Bismarck gained his point and a refusal was sent. He had threatened to resign if his advice were not taken. As soon as the letter was sealed and despatched, Bismarck turned to a tray with glasses which stood on the table and smashed them in pieces. "Are you ill?" asked a friend who was in the room. "No," was the answer; "I was, but I am better now. I felt I must break something." So much were his nerves affected by the struggle.

The Congress went on without the representative of Prussia.

The Kings and Princes discussed the proposals in secret session. They enjoyed this unaccustomed freedom; for the first time they had been able to discuss the affairs of their own country without the intervention of their Ministers. The Ministers had, of course, come to Frankfort, but they found themselves excluded from all participation in affairs. With what admiration and jealousy must they have looked on Bismarck, but there was none of them who had done for his Prince what Bismarck had for the King of Prussia.

Perhaps it was his intention at once to press forward the struggle with Austria for supremacy in Germany. If so, he was to be disappointed. A new difficulty was now appearing in the diplomatic world: the Schleswig-Holstein question, which had been so long slumbering, broke out into open fire, and nearly three years were to pass before Bismarck was able to resume the policy on which he had determined. Men often speak as though he were responsible for the outbreak of this difficulty and the war which followed; that was far from being the case; it interrupted his plans as much as did the Polish question. We shall have to see with what ingenuity he gained for his country an advantage from what appeared at first to be a most inconvenient situation.

We must shortly explain the origin of this question, the most complicated that has ever occupied European diplomacy.

The Duchy of Holstein had been part of the German Empire; for many hundreds of years the Duke of Holstein had also been King of Denmark; the connection at first had been a purely personal union; it was, however, complicated by the existence of the Duchy of Schleswig. Schleswig was outside the Confederation, as it had been outside the German Empire, and had in old days been a fief of the Kingdom of Denmark. The nobles of Holstein had, however, gradually succeeded in extending German influence and the German language into Schleswig, so that this Duchy had become more than half German. Schleswig and Holstein were also joined together by very old customs, which were, it is said, founded on charters given by the Kings of Denmark; it was claimed that the two Duchies were always to be ruled by the same man, and also that they were to be kept quite distinct from the Kingdom of Denmark. These charters are not undisputed, but in this case, as so often happens in politics, the popular belief in the existence of a right was to be more important than the legal question whether the right really existed.

The trouble began about 1830. There was a double question, the question of constitution and the question of inheritance. The Danes, desirous to consolidate the Monarchy, had neglected the rights of the old local Estates in the Duchies; this led to an agitation and a conflict. It was a struggle for the maintenance of local privileges against the Monarchy in Copenhagen. Moreover, a vigorous democratic party had arisen in Denmark; their object was to incorporate the whole of Schleswig in the Danish Monarchy; they did not care what happened to Holstein. This party were called the Eider Danes, for they wished Denmark to be extended to the Eider. Against this proposed separation of the two Duchies violent protests were raised, and in 1848 a rebellion broke out. This was the rebellion which had been supported in that year by Prussia, and it had the universal sympathy of everyone in Germany, Princes and people alike.

The question of constitution was complicated by one of succession. The male line of the Royal House which ruled in Denmark was dying out; according to a law introduced in 1660, descendants of the female branch might succeed in the Kingdom. This law had probably never been legally enacted for the Duchies; in Schleswig and Holstein the old Salic law prevailed. In the ordinary course of things, on the death of Frederick VII., who had succeeded in 1847, the long connection between Holstein and Denmark would cease. Would, however, Schleswig go with Holstein or with Denmark? Every Schleswig-Holsteiner and every German declared that the two Duchies must remain for ever "unvertheilt"; the majority of the Danes determined, whatever the law might be, that they would keep Schleswig, which had once been Danish. The King took a different line; he wished to maintain all the possessions in his House, and that the same man should succeed both in the Kingdom and the Duchies. There was no authority qualified to decide the legal question; and therefore the question of right was sure to become one of power. At first, strange as it may seem, the power was on the side of the Danes. Germany was weak and disunited, the Prussian troops who had been sent to help the rebellion were withdrawn, and the surrender of Olmütz was fatal to the inhabitants of the Duchies. The whole question was brought before a European Congress which met at London. The integrity of the Danish Monarchy was declared to be a European interest; and the Congress of the Powers presumed to determine who should succeed to the ducal and royal power. They chose Christian of Glucksburg, and all the Powers pledged themselves to recognise him as ruler over all the dominions of the King of Denmark.

Prussia and Austria were among the Powers who signed the Treaty of London, but the Diet of Frankfort was not bound by it. At the same time, Denmark had entered into certain engagements pledging itself to preserve the separation between Schleswig-Holstein and Denmark, and also not to oppress the German people in Schleswig. The Danes did not keep their engagement; despising the Germans, they renewed the old policy, attempted to drive back the German language, and introduced new laws which were inconsistent with the local privileges of Holstein and Schleswig. The Holstein Estates appealed for protection to the Diet. The Germans protested, but the Danes were obstinate. As years went on, the excitement of the Germans grew; they believed, and justly believed, that it was a matter of honour to defend the rights of the Duchies. Schleswig-Holstein was the symbol of German weakness and disgrace, and in defence of them the national enthusiasm was again roused.

With this popular enthusiasm Bismarck had no sympathy; and he had no interest for the cause of Schleswig-Holstein. He had originally considered the inhabitants merely as rebels against their lawful sovereign. He had learnt at Frankfort sufficient to make this indifferent to him, but he still regarded them as foreigners and looked on their claims merely from the point of view of Prussian interests. Both his sympathy and his reason led him in fact rather to take the Danish side. "The maintenance of Denmark is in our interest," he wrote in 1857, but Denmark could only continue to exist if it were ruled, more or less arbitrarily, with provincial Estates as it has been for the last hundred years; and in another letter: "We have no reason to desire that the Holsteiners should live very happily under their Duke, for if they do they will no longer be interested in Prussia, and under certain circumstances their interest may be very useful to us. It is important that, however just their cause may be, Prussia should act with great prudence." He recognised that if the complaints of the Duchies led again to a war between Germany and Denmark all the loss would fall on Prussia; the coast of Prussia was exposed to the attacks of the Danish fleet. If the war was successful, the result would be to strengthen the Diet and the Federal Constitution; and, as we know, that was the last thing which Bismarck desired; if it failed, the disgrace and the blame would fall upon Prussia.

The only thing which would have induced him warmly to take up the cause was the prospect of winning the Duchies for Prussia, but of that there seemed little hope.

So long, therefore, as he remained at Frankfort, he had endeavoured to keep the peace, and he continued this policy after he became Minister. The greater number of the German States wished to carry out a Federal execution in Holstein; he tried to avert this and warmly gave his support to Lord Russell in his attempt to settle the question by English mediation. His efforts, however, were unavailing, for the Danish Government, presuming on the weakness of Germany, continued their provocative action. On March 30, 1863, a new Constitution was proclaimed, completely severing Holstein from the rest of the Monarchy. The Holstein Estates had not been consulted and appealed to the Diet for protection; the law of the Federation enabled the Diet in a case like this to occupy the territory of the offending sovereign in order to compel him to rule according to the Constitution. The national German party wished to go farther, to confuse the questions of Schleswig and of Holstein, and so bring about a war with Denmark. Bismarck wrote to the Duke of Oldenburg to explain his objections to this: it would make the worst impression in England; and he insisted that they should attempt nothing more than Federal execution in Holstein. As Holstein belonged to the Federation, this would be a purely German affair and no ground would be given for interfering to England or France. In consequence, the simple execution in Holstein was voted. Even now, however, Bismarck did not give up hopes of keeping peace. He brought pressure to bear on the Danes and was supported by England. If only they would withdraw the proclamation of March 30th, and accept English mediation for Schleswig, he promised them that he would use all his influence to prevent the execution and would probably be successful.

His moderation, which received the warm approval of Lord Russell, of course only added to his unpopularity in Germany. The Danish Government, however, refused to accept Bismarck's proposal; they brought in still another Constitution by which the complete incorporation of Schleswig with the Monarchy was decreed. This was an overt breach of their treaty engagements and a declaration of war with Germany. At the beginning of November, it was carried through the Rigsrad by the required majority of two-thirds, and was sent up to the King to receive his signature. Before he had time to sign it the King died.

It was expected that the death of the King would make little difference in the situation, for it had been agreed that Christian of Glucksburg should succeed to all the provinces of the Monarchy. The first act he had to perform was the signature of the new Constitution; it is said that he hesitated, but was told by the Ministers that if he refused they would answer neither for his crown nor his head. On November 23d he signed.

Before this had happened the situation had received an unexpected change. A new claimant appeared to dispute his title to the Duchies. The day after the death of the King, Frederick, eldest son of the Duke of Augustenburg, published a proclamation announcing his succession to the Duchy under the title of Frederick VIII. No one seems to have foreseen this step; it was supposed that after the agreement of 1853 the question of succession had been finally settled. The whole of the German nation, however, received with enthusiasm the news that it was again to be raised.

They believed that the Prince was the lawful heir; they saw in his claim the possibility of permanently separating the Duchies from Denmark. Nothing seemed to stand between this and accomplishment except the Treaty of London. Surely the rights of the Duchies, and the claim of Augustenburg, supported by united Germany, would be strong enough to bear down this treaty which was so unjust.

The question will be asked, was the claim of Augustenburg valid? No positive answer can be given, for it has never been tried by a competent court of law. It may, however, I think, be said that although there were objections, which might invalidate his right to at least a part of the Duchies, it is almost certain that a quite impartial tribunal would have decided that he had at least a better claim than any of his rivals. This at least would have been true fifteen years before. When, however, the Treaty of London was arranged it was necessary to procure the renunciation of all the different claimants. That of the Emperor of Russia, the Duke of Oldenburg, and others was obtained without much difficulty; the Duke of Augustenburg long refused. In order to compel him to renounce, the Danish Government refused to restore to him his private property, which had been confiscated owing to the part he had taken in the late rebellion. He had been enormously wealthy, but was now living in exile and deprived of his revenues. By this means they had at last induced him to sign a document, in which he promised, for himself and his successors, not to make any attempt to enforce his claims to the succession. The document was curiously worded; there was no actual renunciation, only a promise to abstain from action. In return for this a sum of money, not equal, however, to that which he had lost, was handed over to him. Now it was Bismarck who, while envoy at Frankfort, had carried on the negotiations; he had taken much trouble about the matter, and earned the warm gratitude both of the King of Denmark and of the Duke. There is, I think, no doubt that he believed that the agreement was a bona fide one and would be maintained. Since then the Duke had renounced all his claims in favour of his eldest son; Prince Frederick had not signed the contract and maintained that he was not bound by it. Of course Bismarck could not admit this, and his whole attitude towards the Prince must from the beginning be hostile.

It is only fair to point out that there was no reason whatever why the Augustenburgs should do anything more than that to which they were bound by the strict letter of the agreement; they had no ties of gratitude towards Denmark; they had not, as is often said, sold their rights, for they had received only a portion of their own possessions. However this may be, his claim was supported, not only by the people and Parliaments, but by leaders of the German Governments, headed by the King of Bavaria.

Bismarck was now asked to denounce the Treaty of London to which Prussia had given her assent; to support the claims of Augustenburg; to carry out the policy of the Diet, and if necessary to allow the Prussian army to be used in fighting for Prince Frederick against the King of Denmark. This he had not the slightest intention of doing. He had to consider first of all that Prussia was bound by treaties. As he said: "We may regret that we signed, but the signature took place. Honour as well as wisdom allows us to leave no doubt as to our loyalty to our engagements." He had moreover to consider that if he acted as the Germans wished he would find himself opposed, not only by

Denmark, but also by Russia and England, and in military operations on the narrow peninsula the power of the English fleet would easily outbalance the superiority of the Prussian army. Moreover, and this was the point which affected him most, what good would come to Prussia even if she were successful in this war? "I cannot regard it as a Prussian interest to wage war in order in the most favourable result to establish a new Grand Duke in Schleswig-Holstein, who out of fear of Prussian aggression would vote against us at the Diet."

His policy, therefore, was clearly marked out for him: he must refuse to recognise the claims of Augustenburg; he must refuse to break the Treaty of London. This, however, would not prevent him from bringing pressure to bear on the new King of Denmark, as he had done on his predecessor, to induce him to abide by his treaty engagements, and, if he did not do so, from declaring war against him.

There was even at this time in his mind another thought. He had the hope that in some way or other he might be able to gain a direct increase of territory for Prussia. If they recognised the Augustenburg claims this would be always impossible, for then either the Duchies would remain under the King of Denmark or, if the Danes were defeated, they would have to be given to the Prince.

In this policy he was supported by Austria. The Austrian Government was also bound by the Treaty of London; they were much annoyed at the violent and almost revolutionary agitation which had broken out in Germany; it was with much relief that they learned that Prussia, instead of heading the movement as in 1849, was ready to oppose it.

The two great Powers so lately in opposition now acted in close union.

Issue was joined at the Diet between the two parties. The Prince brought his claim before it, and those who supported him proposed that, as the succession to the Duchies was in dispute, they should be occupied by a Federal army until the true ruler had been determined. Against this Austria and Prussia proposed that the Federal execution in Holstein, which had before been resolved on, should be at once carried out. If the execution were voted it would be an indirect recognition of Christian as ruler, for it would be carried out as against his Government; on this point, execution or occupation, the votes were taken.

Bismarck was, however, greatly embarrassed by the strong influence which the Prince of Augustenburg had in the Prussian Royal Family; he was an intimate friend of the Crown Princess, and the Crown Princess and the King himself regarded his claims with favour. Directly after his proclamation the pretender came to Berlin; he had a very friendly reception from the King, who expressed his deep regret that he was tied by the London Convention, but clearly shewed that he hoped this difficulty might be overcome. Bismarck took another line; he said that he was trying to induce the new King not to sign the Constitution; the Prince, to Bismarck's obvious annoyance, explained that that would be no use; he should maintain his claims just the same.

The King disliked the Treaty of London as much as everyone else did; he had to agree to Bismarck's arguments that it would not be safe to denounce it, but he would have been quite willing, supposing Prussia was outvoted in the Diet, to accept the vote and obey the decision of the majority; he even hoped that this would be the result. Bismarck would have regarded an adverse vote as a sufficient reason for retiring from the Federation altogether. Were Prussia outvoted, it would be forced into a European war, which he wished to avoid, and made to fight as a single member of the German Confederation. Rather than do this he would prefer to fight on the other side; "Denmark is a better ally than the German States," he said. The two parties were contending as keenly at the Prussian Court as at Frankfort; Vincke wrote a long and pressing letter to the King; Schleinitz appeared again, supported as of old by the Queen; the Crown Prince was still in England, but he and his wife were enthusiastic on the Prince's side.

How much Bismarck was hampered by adverse influences at Court we see from a letter to Roon:

"I am far removed from any hasty or selfish resolution, but I have a feeling that the cause of the King against the Revolution is lost; his heart is in the other camp and he has more confidence in his opponents than his friends. For us it will be indifferent, one year or thirty years hence, but not for our children. The King has ordered me to come to him before the sitting to discuss what is to be said; I shall not say much, partly because I have not closed my eyes all night and am wretched, and then I really do not know what to say. They will certainly reject the loan, and his Majesty at the risk of breaking with Europe and experiencing a second Olmütz will at last join the Democracy, and work with it in order to set up Augustenburg and found a new State. What is the good of making speeches and scolding? Without some miracle of God the game is lost. Now and with posterity the blame will be laid upon us. As God will. He will know how long Prussia has to exist. But God knows I shall be sorry when it ceases."

The only ally that Bismarck had was Austria. Their combined influence was sufficiently strong by a majority of one to carry through the Diet execution instead of occupation; though there was appended to the motion a rider that the question of succession was not thereby prejudiced.

The execution took place. During the month of December the Hanoverians and Saxons occupied Holstein; the Danes did not resist but retreated across the Eider. At the end of the year the occupation was complete. In the rear of the German troops had come also the Prince of Augustenburg, who had settled himself in the land of which he claimed to be ruler.

What was now to be done? The Augustenburg party wished at once to press forward with the question of the succession; let the Diet decide this immediately; then hand over Holstein to the new Duke and immediately seize Schleswig also and vindicate it from Christian, the alien usurper. Bismarck would not hear of this; he still maintained his policy that Prussia should not denounce the London Convention, should recognise the sovereignty of Christian, and should demand from him as lawful ruler of all the Danish possessions the repeal of the obnoxious November Constitution. In this he was still supported by Austria; if the Danes did not acquiesce in these very moderate demands, the Germans should enter Schleswig and seize it as a security. Then he would be able when he wished to free himself from the Treaty of London, for war dissolves all treaties.

The advantage of this plan was that it entirely deprived England of any grounds for interference; Prussia alone was now defending the London Convention; Prussia was preventing the Diet from a breach of treaty; the claim of Denmark was one in regard to which the Danes were absolutely wrong. Bismarck had therefore on his side Austria, Russia, probably France, and averted the hostility of England. Against him was German public opinion, the German Diet, and the Prussian Parliament; everyone, that is, whom he neither feared nor regarded. So long as the King was firm he could look with confidence to the future, even though he did not know what it would bring forth.

With the Parliament indeed nothing was to be done; they, of course, strongly supported Augustenburg. They refused to look at the question from a Prussian point of view. "On your side," Bismarck said, "no one dares honestly to say that he acts for the interests of Prussia and as a Prussian." They feared that he proposed to hand back the Duchies to Denmark; they refused to consider him seriously as Foreign Minister; they spoke of him as a rash amateur. It was to attack him on his most sensitive point. Here, at least, he felt on completely secure ground; diplomacy was his profession; what did the professors and talkers in the Chamber know of it? They were trying to control the policy of the State, but, he said, "in these days an Assembly of 350 members cannot in the last instance direct the policy of a great Power." The Government asked for a loan for military operations; he appealed to their patriotism, but it was in vain; the House voted an address to the King, remonstrating against the conduct of foreign affairs, and threw out the loan by a majority of 275 to 51. "If you do not vote the money, we shall take it where we can get it," Bismarck had warned them. The House was immediately prorogued after a session of only two months, not to meet again till January, 1865.

This policy of Bismarck was proposed by Austria and Prussia at the Diet; the other States refused to adopt it, as they wished to raise the question of succession; on a division Prussia was outvoted. The two great Powers therefore entered into a separate agreement in which, while still recognising the integrity of the Danish Monarchy, they undertook to force the King to withdraw the obnoxious Constitution, and, if he did not consent to do so, they agreed to occupy Schleswig.

The Prussian House, in its address to the King, had declared that the only result of this policy would be to give back the Duchies to Denmark. Was there no fear of this? What would have happened had Denmark after all given in, as England strongly pressed her to do? Had she withdrawn the obnoxious Constitution, and granted all that Bismarck asked, why then Prussia and Austria would have been bound to support the integrity of Denmark, and, if necessary, by force of arms to eject the Federal troops from Holstein. Bismarck had considered this contingency, and guarded himself against it. Many years later Beust put the question to him. "Oh, I was all right," he answered; "I had assured myself that the Danes would not give in. I had led them to think that England would support them, though I knew this was not the case." He had, however, even a surer guarantee than this; the ultimatum presented to Denmark was couched in such a form that even if he would the King could not comply with it. The requirement was that the Constitution should be revoked before the 1st of January. By the Constitution the King could not do this of his own prerogative; he must have the assent of the Rigsrad. This assent could not be obtained for the following reasons: the Rigsrad of the old Constitution had been dissolved and had no longer a legal existence; a new assembly could not be summoned before the 1st of January—there was not time.

If an assembly were summoned after that date, it must be of course summoned according to the new Constitution. To do this, however, would be to bring the obnoxious Constitution actually into force, and would mean, so to speak, a declaration of war against Prussia. If the King wished to give in he must have time; he must be allowed to summon the new assembly, lay before it the German demands, and require it to declare its own revocation. The English Government, still anxious to keep the peace, represented to Bismarck the dilemma in which he had placed the Danes. Lord Wodehouse, who was in Berlin in December, requested that at least more time should be allowed. Bismarck refused to listen to the request.

"These constitutional questions," he said, "had nothing to do with him; the Danes had put off the Germans for years; they could not wait any longer. The King could always make a coup d'état; he would have to do so sooner or later. Germany and Denmark could never be at peace so long as the Democratic party had the authority."

Denmark did not give way; the help from England, on which they had reckoned, was not forthcoming; the fatal day passed; the Austrians and Prussians entered Holstein, marched across that Duchy, and in the early part of February began the invasion of Schleswig. The relations of the Allied troops to the Federal army of occupation were very remarkable. Both were opposed to the Danes, but they were equally opposed to one another; had they dared to do so, the Saxons would have opposed the Prussian advance. As it was they sullenly watched the Prussian and Austrian columns marching north to the invasion of Denmark.

It was the first time that the remodelled Prussian army had been tested on the field of battle; Bismarck had brought it about that they were fighting for the cause of Germany and in alliance with Austria. As soon as war began, his own position improved. The King and the army were, of course, all the more confident in a Minister who had given them so good a cause of war and allowed them to take the field side by side with their old ally. Their superiority in number and discipline ensured success in the military operations; the Danes evacuated their first position at the Dannewirk; the German troops occupied the whole of Schleswig, then after some further delay advanced into Jutland, and finally began the siege of the strong fortification of the Düppel. The taking of this was a difficult piece of work, which, after some delay, was successfully carried out at the beginning of April.

Meanwhile the diplomatic difficulties had continued. There had now come from England the proposal of a Conference. This Bismarck, always wishing to preserve the appearance of moderation, accepted. Before doing so, he knew that he had gained a very important ally. Napoleon was displeased with the English Government; he it was who suggested to Bismarck that the best solution of the difficulty would be the annexation of the Duchies to Prussia. It was just what Bismarck himself desired. Would he be able to bring it about? This was what was in his mind when he had to consider the attitude he should adopt at the Conference.

He could not, of course, propose it openly; he might be able to arrange affairs so that in the universal confusion this solution should be welcomed. He first of all began to change his attitude towards the German agitation for Augustenburg; hitherto he had opposed and discouraged it; now he let it have free course. He wrote:

"The present situation is such that it seems to me desirable to let loose the whole pack against the Danes at the Congress; the joint noise will work in the direction of making the subjugation of the Duchies to Denmark appear impossible to foreigners; they will have to consider programmes which the Prussian Government cannot lay before them."

What this means is that England and Russia were to be convinced that Denmark could not regain the Duchies; then they would have to consider who should have them. Bismarck believed that Austria was irrevocably opposed to Augustenburg. "She would rather see the Duchies in our hands than in those of the Prince," he wrote. Austria and Russia would, therefore, oppose this solution; if both Denmark and Augustenburg were impossible, then would be the time for France to ask why should they not be given to Prussia, and to join this proposal with another one for the division of the Duchies according to nationality.

Napoleon, in accordance with his principles, wished entirely to disregard the question of law; he was equally indifferent to the Treaty of London, the hereditary rights of Augustenburg, or the chartered privileges of the Duchies. He wished to consult the inhabitants and allow each village to vote whether it wished to be German or Danish; thus, districts in the north where Danish was spoken would then be incorporated in Denmark; the whole of Holstein and the south of Schleswig would be permanently united to Germany, and by preference to Prussia. These revolutionary principles of Napoleon were in the eyes of the Austrian statesmen criminal, for if applied consistently not only would Austria be deprived of Venetia, but the whole Empire would be dissolved.

It required all Bismarck's ingenuity to maintain the alliance with Austria, which was still necessary to him, and at the same time to keep Napoleon's friendship by giving his assent to doctrines that would be so convenient to Prussia.

In considering Bismarck's diplomatic work we must not suppose that he ever deceived himself into thinking that he would be able clearly to foresee all that would happen; he knew too well the uncertain nature of the pieces with which he had to deal: no one could quite foretell, for instance, the result of the struggle which was going on in the English Ministry or the votes of the House of Commons; equally impossible was it to build on the assurances of Napoleon.

"The longer I work at politics," he said, "the smaller is my belief in human calculation. I look at the affair according to my human understanding, but gratitude for God's assistance so far, raises in me the confidence that the Lord is able to turn our errors to our own good; that I experience daily to my wholesome humiliation."

This time he had been mistaken in his forecast. In a despatch of May 23d to Austria he suggested two solutions,—the Augustenburg succession, and annexation by Prussia; he inclined towards the former, though, as he said, if the Prince was to be recognised,

"it would be imperatively necessary to obtain guarantees for a Conservative administration, and some security that the Duchies should not become the home of democratic agitations."

As he said elsewhere, "Kiel must not become a second Gotha." He no doubt anticipated that Austria would refuse this first alternative; then the annexation by Prussia would naturally arise for discussion. Had Austria been consistent, all would have been well, but a change had taken place there; the Government was not disinclined to win the popularity that would accrue to them if they took up the Augustenburg cause; after all, Austria would be rather strengthened than weakened by the establishment of a new Federal State, which, as all the other smaller Princes, would probably be inclined to take the Austrian side. In answer, therefore, to this despatch the Austrians, throwing aside all attempt at consistency, proposed vigorously to press the Augustenburg claim. "It is just what we were going to suggest ourselves," they said. Bismarck therefore was compelled now, as best he could, to get out of the difficulty, and, as Austria had not rejected it, he begins to withdraw the proposal he had himself made. To Bernstorff, his envoy at the Congress, he writes:

"Austria is endeavouring to establish irrevocably the candidacy of Augustenburg in order by this means to render it difficult for Prussia to impose special conditions. We cannot consent to this. The dynastic questions must be discussed with special consideration for Prussian interests, and, consequently, other possibilities cannot be ruled out, until we have negotiated with Augustenburg and ascertained in what relation to Prussia he intends to place himself and his country. If the person of Augustenburg meets with more opposition in the Conference than the project of a division, then let the former drop."

The proposal, however, had to be made; for once, all the German Powers appeared in agreement when they demanded from the neutrals the recognition of Augustenburg; but Bismarck proposed it in such words as to avoid pledging himself to the legality. Of course the proposal was rejected by the Danes and Russians and it was allowed to fall to the ground. For Bismarck the interest is for the moment diverted from London to Berlin.

The time had come when Bismarck should definitely decide on the attitude he was to adopt toward Augustenburg. Hitherto he had avoided committing himself irrevocably; it was still open to him either to adopt him as the Prussian candidate on such conditions as might seem desirable, or to refuse to have any dealings with him. He had, in fact, kept both plans open, for it was characteristic of his diplomatic work that he would generally keep in his mind, and, to some extent, carry out in action, several different plans at the same time. If one failed him he could take up another. In this case he intended, if possible, to get the Duchies for Prussia; it was always to be foreseen that the difficulties might be insurmountable; he had therefore to consider the next best alternative. This would be the creation of a new State, but one which was bound to Prussia by a special and separate treaty. There were many demands, some of them legitimate, which Prussia was prepared to make. Bismarck attributed great importance to the acquisition of Kiel, because he wanted to found a Prussian navy. Then he was very anxious to have a canal made across Holstein so that Prussian vessels could reach the North Sea without passing the Sound; and of course he had to consider the military protection on the north. It would therefore be a condition that, whoever was made Duke, certain military and other privileges should be granted to Prussia. On this, all through the summer, negotiations were carried on unofficially between the Prince of Augustenburg and the Prussian authorities. We cannot here discuss them in detail, but the Prince seems to have been quite willing to acquiesce in these naval and military requirements. He made several suggestions and objections in detail, and he also pointed out that constitutionally he could not enter into a valid treaty until after he had been made Duke and received the assent of the Estates. I think, however, that no one can doubt that he was quite loyal to Prussia and really wished to bring the matter to a satisfactory issue. As might be expected, he was very cautious in his negotiations with Bismarck, but his letters to the King are more open. Had Bismarck wished he could at any time have come to an agreement with the Prince, but he never gave the opportunity for a serious and careful discussion on the detailed wording of the conditions. He did not wish to be bound by them, but he kept the negotiations open in case events occurred which might compel him to accept this solution.

In his treatment of the question he was, to some extent, influenced by the personal dislike he always felt for the Prince.

What was the cause of this enmity? There was nothing in the Prince's character to justify it; he was a modest, honourable, and educated man; though deficient in practical ability, he had at a very critical time announced his claims to a decision and maintained them with resolution. Bismarck, who in private life was always able to do justice to his enemies, recognised this: "I should have acted in just the same way myself had I been in your place," he said. He always himself said that his distrust of the Prince was caused by his dislike of the men whom the latter relied upon for advice. He was too closely connected with the Progressive party. He had surrounded himself with a kind of ministry, consisting chiefly of men who, though by birth inhabitants of the Duchies, had for some years been living at Gotha under the protection of the Duke of Coburg. They were strong Liberals and belonged to that party in Germany of which the Court of Coburg was the centre, who maintained a close connection with the Crown Prince, and who undoubtedly were looking forward to the time when the Crown Prince would become King of Prussia, Bismarck would be dismissed, and their party would come into office. This is probably quite sufficient reason to explain Bismarck's personal dislike of Augustenburg, though it is probable that he laid more stress on this aspect of the matter than he otherwise would have done, for he hoped thereby to prejudice the King against the Prince; as long as the King recognised Augustenburg's claims, his own hands would be tied in the attempt to win the Duchies for Prussia.

He had, as we have seen, had a short interview with the Prince at the end of the previous year now a new meeting was arranged, avowedly to discuss the conditions which Prussia would require if she supported the Prince. The Crown Prince, who was very anxious to help his friend, persuaded him to go to Berlin and if possible come to some clear understanding with the King and Bismarck. Augustenburg was reluctant to take this step. Loyal as he was to Prussia he much distrusted Bismarck. He feared that if he unreservedly placed his cause in Prussia's hands, Bismarck would in some way betray him. The position he took up was perfectly consistent. He was, by hereditary right, reigning Duke; he only wished to be left alone with the Duchies; he knew that if he was, they would at once recognise him and he would enter into government. In order to win his dominions, he had required the help of Germany; it was comparatively indifferent to him whether the help came from Prussia, Austria, or the Federation. But he quite understood that Prussia must have some recompense for the help it had given. What he had to fear was that, if he entered into any separate and secret engagements with Prussia, he would thereby lose the support he enjoyed in the rest of Germany, and that then Bismarck would find some excuse not to carry out his promises, so that at the end he would be left entirely without support. We know that his suspicions were unfounded, for Bismarck was not the man in this way to desert anyone who had entered into an agreement with him, but Augustenburg could not know this and had every reason for distrusting Bismarck, who was his avowed enemy.

On the 30th of May, the Prince, with many misgivings, came to Berlin. The evening of the next day he had a long interview with Bismarck; it began about nine o'clock and lasted till after midnight. There is no doubt that this interview was decisive against his chances. From that time Bismarck was determined that under no circumstances should he succeed, and we shall see that when Bismarck wished for anything he usually attained it. We would gladly, therefore, know exactly what happened; both Bismarck and the Prince have given accounts of what took place, but unfortunately they differ on very important points, and no one else was present at the interview. It is clear that the Prince throughout, for the reasons we have named, observed great reserve. It would undoubtedly have been wiser of him openly to place himself entirely in Bismarck's hands, to throw himself on the generosity of Prussia, and to agree to the terms which Bismarck offered. Why he did not do this we have explained. The conversation chiefly turned on the Prussian demands for the harbour of Kiel and certain other concessions; the Prince expressed himself quite willing to grant most of what was required, but he could not enter into any formal treaty without the consent of the Estates of the Duchies. When he left the room he seems to have been fairly satisfied with what had been said. If so he deceived himself grievously. Scarcely had he gone (it was already midnight) when Bismarck sent off despatches to St. Petersburg, Paris, and London, explaining that he was not inclined to support Augustenburg any longer, and instructing the Ambassadors to act accordingly. Not content with this he at once brought forward an alternative candidate. Among the many claimants to the Duchies had been the Duke of Oldenburg and the Czar, who both belonged to the same branch of the family. The Czar had, at the end of May, transferred his claims to the Duke, and Bismarck now wrote to St. Petersburg that he would also be prepared to support him. We must not suppose that in doing this he had the slightest intention of allowing the Duke to be successful. He gained, however, a double advantage. First of all he pleased the Czar and prevented any difficulties from Russia; secondly, the very fact of a rival candidate coming forward would indefinitely postpone any settlement. So long as Augustenburg was the only German candidate there was always the danger, as at the Congress of London, that he might suddenly be installed and Bismarck be unable to prevent it. If, however, the Duke of Oldenburg came forward, Bismarck would at once take up the position that, as there were rival claimants, a proper legal verdict must be obtained and that Prussia could not act so unjustly as to prejudice the decision by extending her support to either. It was not necessary for anyone to know that he himself had induced the Duke of Oldenburg to revive his claim.

At the same time he took other steps to frustrate Augustenburg's hopes; he caused the statement to be published in the Prussian papers that during the conversation of May 31st the Prince had said that he had never asked the Prussians for help, and that he could have got on very well without them. It was just the sort of thing which would strongly prejudice the King against him, and

Bismarck was very anxious to destroy the influence which the Prince still had with the King and with many other Prussians. At that time, and always later, the Prince denied that he had said anything of the kind. Even if, in the course of a long conversation, he had said anything which might have been interpreted to mean this, it was a great breach of confidence to publish these words from a private discussion taken out of their context. The Prussian Press received the word, and for years to come did not cease to pour out its venom against the Prince. This action of Bismarck's seemed quite to justify the apprehension with which the Prince had gone to Berlin.

It is not necessary to look for any far-fetched explanation of Bismarck's action; the simplest is the most probable. He had not arranged the interview with any intention of entrapping Augustenburg; he had really been doubtful whether, after all, it might not be wiser to accept the Prince and make a separate treaty with him. All depended on his personal character and the attitude he adopted towards Prussia. Bismarck, who had great confidence in his own judgment of mankind, regarded a personal interview as the best means of coming to a conclusion; the result of it was that he felt it impossible to rely on the Prince, who, instead of being open, positive, and ready to do business, was reserved, hesitating, distrustful, and critical. Bismarck had given him his chance; he had failed to seize it. Instead of being a grateful client he was a mere obstacle in the road of Prussian greatness, and had to be swept away. Against him all the resources of diplomacy were now directed. His influence must be destroyed, but not by force, for his strength came from his very weakness; the task was to undermine the regard which the German people had for him and their enthusiasm for his cause—work to be properly assigned to the Prussian Press.

The Conference in London separated at the end of June without coming to any conclusion; it had, however, enabled Bismarck formally to dissociate himself from the former Treaty of London, and henceforward he had a free hand in his dealings with Denmark.

Another brilliant feat of arms, the transference of the Prussian troops across the sea to the island of Alsen, completed the war. Denmark had to capitulate, and the terms of peace, which were ultimately decided at Vienna, were that Schleswig, Holstein, and also Lauenburg should be given up. Christian transferred to the Emperor of Austria and the King of Prussia all the rights which he possessed. As to Lauenburg the matter was simple—the authority of the King of Denmark over this Duchy was undisputed; as to Schleswig-Holstein all the old questions still continued; the King had transferred his rights, but what were his rights? He could only grant that which belonged to him; if the Prince of Augustenburg was Duke, then the King of Denmark could not confer another man's throne. There was, however, this difference: hitherto the question had been a European one, but since the London Congress no other State had any claim to interfere. The disputed succession of the Duchies must be settled between Austria and Prussia. It was a special clause in the terms of peace that it should be decided by agreement between them and not referred to the Diet.

CHAPTER IX.

THE TREATY OF GASTEIN.

1864-1865.

Bismarck always looked back with peculiar pleasure on the negotiations which were concluded by the Peace of Vienna. His conduct of the affair had in fact been masterly; he had succeeded in permanently severing the Duchies from Denmark; he had done this without allowing foreign nations the opportunity for interfering; he had maintained a close alliance with Austria; he had pleased and flattered the Emperors of Russia and France. What perhaps gave him most satisfaction was that, though the result had been what the whole of the German nation desired, he had brought it about by means which were universally condemned, and the rescue of the Duchies had been a severe defeat to the Democratic and National party.

With the Peace a new stage begins; the Duchies had been transferred to the Allied Powers; how were they now to be disposed of? We have seen that Bismarck desired to acquire them for Prussia; if it were absolutely necessary, he would accept an arrangement which would leave them to be ruled by another Prince, provided very extensive rights were given to Prussia. He would acquiesce in this arrangement if annexation would involve a war with one of the European Powers. If, however, a Duke of Schleswig-Holstein was to be created he was determined that it should not be the Prince of Augustenburg, whom he distrusted and disliked. The real object of his diplomacy must be to get the Duchies offered to Prussia; it was, however, very improbable, as the Czar once said to him, that this would happen.

He wished for annexation, but he wished to have it peacefully; he had not forgotten his own resolution to have a war with Austria, but he did not wish to make the Duchies the occasion of a war. Austria, however, refused to assent to annexation unless the King of Prussia would give her a corresponding increase of territory; this the King positively refused. It was an unchangeable principle with him that he would not surrender a single village from the Prussian Monarchy; his pride revolted from the idea of bartering old provinces for new. If Austria would not offer the Duchies to Prussia, neither would the Diet; the majority remained loyal to Augustenburg. The people of the Duchies were equally determined in their opposition to the scheme; attempts were made by Bismarck's friends and agents to get up a petition to incorporate them with Prussia, but they always failed. Even the Prussian people were not really very anxious for this acquisition, and it required two years of constant writing in the inspired Press to bring them into such a state of mind that they would believe that it was, I will not say the most honourable, but the most desirable solution. The King himself hesitated. It was true that ever since the taking of the Düppel the lust of conquest had been aroused in his mind; he had visited the place where so many Prussian soldiers had laid down their lives; and it was a natural feeling if he wished that the country they had conquered should belong to their own State. On the other hand, he still felt that the rights of Augustenburg could not be neglected; when he discussed the matter with the Emperor of Austria and the subject of annexation was raised, he remained silent and was ill at ease.

If Bismarck was to get his way, he must first of all convince the King; this done, an opportunity might be found. There was one man who was prepared to offer him the Duchies, and that man was Napoleon. It is instructive to notice that as soon as the negotiations at Vienna had been concluded, Bismarck went to spend a few weeks at his old holiday resort of Biarritz. He took the opportunity of having some conversation with both the Emperor and his Ministers.

He required rest and change after the prolonged anxieties of the two years; at no place did he find it so well as in the south of France:

"It seems like a dream to be here again," he writes to his wife. "I am already quite well, and would be quite cheerful if I only knew that all was well with you. The life I lead at Berlin is a kind of penal servitude, when I think of my independent life abroad." Seabathing, expeditions across the frontier, and sport passed three weeks. "I have not for a long time found myself in such comfortable conditions, and yet the evil habit of work has rooted itself so deeply in my nature, that I feel some disquiet of conscience at my laziness. I almost long for the Wilhelmstrasse, at least if my dear ones were there."

On the 25th he left "dear Biarritz" for Paris, where he found plenty of politics awaiting him; here he had another of those interviews with Napoleon and his Ministers on which so much depended, and then he went back to his labours at Berlin.

At that time he was not prepared to break with Austria, and he still hoped that some peaceful means of acquisition might be found, as he wrote some months later to Goltz,

"We have not got all the good we can from the Austrian alliance." Prussia had the distinct advantage that she was more truly in possession of the Duchies than Austria. This possession would more and more guarantee its own continuance; it was improbable that any Power would undertake an offensive war to expel her. On the whole, therefore, Bismarck seems to have wished for the present to leave things as they were; gradually to increase the hold of Prussia on the Duchies, and wait until they fell of themselves into his hands. In pursuit of this policy it was necessary, however, to expel all other claimants, and this could not be done without the consent of Austria; this produced a cause of friction between the two great Powers which made it impossible to maintain the co-dominium.

There were in Holstein the Confederate troops who had gone there a year ago and had never been withdrawn; Augustenburg was still living at Kiel with his phantom Court; and then there were the Austrian soldiers, Prussia's own allies. One after another they had to be removed. Bismarck dealt first with the Confederate troops.

He had, as indeed he always was careful to have, the strict letter of the law on his side; he pointed out that as the execution had been directed against the government of Christian, and Christian had ceased to have any authority, the execution itself must ipso facto cease; he therefore wrote asking Austria to join in a demand to Saxony and Hanover; he was prepared, if the States refused, to expel their troops by force. Hanover—for the King strongly disliked Augustenburg—at once acquiesced; Saxony refused. Bismarck began to make military preparations; the Saxons began to arm; the Crown treasures were taken from Dresden to Königstein. Would Austria support Saxony or Prussia? For some days the question was in debate; at last

Austria determined to support a motion at the Diet declaring the execution ended. It was carried by eight votes to seven, and the Saxons had to obey. The troops on their return home refused to march across Prussian territory; and from this time Beust and the King of Saxony must be reckoned among the determined and irreconcilable enemies of Bismarck.

The first of the rivals was removed; there remained Austria and the Prince.

Just at this time a change of Ministry had taken place in Austria; Rechberg, who had kept up the alliance, was removed, and the anti-Prussian party came to the front. It was, therefore, no longer so easy to deal with the Prince, for he had a new and vigorous ally in Austria. Mensdorf, the new Minister, proposed in a series of lengthy despatches his solution of the question; it was that the rights of the two Powers should be transferred to Augustenburg, and that Schleswig-Holstein should be established as an independent Confederate State. The Austrian position was from this time clearly defined, and it was in favour of that policy to which Bismarck would never consent. It remained for him to propose an alternative. Prussia, he said, could only allow the new State to be created on condition that large rights were given to Prussia; what these were would require consideration; he must consult the different departments. This took time, and every month's delay was so much gain for Prussia; it was not till February, 1865, that Bismarck was able to present his demands, which were, that Kiel should be a Prussian port, Rendsburg a Prussian fortress; that the canal was to be made by Prussia and belong to Prussia, the management of the post and telegraph service to be Prussian and also the railways; the army was to be not only organised on the

Prussian system but actually incorporated with the Prussian army, so that the soldiers would take the oath of allegiance not to their own Duke but to the King of Prussia. The Duchies were to join the Prussian Customs' Union and assimilate their system of finance with that of Prussia. The proposals were so drawn up that it would be impossible for Austria to support, or for the Prince of Augustenburg to accept them. They were, in fact, as Bismarck himself told the Crown Prince, not meant to be accepted. "I would rather dig potatoes than be a reigning Prince under such conditions," said one of the Austrian Ministers. When they were officially presented, Karolyi was instructed to meet them with an unhesitating negative, and all discussion on them ceased.

Prussia and Austria had both proposed their solution; each State even refused to consider the suggestion made by the other. Meanwhile, since the departure of the Confederate troops the administration of the Duchies was in their hands; each Power attempted so to manage affairs as to prepare the way for the final settlement it desired, Prussia for annexation, Austria for Augustenburg. Prince Frederick was still living at Kiel. His position was very anomalous: he assumed the style and title of a reigning Prince, he was attended by something like a Court and by Ministers; throughout Holstein, almost without exception, and to a great extent also in Schleswig, he was looked upon and treated by the population as their lawful sovereign; his birthday was celebrated as a public holiday; he was often prayed for in church. All this the Austrians regarded with equanimity and indirectly supported; Bismarck wished to expel him from the country, but could not do so without the consent of Austria. At the end of March the matter again came up in the Diet; Bavaria and Saxony brought in a motion that they expected that Austria and Prussia would transfer the administration to Frederick. The Prussian Envoy rose and explained that they might expect it, but that Prussia would not fulfil their expectations; he moved that the claims of all candidates should be considered by the Diet, not only those of Augustenburg and of the Duke of Oldenburg, but also of Brandenburg.

The claims of Brandenburg were a new weapon of which Bismarck was glad to avail himself. No one supposed that they had really any foundation; they were not seriously put forward; but if the motion was carried, the Diet would be involved in the solution of a very complicated and necessarily very lengthy legal discussion. What the result was would be known from the beginning, but the Diet and its committees always worked slowly, and Bismarck could with much force maintain that, until they had come to a decision, there was no reason for handing over the administration to Augustenburg; it was at least decent not to do this till the claims of the rivals had been duly weighed. In the months that must elapse many things might happen. In the meantime the Diet would be helpless. When it had come to a decision he would then be able to point out, as he had already done, that they had no legal power for determining who was the ruler of any State, and that their decision therefore was quite valueless, and everything would have been again exactly as it was before. Austria supported the motion of Saxony, which was carried by nine votes to six. Prussia answered by sending her fleet from Danzig to Kiel, and occupying the harbour; the Government asked for a vote for the erection of fortifications and docks and for the building of a fleet; the Chamber refused the money, but Roon declared publicly in the House that Prussia would retain Kiel,—they had gone there and did not intend to leave. The occupation of Kiel was an open defiance to Austria; that it was intended to be so is shewn by the fact that a few days later Bismarck wrote to Usedom, the Prussian Minister at Florence, instructing him to sound the Italian Government as to whether they would be willing to join Prussia in war against Austria. At the same time he wrote to Goltz to find out in Paris whether there was any alliance between Austria and France. It would be some time before foreign relations could be sufficiently cleared up for him to determine whether or not war would be safe. He occupied the intervening period by continuing the negotiations as to the principles on which the joint administration should be conducted. He came forward with a new proposal and one which was extremely surprising, that the Estates of the Duchies should be summoned, and negotiations entered into with them. It is one of the most obscure of all his actions; he did it contrary to the advice of those on the spot. Everyone warned him that if the Estates were summoned their first action would be to proclaim Augustenburg as Duke. Some suppose that the King insisted on his taking this step; that is, however, very improbable; others that he proposed it in order that it might be rejected by Austria, so that Austria might lose the great influence which by her support of Augustenburg she was gaining in Germany. Austria, however, accepted the proposal, and then negotiations began as to the form in which the Estates should be called together; what should be the relations to them of the two Powers? This gave rise to a minute controversy, which could not be settled, and no doubt Bismarck did not wish that it should be settled. One of his conditions, however, was that, before the Estates were summoned, Augustenburg should be compelled to leave Holstein. Of course the Prince refused, for he well knew that, if he once went away, he would never be allowed to return. The Duke of Oldenburg, who was always ready to come forward when Bismarck wished it, himself demanded the expulsion of the Prince. The King of Prussia wrote a severe letter to Augustenburg, intimating his displeasure at his conduct and warning him to leave the country. The Prince answered, as he always did to the King, expressing his gratitude and his constant loyalty to Prussia, but refused, and his refusal was published in the papers. It was still impossible to remove him except by force, but before he ventured on that Bismarck had to make secure the position of Prussia.

At the beginning of July events began to move towards a crisis. Bismarck had appointed a commission of Prussian lawyers to report on the legal claim of the different candidates for the Ducal throne; their report was now published. They came to the conclusion, as we might anticipate that they would, that Augustenburg had absolutely no claim, and that legally the full authority was possessed by the two Powers who had the de facto government. Their opinion did not carry much weight even in Prussia itself, but they seem to have succeeded in convincing the King. Hitherto he had always been haunted by the fear lest, in dispossessing Augustenburg, he would be keeping a German Prince from the throne which was his right, and that to him was a very serious consideration. Now his conscience was set at rest. From this time the last support which Augustenburg had in Prussia was taken from him, for the Crown Prince, who always remained faithful to him, was almost without influence. Bismarck was henceforward able to move more rapidly. On the 5th of July the Prince's birthday was celebrated throughout the Duchy with great enthusiasm; this gave bitter offence to the King; shortly afterwards Bismarck left Berlin and joined the King, who was taking his annual cure at Carlsbad, and for July 28th a Council of State was summoned to meet at Regensburg. Probably this is the only instance of a King coming to so important a decision outside his own territories. The Council was attended not only by the Ministers, but also by some of the generals and by Goltz, who was summoned from Paris for the purpose. It was determined to send an ultimatum to Austria; the chief demand was that Austria should withdraw all support from Augustenburg, and agree immediately to eject him from the Duchies. If Austria refused to agree, Prussia would do so herself; he was to be seized, put on board a ship, and carried off to East Prussia. To shew that they were in earnest, a beginning was made by seizing in Holstein Prussian subjects who had written in the newspapers in a sense opposed to the wishes of the Prussian Government, and carrying them off to be tried at Berlin. In order to be prepared for all possibilities, an official request was sent to Italy to ask for her assistance in case of an outbreak of war. After these decisions were arrived at, the King continued his journey to Gastein to complete his cure; there, on Austrian territory in company with Bismarck, he awaited the answer.

In Austria opinions were divided; the feeling of annoyance with Prussia had been steadily growing during the last year. The military party was gaining ground; many would have been only too glad to take up the challenge. It would indeed have been their wisest plan to do so—openly to support the claim of Augustenburg, to demand that the Estates of Holstein should be at once summoned, and if Bismarck carried out his threats, to put herself at the head of Germany and in the name of the outraged right of a German Prince and a German State to take up the Prussian challenge.

There were, however, serious reasons against this. The Emperor was very reluctant to go to war, and, as so often, the personal feelings of the rulers had much to do with the policy of the Government. Then the internal condition of Austria both politically and financially was very unsatisfactory; it would have been necessary to raise a loan and this could not be easily done. There was also the constant danger from Italy, for Austria knew that, even if there were no alliance, as soon as she was attacked on one side by Prussia, the Italians on the other side would invade Venetia. Count Metternich was instructed to ask Napoleon, but received as an answer that they could not hope for a French alliance; the Austrians feared that he might already be engaged on the side of Prussia. For all these reasons it was determined to attempt to bring about a compromise. A change of Ministry took place, and Count Blome, one of the new Ministers, was sent to Gastein. He found both the King and Bismarck not disinclined to some compromise. The reports both from Florence and Paris did not seem to Bismarck to be entirely satisfactory: he did not find such readiness as he had hoped for; he feared that some secret understanding might be arrived at between Austria and Napoleon; and then, as we have seen, he was really anxious to avoid war for the sake of the Duchies; he had not given up his intention of war with Austria some day, but it would be impossible to find a less agreeable excuse for it.

"Halbuber and Augustenburg are acting so that we shall soon have to apply force; this will cause bad blood in Vienna; it is not what I wish, but Austria gives us no choice,"

he had written a few days before. After a few days of indecision a compromise therefore was agreed upon. The joint administration of the Duchies was to be given up; Austria was to administer Holstein, Prussia, Schleswig;

they both undertook not to bring the question before the Diet; the Duchy of Lauenburg was to be handed over absolutely to the King of Prussia, the Emperor of Austria receiving two million thalers for his share. Lauenburg was the first new possession which Bismarck was able to offer to the King; the grateful monarch conferred on him the title of Count, and in later years presented to him large estates out of the very valuable royal domains. It was from Lauenburg that in later years the young German Emperor took the title which he wished to confer on the retiring Chancellor.

CHAPTER X.

OUTBREAK OF WAR WITH AUSTRIA.

1865-1866.

The arrangement made at Gastein could not be permanent; it was only a temporary expedient to put off the conflict which henceforward was inevitable—inevitable, that is, if the Emperor of Austria still refused to sell Holstein to Prussia. It was, however, so far as it went, a great gain to Prussia, because it deprived Austria of the esteem of the other German States. Her strength had hitherto lain in her strict adhesion to popular feeling and to what the majority of the Germans, Princes and people alike, believed was justice; by coming to a separate agreement with Prussia, she had shaken their confidence. Bavaria especially was much annoyed by this change of front, and it seemed probable that the most important of the southern States would soon be ranged on the side of Prussia. This was a consummation which Bismarck ardently desired, and to which he addressed himself with much energy.

The attitude of France was more important than that of the German States, and in the autumn Bismarck made a fresh visit to that country. Just as he had done the year before, he went to take the sea-baths at Biarritz. This step was the more remarkable because Napoleon had received the news of the Treaty of Gastein with marked displeasure, and had given public expression to his opinions. Bismarck saw Drouyn de Lhuys at Paris and then went on to Biarritz where the Emperor was; for ten days he lived there in constant association with the Imperial family. The personal impression which he made was very favourable: "A really great man," wrote Mérimée, "free from feeling and full of esprit." He saw Napoleon again on his return through Paris; the two succeeded in coming to an understanding. Napoleon assured him that he might depend on the absolute neutrality of France, in case of a war between Prussia and Austria; it was agreed also that the annexation of the Duchies to Prussia would not be an increase of territory which would cause any uneasiness at Paris; Napoleon would view it with favour. Bismarck went farther than this; he opened the subject of a complete reform of the German Constitution on the lines that Prussia was to have a free hand in the north of Germany; he pointed out

"that the acquisition of the Duchies would only be an earnest for the fulfilment of the pledge which history had laid upon the State of Prussia; for the future prosecution of it we need the most friendly relations with France. It seems to me in the interest of France to encourage Prussia in the ambitious fulfilment of her national duty."

The Emperor acquiesced; as we know, the division of Europe into large national States was what he meant by Napoleonic ideas; he was willing enough to help in Germany a change such as that he had brought about in Italy. It was agreed that events should be allowed to develop themselves; when the time came it would be easy enough to come to some definite agreement.

This however was not all; it was not to be expected that Napoleon should render Prussia so valuable a service without receiving something in exchange; we know Bismarck's opinion of a statesman who, out of sympathy for another country, would sacrifice the interests of his own. The creation of a strong consolidated State in the north of Germany could not be in the interests of France; the power of France had always been founded on the weakness of Germany. Even if Napoleon himself, with his generous and cosmopolitan sympathies, was willing to make the sacrifice, France was not; Napoleon knew, and Bismarck knew, that Napoleon could not disregard the feeling of the country; his power was based on universal suffrage and the popularity of his name; he could not, as a King of Prussia could, brave the displeasure of the people. France must then have some compensation. What was it to be? What were to be the terms of the more intimate and special understanding? We do not know exactly what was said; we do know that Bismarck led both the Emperor and his Ministers to believe that Prussia would support them in an extension of the frontier. He clearly stated that the King would not be willing to surrender a single Prussian village; he probably said that they would not acquiesce in the restoration to France of any German territory. France therefore must seek her reward in a French-speaking people. It was perhaps an exaggeration if Drouyn de Lhuys said "he offered us all kinds of things which did not belong to him," but Napoleon also in later years repeated that Bismarck had promised him all kinds of recompenses. No written agreement was made; that was reserved for later negotiations, but there was a verbal understanding, which both parties felt was binding. This was the pendant to the interview of Plombières. But Bismarck had improved on Cavour's example; he did not want so much, he asked only for neutrality: the King of Prussia would not be called upon, like Victor Emmanuel, to surrender the old possessions of his House.

Bismarck returned to Berlin with his health invigorated by the Atlantic winds and his spirits raised by success. The first step now was to secure the help of Italy; he had seen Nigra, the Italian Minister, at Paris, and told him that war was inevitable; he hoped he could reckon on Italian alliance, but there was still, however, much ground for anxiety that Austria might succeed in arranging affairs with Italy.

The relations of the four Powers at this time were very remarkable. All turned on Venetia. The new Kingdom of Italy would not rest until it had secured this province. Napoleon also was bound by honour to complete his promise and "free Italy to the Adriatic"; neither his throne nor that of his son would be secure if he failed to do so. A war between Austria and Prussia would obviously afford the best opportunity, and his whole efforts were therefore directed to preventing a reconciliation between the two German Powers. His great fear was that Austria should come to terms with Prussia, and surrender the Duchies on condition that Prussia should guarantee her Italian possessions. When Bismarck visited Napoleon at Biarritz, the first question of the Emperor was, "Have you guaranteed Venetia to Austria?" It was the fear of this which caused his anger at the Treaty of Gastein. On the other hand, Bismarck had his reasons for anxiety. It was always possible that Austria, instead of coming to terms with Prussia, might choose the other side; she might surrender Venetia in order to obtain French and Italian support in a German war. The situation indeed was this: Austria was liable at any moment to be attacked by both Italy and Prussia; it would probably be beyond her strength to resist both assailants at the same time. A wise statesman would probably have made terms with one or the other. He would have either surrendered Venetia, which was really a source of weakness, to Italy, or agreed with Prussia over the Duchies and the German problem, thereby gaining Prussian support against Italy. The honourable pride of Mensdorf and the military party in Austria refused to surrender anything till it was too late.

None the less, the constant fear lest Austria should make terms with one of her enemies for a long time prevented an alliance between Prussia and Italy. The Italians did not trust Bismarck; they feared that if they made a treaty with him, he would allow them to get entangled in war, and then, as at Gastein, make up his quarrel with Austria. Bismarck did not trust the Italians; he feared that they and Napoleon would even at the last moment take Venetia as a present, and, as very nearly happened, offer Austria one of the Prussian provinces instead. It was impossible to have any reliance on Napoleon's promises, for he was constantly being pulled two ways; his own policy and sympathies would lead him to an alliance with Prussia; the clerical party, which was yearly growing stronger and had the support of the Empress, wished him to side with the Catholic power. In consequence, even after his return from France, Bismarck could not pass a day with full security that he might not find himself opposed by a coalition of Austria, France, and Italy; the Austrians felt that they were to be made the victims of a similar coalition between Prussia, France, and Italy; France always feared a national union between the two great German Powers.

Bismarck began by completing and bringing to a conclusion the arrangements for a commercial treaty with Italy; at the beginning of January the King of Prussia sent Victor Emmanuel the order of the Black Eagle; Bismarck also used his influence to induce Bavaria to join in the commercial treaty and to recognise the Kingdom of Italy. Then on January 13th he wrote to Usedom that the eventual decision in Germany would be influenced by the action of Italy; if they could not depend on the support of Italy, he hinted that peace would be maintained; in this way he hoped to force the Italians to join him.

Affairs in the Duchies gave Bismarck the opportunity for adopting with good grounds a hostile attitude towards Austria; Gablenz, the new Governor of Holstein, continued to favour the Augustenburg agitation. Many had expected that Austria would govern Holstein as a part of the Empire; instead of doing so, with marked design the country was administered as though it were held in trust for the Prince; no taxes were levied, full freedom was allowed to the Press, and while the Prussians daily became more unpopular in Schleswig the Austrians by their leniency won the affection of Holstein. At the end of January, they even allowed a mass meeting, which was attended by over 4000 men, to be held at Altona. This made a very unfavourable impression on the King, and any action of Austria that offended the King was most useful to Bismarck. "Bismarck is using all his activity to inspire the King with his own views and feelings," wrote Benedetti, the French Ambassador, at this time. At the end of January he felt sufficiently secure to protest seriously against the Austrian action in Holstein. "Why," he asked, "had they left the alliance against our common enemy, the Revolution?" Austria, in return, refused peremptorily to allow Bismarck any voice in the administration of Holstein. Bismarck, when the despatch was read to him, answered curtly that he must consider that henceforth the relations of the two Powers had lost their intimate character; "we are as we were before the Danish war, neither worse nor better." He sent no answer to the Austrian despatch and ceased to discuss with them the affairs of the Duchies.

This was a fair warning to Austria and it was understood; they took it as an intimation that hostilities were intended, and from this day began quietly to make their preparations. As soon as they did this, they were given into Bismarck's hands; the Prussians, owing to the admirable organisation of the army, could prepare for war in a fortnight or three weeks' time less than the Austrians would require; Austria to be secure must therefore begin to arm first; as soon as she did so the Prussian Government would be able, with full protestation of innocence, to point to the fact that they had not moved a man, and then to begin their own mobilisation, not apparently for offence but, as it were, to protect themselves from an unprovoked attack. In a minute of February 22d Moltke writes that it would be better for political reasons not to mobilise yet; then they would appear to put Austria in the wrong; Austria had now 100,000 men in Bohemia and it would be impossible to undertake any offensive movement against Prussia with less than 150,000 or 200,000; to collect these at least six weeks would be required, and the preparations could not be concealed. Six days later a great council was held in Berlin. "A war with Austria must come sooner or later; it is wiser to undertake it now, under these most favourable circumstances, than to leave it to Austria to choose the most auspicious moment for herself," said Bismarck. The rupture, he explained, had already really been effected; that had been completed at his last interview with Karolyi. Bismarck was supported by most of the Ministers; the King said that the Duchies were worth a war, but he still hoped that peace would be kept. The arrangement of the foreign alliances was now pushed on. The King wrote an autograph letter to Napoleon saying that the time for the special understanding had come; Goltz discussed with him at length the terms of French compensation. Napoleon did not ask for any definite promise, but suggested the annexation of some German territory to France; it was explained to him that Prussia would not surrender any German territory, but that, if France took part of Belgium, the Prussian frontier must be extended to the Maas, that is, must include the north-east of Belgium.

Again no definite agreement was made, but Napoleon's favouring neutrality seemed secure. There was more difficulty with Italy, for here an active alliance was required, and the Italians still feared they would be tricked. It was decided to send Moltke to Florence to arrange affairs there; this, however, was unnecessary, for Victor Emmanuel sent one of his generals, Govone, nominally to gain some information about the new military inventions; for the next three weeks, Govone and Barrel, the Italian Minister, were engaged in constant discussions as to the terms of the treaty. Of course the Austrians were not entirely ignorant of what was going on.

The negotiations with Italy roused among them intense bitterness; without actually mobilising they slowly and cautiously made all preliminary arrangements; a despatch was sent to Berlin accusing the Prussians of the intention of breaking the Treaty of Gastein, and another despatch to the German Courts asking for their assistance. Karolyi waited on Bismarck, assured him that their military preparations, were purely defensive, and asked point-blank whether Prussia proposed to violate the treaty. The answer, of course, was a simple "No," but according to the gossip of Berlin, Bismarck added, "You do not think I should tell you if I did intend to do so." On March 24th a despatch was sent to the envoys at all the German Courts drawing their attention to the Austrian preparations, for which it was said there was no cause; in view of this obvious aggression Prussia must begin to arm. That this was a mere pretext is shewn by a confidential note of Moltke of this same date; in it he states that all the Austrian preparations up to this time were purely defensive; there was as yet no sign of an attempt to take the offensive. Two days later, a meeting of the Prussian Council was held and the orders for a partial mobilisation of the army were given, though some time elapsed before they were actually carried out.

Under the constant excitement of these weeks Bismarck's health again began to break down; except himself, there was in fact scarcely a single man who desired the war; the King still seized every opportunity of preserving the peace; England, as so often, was beginning to make proposals for mediation; all the Prussian diplomatists, he complained, were working against his warlike projects. He made it clear to the Italians that the result would depend on them; if they would not sign a treaty there would be no war. The great difficulty in arranging the terms of the treaty was to determine who should begin. The old suspicion was still there: each side expected that if they began they would be deserted by their ally. The suspicion was unjust, for on both sides there were honourable men. The treaty was eventually signed on April 9th; it was to the effect that if Prussia went to war with Austria within the next three months, Italy would also at once declare war; neither country was to make a separate peace; Prussia would continue the war till Venetia was surrendered. On the very day that this treaty was signed, Bismarck, in answer to an Austrian despatch, wrote insisting that he had no intention of entering on an offensive war against Austria. In private conversation he was more open; to Benedetti he said: "I have at last succeeded in determining a King of Prussia to break the intimate relations of his House with that of Austria, to conclude a treaty of alliance with Italy, to accept arrangements with Imperial France; I am proud of the result."

Suddenly a fresh impediment appeared: the Austrians, on April 18th, wrote proposing a disarming on both sides; the Prussian answer was delayed for many days; it was said in Berlin that there was a difference of opinion between Bismarck and the King; Bismarck complained to Benedetti that he was wavering: when at last the answer was sent it was to accept the principle, but Bismarck boasted that he had accepted it under such conditions that it could hardly be carried out.

The reluctance of the King to go to war caused him much difficulty; all his influence was required; it is curious to read the following words which he wrote at this time:

"It is opposed to my feelings, I may say to my faith, to attempt to use influence or pressure on your paternal feelings with regard to the decision on peace or war; this is a sphere in which, trusting to God alone, I leave it to your Majesty's heart to steer for the good of the Fatherland; my part is prayer, rather than counsel"; and then he again lays before the King the insuperable arguments in favour of war.

Let us not suppose that this letter was but a cunning device to win the consent of the King. In these words more than in anything else we see his deepest feelings and his truest character. Bismarck was no Napoleon; he had determined that war was necessary, but he did not go to the terrible arbitrament with a light heart. He was not a man who from personal ambition would order thousands of men to go to their death or bring his country to ruin. It was his strength that he never forgot that he was working, not for himself, but for others. Behind the far-sighted plotter and the keen intriguer there always remained the primitive honesty of his younger years. He may at times have complained of the difficulties which arose from the reluctance of the King to follow his advice, but he himself felt that it was a source of strength to him that he had to explain, justify, and recommend his policy to the King.

All anxiety was, however, removed by news which came the next day. A report was spread throughout the papers that Italy had begun to mobilise, and that a band of Garibaldians had crossed the frontier. The report seems to have been untrue. How it originated we know not; when Roon heard of it he exclaimed, "Now the Italians are arming, the Austrians cannot disarm." He was right. The Austrian Government sent a message to Berlin that they would withdraw part of their northern army from Bohemia, but must at once put the whole of their southern army on a war footing. Prussia refused to accept this plea, and the order for the mobilisation of the Prussian army went out.

As soon as Austria had begun to mobilise, war was inevitable; the state of the finances of the Empire would not permit them to maintain their army on a war footing for any time. None the less, another six weeks were to elapse before hostilities began.

We have seen how throughout these complications Bismarck had desired, if he fought Austria, to fight, not for the sake of the Duchies, but for a reform of the German Confederation.

In March he had said to the Italians that the Holstein question was not enough to warrant a declaration of war. Prussia intended to bring forward the reform of the Confederation. This would take several months. He hoped that among other advantages, he would have at least Bavaria on his side; for the kind of proposal he had in his mind, though at this time he seems to have had no clear plan, was some arrangement by which the whole of the north of Germany should be closely united to Prussia, and the southern States formed in a separate union with Bavaria at the head. He had always pointed out, even when he was at Frankfort, that Bavaria was a natural ally of Prussia. In a great war the considerable army of Bavaria would not be unimportant.

At the beginning of April Bismarck instructed Savigny, his envoy at the Diet, to propose the consideration of a reform in the Constitution. The proposal he made was quite unexpected. No details were mentioned as to changes in the relations of the Princes, but a Parliament elected by universal suffrage and direct elections was to be chosen, to help in the management of common German affairs. It is impossible to exaggerate the bewilderment and astonishment with which this proposal was greeted. Here was the man who had risen into power as the champion of monarchical government, as the enemy of Parliaments and Democracy, voluntarily taking up the extreme demand of the German Radicals. It must be remembered that universal suffrage was at this time regarded not as a mere scheme of voting,—it was a principle; it was the cardinal principle of the Revolution; it meant the sovereignty of the people. It was the basis of the French Republic of 1848, it had been incorporated in the German Constitution of 1849, and this was one of the reasons why the King of Prussia had refused then to accept that Constitution. The proposal was universally condemned. Bismarck had perhaps hoped to win the Liberals; if so, he was disappointed; their confidence could not be gained by this sudden and amazing change—they distrusted him all the more; "a Government that, despising the laws of its own country, comes forward with plans for Confederate reform, cannot have the confidence of the German people," was the verdict of the National party. The Moderate Liberals, men like Sybel, had always been opposed to universal suffrage; even the English statesmen were alarmed; it was two years before Disraeli made his leap in the dark, and here was the Prussian statesman making a far bolder leap in a country not yet accustomed to the natural working of representative institutions. He did not gain the adhesion of the Liberals, and he lost the confidence of his old friends. Napoleon alone expressed his pleasure that the institutions of the two countries should become so like one another.

There was, indeed, ample reason for distrust; universal suffrage meant not only Democracy,—it was the foundation on which Napoleon had built his Empire; he had shewn that the voice of the people might become the instrument of despotism. All the old suspicions were aroused; people began to see fresh meaning in these constant visits to France; Napoleon had found an apt pupil not only in foreign but in internal matters. It could mean nothing more than the institution of a democratic monarchy; this was Bonapartism; it seemed to be the achievement of that change which, years ago, Gerlach had foreboded. No wonder the King of Hanover began to feel his crown less steady on his head.

What was the truth in the matter? What were the motives which influenced Bismarck? The explanation he gave was probably the true one: by universal suffrage he hoped to attain a Conservative and monarchical assembly; he appealed from the educated and Liberal middle classes to the peasants and artisans. We remember how often he had told the Prussian House of Commons that they were not the true representatives of the people.

"Direct election and universal suffrage I consider to be greater guarantees of Conservative action than any artificial electoral law; the artificial system of indirect election and elections by classes is a much more dangerous one in a country of monarchical traditions and loyal patriotism. Universal suffrage, doing away as it does with the influence of the Liberal bourgeoisie, leads to monarchical elections."

There was in his mind a vague ideal, the ideal of a king, the father of his country, supported by the masses of the people. He had a genuine interest in the welfare of the poorest; he thought he would find in them more gratitude and confidence than in the middle classes. We know that he was wrong; universal suffrage in Germany was to make possible the Social Democrats and Ultramontanes; it was to give the Parliamentary power into the hands of an opponent far more dangerous than the Liberals of the Prussian

Assembly. Probably no one had more responsibility for this measure than the brilliant founder of the Socialist party. Bismarck had watched with interest the career of Lassalle; he had seen with admiration his power of organisation; he felt that here was a man who in internal affairs and in the management of the people had something of the skill and courage which he himself had in foreign affairs. He was a great demagogue, and Bismarck had already learnt that a man who aimed at being not only a diplomatist, but a statesman and a ruler, must have something of the demagogic art. From Lassalle he could learn much. We have letters written two years before this in which Lassalle, obviously referring to some previous conversation, says: "Above all, I accuse myself of having forgotten yesterday to impress upon you that the right of being elected must be given to all Germans. This is an immense means of power; the moral conquest of Germany." Obviously there had been a long discussion, in which Lassalle had persuaded the Minister to adopt universal suffrage. The letters continue with reference to the machinery of the elections, and means of preventing abstention from the poll, for which Lassalle professes to have found a magic charm.

One other remark we must make: this measure, as later events were to prove, was in some ways characteristic of all Bismarck's internal policy. Roon once complained of his strokes of genius, his unforeseen decisions. In foreign policy, bold and decisive as he could be, he was also cautious and prudent; to this he owes his success; he could strike when the time came, but he never did so unless he had tested the situation in every way; he never began a war unless he was sure to win, and he left nothing to chance or good fortune. In internal affairs he was less prudent; he did not know his ground so well, and he exaggerated his own influence. Moreover, in giving up the simpler Conservative policy of his younger years, he became an opportunist; he would introduce important measures in order to secure the support of a party, even though he might thereby be sacrificing the interests of his country to a temporary emergency. He really applied to home affairs the habits he had learned in diplomacy; there every alliance is temporary; when the occasion of it has passed by, it ceases, and leaves no permanent effect. He tried to govern Germany by a series of political alliances; but the alliance of the Government with a party can never be barren; the laws to which it gives birth remain. Bismarck sometimes thought more of the advantage of the alliance than of the permanent effect of the laws.

Even after this there was still delay; there were the usual abortive attempts at a congress, which, as in 1859, broke down through the refusal of Austria to give way. There were dark intrigues of Napoleon, who even at the last moment attempted to divert the Italians from their Prussian alliance. In Germany there was extreme indignation against the man who was forcing his country into a fratricidal war. Bismarck had often received threatening letters; now an attempt was made on his life; as he was walking along Unter den Linden a young man approached and fired several shots at him. He was seized by Bismarck, and that night put an end to his own life in prison. He was a South German who wished to save his country from the horrors of civil war. Moltke, now that all was prepared, was anxious to begin. Bismarck still hesitated; he was so cautious that he would not take the first step. At last the final provocation came, as he hoped it would, from Austria. He knew that if he waited long enough they would take the initiative. They proposed to summon the Estates of Holstein, and at the same time brought the question of the Duchies before the Diet. Bismarck declared that this was a breach of the Treaty of Gastein, and that that agreement was therefore void; Prussian troops were ordered to enter Holstein. Austria appealed for protection to the Diet, and moved that the Federal forces should be mobilised. The motion was carried by nine votes to seven. The Prussian Envoy then rose and declared that this was a breach of the Federal law; Prussia withdrew from the Federation and declared war on all those States which had supported Austria. Hanover and Hesse had to the end attempted to maintain neutrality, but this Bismarck would not allow; they were given the alternative of alliance with Prussia or disarmament. The result was that, when war began, the whole of Germany, except the small northern States, was opposed to Prussia. "I have no ally but the Duke of Mecklenburg and Mazzini," said the King.

CHAPTER XI.

THE CONQUEST OF GERMANY.

1866.

Bismarck had no part in the management of the army. This the King always kept in his own hands. He was himself Commander-in-Chief, and on all military questions he took the advice of his Minister of War and the chief of the staff. When his power and influence in the State were greatest, Bismarck's authority always ceased as soon as technical and military matters arose for consideration. He often chafed at this limitation and even in a campaign was eager to offer his advice; there was soldier's blood in his veins, and he would have liked himself to bear arms in the war. At least he was able to be present on the field of battle with the King and witness part of the campaign.

With the King he left Berlin on June 30th to join the army in Bohemia. Already the news had come of the capitulation of the Hanoverians; the whole of North-West Germany had been conquered in a week and the Prussian flank was secure. The effect of these victories was soon seen: his unpopularity was wiped out in blood. Night by night as the bulletins arrived, crowds collected to cheer and applaud the Minister.

The King and his suite reached the army on July 1st; they were just in time to be present at the decisive battle. At midnight on July 2d it was known that the Austrians were preparing to give battle near Königgrätz with the Elbe in their rear. Early the next morning the King with Bismarck, Roon, and Moltke rode out and took up their positions on the hill of Dub, whence they could view what was to be the decisive battle in the history of Germany. Here, after the lapse of more than a hundred years, they were completing the work which Frederick the Great had begun. The battle was long and doubtful. The army of Prince Frederick Charles attacked the Austrian division under the eyes of the King, but could make no advance against their powerful artillery. They had to wait till the Crown Prince, who was many miles away, could come up and attack the right flank of the Austrians. Hour after hour went by and the Crown Prince did not come; if he delayed longer the attack would fail and the Prussians be defeated. We can easily imagine what must have been Bismarck's thoughts during this crisis. On the result depended his position, his reputation, perhaps his life; into those few hours was concentrated the struggle to which he had devoted so much of his lifetime, and yet he was quite helpless. Success or failure did not depend on him. It is the crudest trial to the statesman that he must see his best plans undone by the mistakes of the generals. Bismarck often looked with anxiety at Moltke's face to see whether he could read in it the result of the battle. The King, too, was getting nervous. Bismarck at last could stand it no longer; he rode up to Moltke, took out a cigar case, and offered it to the General; Moltke looked at the cigars carefully and took the best; "then I knew we were all right," said Bismarck in telling this story. It was after two when at last the cannon of the Crown Prince's army came into action, and the Austrian army, attacked on two sides, was overthrown.

"This time the brave grenadiers have saved us," said Roon. It was true; but for the army which he and the King had made, all the genius of Moltke and Bismarck would have been unavailing.

"Our men deserve to be kissed," wrote Bismarck to his wife. "Every man is brave to the death, quiet, obedient; with empty stomachs, wet clothes, little sleep, the soles of their boots falling off, they are friendly towards everyone; there is no plundering and burning; they pay what they are able, though they have mouldy bread to eat. There must exist a depth of piety in our common soldier or all this could not be."

Bismarck might well be proud of this practical illustration which was given of that which he so often in older days maintained. This was a true comment on the pictures of the loyalty of the Prussian people and the simple faith of the German peasants, which from his place in Parliament he had opposed to the new sceptical teaching of the Liberals. As soon as he was able he went about among the wounded; as he once said, the King of Prussia was accustomed to look into the eyes of wounded men on the field of battle and therefore would never venture on an unjust or unnecessary war, and in this Bismarck felt as the King. He writes home for cigars for distributing among the wounded. Personally he endured something of the hardships of campaigning, for in the miserable Bohemian villages there was little food and shelter to be had. He composed himself to sleep, as best he could, on a dung-heap by the roadside, until he was roused by the Prince of Mecklenburg, who had found more acceptable quarters.

It was not for long that this life, which was to him almost a welcome reminiscence of his sporting days, could continue. Diplomatic cares soon fell upon him.

Not two days had passed since the great battle, when a telegram from Napoleon was placed in the King's hands informing him that Austria had requested France's mediation, that Venetia had been surrendered to France, and inviting the King to conclude an armistice. Immediately afterwards came the news that the surrender of Venetia to France had been published in the Moniteur.

If this meant anything, it meant that Napoleon intended to stop the further progress of the Prussian army, to rescue Austria, and to dictate the terms of peace; it could not be doubted that he would be prepared to support his mediation by arms, and in a few days they might expect to hear that the French corps were being stationed on the frontier. What was to be done? Bismarck neither doubted nor hesitated; it was impossible to refuse French mediation. West Germany was almost undefended, the whole of the southern States were still unconquered; however imperfect the French military preparations might be, it was impossible to run such a risk. At his advice the King at once sent a courteous answer accepting the French proposal. He was more disposed to this because in doing so he really bound himself to nothing. He accepted the principle of French mediation; but he was still free to discuss and refuse the special terms which might be offered. He said that he was willing to accept an armistice, but it was only on condition that the preliminaries of peace were settled before hostilities ceased, and to them the King could not agree except after consultation with the King of Italy. It was a friendly answer, which cost nothing, and meanwhile the army continued to advance. An Austrian request for an armistice was refused; Vienna was now the goal; Napoleon, if he wished to stop them, must take the next move, must explain the terms of peace he wished to secure, and shew by what measures he was prepared to enforce them.

By his prompt action, Bismarck, who knew Napoleon well, hoped to escape the threatened danger. We shall see with what address he used the situation, so that the vacillation of France became to him more useful than even her faithful friendship would have been, for now he felt himself free from all ties of gratitude. Whatever services France might do to Prussia she could henceforth look to him for no voluntary recompense. Napoleon had deceived him; he would henceforward have no scruples in deceiving Napoleon. He had entered on the war relying on the friendship and neutrality of France; at the first crisis this had failed him; he never forgot and he never forgave; years later, when the news of Napoleon's death was brought to him, this was the first incident in their long connection which came into his mind.

Intercourse with Paris was slow and uncertain; the telegraph wires were often cut by the Bohemian peasants; some time must elapse before an answer came. In the meanwhile, as the army steadily advanced towards the Austrian capital, Bismarck had to consider the terms of peace he would be willing to accept. He had to think not only of what he would wish, but of what it was possible to acquire. He wrote to his wife at this time:

"We are getting on well. If we are not extreme in our claims and do not imagine that we have conquered the world, we shall obtain a peace that is worth having. But we are as easily intoxicated as we are discouraged, and I have the thankless task of pouring water into the foaming wine and of pointing out that we are not alone in Europe, but have three neighbours."

Of the three neighbours there was little to fear from England. With the death of Lord Palmerston, English policy had entered on a new phase; the traditions of Pitt and Canning were forgotten; England no longer aimed at being the arbitress of Europe; the leaders of both parties agreed that unless her own interests were immediately affected, England would not interfere in Continental matters. The internal organisation of Germany did not appear to concern her; she was the first to recognise the new principle that the relations of the German States to one another were to be settled by the Germans themselves, and to extend to Germany that doctrine of non-intervention which she had applied to Spain and Italy.

Neither France nor Russia would be so accommodating; France, we have already seen, had begun to interfere, Russia would probably do so; if they came to some agreement they would demand a congress; and, as a matter of fact, a few days later the Czar proposed a congress, both in Paris and in London. Of all issues this was the one which Bismarck dreaded most. A war with France he would have disliked, but at the worst he was not afraid of it. But he did not wish that the terms of peace he proposed to dictate should be subjected to the criticism and revision of the European Powers, nor to undergo the fate which fell on Russia twelve years later. Had the congress, however, been supported by Russia and France he must have accepted it. It is for this reason that he was so ready to meet the wishes of France, for if Napoleon once entered into separate and private negotiations, then whatever the result of them might be, he could not join with the other Powers in common action.

With regard to the terms of peace, it was obvious that Schleswig-Holstein would now be Prussian; it could scarcely be doubted that there must be a reform in the Confederation, which would be reorganised under the hegemony of Prussia, and that Austria would be excluded from all participation in German affairs. It might, in fact, be anticipated that the very great successes of Prussia would enable her to carry out the programme of 1849, and to unite the whole of Germany in a close union. This, however, was not what Bismarck intended; for him the unity of Germany was a matter of secondary importance; what he desired was complete control over the north. In this he was going back to the sound and true principles of Prussian policy; he, as nearly all other Prussian statesmen, looked on the line of the Main as a real division. He, therefore, on the 9th of July, wrote to Goltz, explaining the ideas he had of the terms on which peace might be concluded.

"The essential thing," he said, was that they should get control over North Germany in some form or other.

"I use the term North German Confederation without any hesitation, because I consider that if the necessary consolidation of the Federation is to be made certain it will be at present impossible to include South Germany in it. The present moment is very favourable for giving our new creation just that delimitation which will secure it a firm union."

The question remained, what form the Union should take. On this he writes: "Your Excellency must have the same impression as myself, that public opinion in our country demands the incorporation of Hanover, Saxony, and Schleswig." He adds that this would undoubtedly be the best solution of the matter for all concerned, if it could be effected without the cession of other Prussian territory, but he did not himself consider the difference between a satisfactory system of reform and the acquisition of these territories sufficient to justify him in risking the fate of the whole monarchy. It was the same alternative which had presented itself to him about Schleswig-Holstein; now, as then, annexation was what he aimed at, and he was not the man easily to reconcile himself to a less favourable solution. At the same time that he wrote this letter he sent orders that Falkenstein should quickly occupy all the territory north of the Main.

It is important to notice the date at which this letter was sent. It shews us that these proposals were Bismarck's own. Attempts have often been made since to suggest that the policy of annexation was not his, but was forced on him by the King, or by the military powers, or by the nation. This was not the case. He appeals indeed to public opinion, but public opinion, had it been asked, would really have demanded, not the dethronement of the Kings of Hanover and Saxony, but the unity of all Germany; and we know that Bismarck would never pursue what he thought a dangerous policy simply because public opinion demanded it. It has also been said that the dethronement of the King of Hanover was the natural result of the obstinacy of himself and his advisers, and his folly in going to Vienna to appeal there to the help of the Austrian Emperor.

This also is not true. We find that Bismarck has determined on this policy some days before the King had left Thuringia. This, like all he did, was the deliberate result of the consideration: What would tend most to the growth of Prussian power? He had to consider three alternatives: that these States should be compelled to come into a union with Prussia on the terms that the Princes should hand over the command of their forces to the Prussian King, but he knew that the King of Hanover would never consent to this, and probably the King of Saxony would also refuse; he might also require the reigning Kings to abdicate in place of their sons; or he might leave them with considerable freedom, but cripple their power by taking away part of their territory. These solutions seemed to him undesirable because they would leave dynasties, who would naturally be hostile, jealous, and suspicious, with the control of large powers of government. Surely it would be better, safer, and wiser to sweep them away altogether. It may be objected that there was no ground in justice for so doing. This is true, and Bismarck has never pretended that there was. He has left it to the writers of the Prussian Press to justify an action which was based purely on policy, by the pretence that it was the due recompense of the crimes of the rival dynasties.

Sybel says that Bismarck determined on these terms because they were those which would be most acceptable to France; that he would have preferred at once to secure the unity of the whole of Germany, but that from his knowledge of French thought and French character he foresaw that this would be possible only after another war, and he did not wish to risk the whole. So far as our information goes, it is against this hypothesis; it is rather true to say that he used the danger of French interference as a means of persuading the King to adopt a policy which was naturally repugnant to him. It is true that these terms would be agreeable to Napoleon. It would appear in France and in Europe as if it was French power which had persuaded Prussia to stop at the Main and to spare Austria; Bismarck did not mind that, because what was pleasant to France was convenient to him. He knew also that the proposal to annex the conquered territories would be very agreeable to Napoleon; the dethronement of old-established dynasties might be regarded as a delicate compliment to the principles he had always maintained and to the traditional policy of his house. If, however, we wish to find Bismarck's own motives, we must remember that before the war broke out he had in his mind some such division of Germany; he knew that it would be impossible at once to unite the whole in a firm union. If Bavaria were to be included in the new Confederation they would lose in harmony what they gained in extent. As he said in his drastic way:

"We cannot use these Ultramontanes, and we must not swallow more than we can digest. We will not fall into the blunder of Piedmont, which has been more weakened than strengthened by the annexation of Naples."

Of course he could not express this openly, and even now German writers obscure the thought, for in Germany, as in Italy, the desire for unity was so powerful that it was difficult to pardon any statesman who did not take the most immediate path to this result. It was fortunate for Germany that Bismarck was strong enough not to do so, for the Confederation of the north could be founded and confirmed before the Catholic and hostile south was included. The prize was in his hands; he deliberately refused to pick it up.

Supposing, however, that, after all, France would not accept the terms he suggested—during the anxious days which passed, this contingency was often before him. It was not till the 14th that Goltz was able to send him any decisive information, for the very good reason that Napoleon had not until then made up his own mind. Bismarck's anxiety was increased by the arrival of Benedetti. He had received instructions to follow the King, and, after undergoing the discomfort of a hasty journey in the rear of the Prussian army, reached headquarters on the 10th at Zwittau. He was taken straight to Bismarck's room although it was far on into the night. He found him sitting in a deserted house, writing, with a large revolver by his side; for as Roon complains, even during the campaign Bismarck would not give up his old custom of working all night and sleeping till midday or later. Bismarck received the French Ambassador with his wonted cordiality and the conversation was prolonged till three or four o'clock in the morning, and continued on the following days. Bismarck hoped that he had come with full powers to treat, or at least with full information on the intentions of his Government; that was not the case; he had no instructions except to use his influence to persuade Prussia to moderation; Napoleon was far too much divided in his own mind to be able to tell him anything further. Bismarck with his usual frankness explained what he wished, laying much stress on the annexations in North Germany; Benedetti, so little did he follow Napoleon's thought, protested warmly against this. "We are not," he said, "in the times of Frederick the Great."

Bismarck then tried to probe him on other matters; as before, he assumed that Napoleon's support and good-will were not to be had for nothing. He took it as a matter of course that if France was friendly to Prussia, she would require some recompense. He had already instructed Goltz to enquire what non-German compensation would be asked; he was much disturbed when Benedetti met his overtures with silence; he feared that Napoleon had some other plan. Benedetti in his report writes:

"Without any encouragement on my part, he attempted to prove to me that the defeat of Austria permitted France and Prussia to modify their territorial limits and to solve the greater part of the difficulties which continued to menace the peace of Europe. I reminded him that there were treaties and that the war which he desired to prevent would be the first result of a policy of this kind. M. de Bismarck answered that I misunderstood him, that France and Prussia united and resolved to rectify their respective countries, binding themselves by solemn engagements henceforth to regulate together these questions, need not fear any armed resistance either from England or from Russia."

What was Bismarck's motive in making these suggestions and enquiries? German writers generally take the view that he was not serious in his proposal, that he was deliberately playing with Napoleon, that he wished to secure from him some compromising document which he might then be able, as, in fact, was to happen, to use against him. They seem to find some pleasure in admiring him in the part of Agent provocateur. Perhaps we may interpret his thought rather differently. We have often seen that it was not his practice to lay down a clear and definite course of action, but he met each crisis as it occurred. The immediate necessity was to secure the friendship of France; believing, as he did, that in politics no one acted simply on principle or out of friendship, he assumed that Napoleon, who had control of the situation, would not give his support unless he had the promise of some important recompense. The natural thing for him, as he always preferred plain dealing, was to ask straight out what the Emperor wanted. When the answer came, then fresh questions would arise; if it was of such a kind that Bismarck would be able to accept it, a formal treaty between the two States might be made; if it was more than Bismarck was willing to grant, then there would be an opportunity for prolonging negotiations with France, and haggling over smaller points, and he would be able to come to some agreement with Austria quickly. If he could not come to any agreement with France, and war were to break out, he would always have this advantage, that he would be able to make it appear that the cause of war arose not in the want of moderation of Prussia, but in the illegitimate claims of France. Finally he had this to consider, that so long as France was discussing terms with him, there was no danger of their accepting the Russian proposal for a congress. Probably the one contingency which did not occur to him was that which, in fact, was nearest to the truth, namely, that Napoleon did not care much for any recompense, and that he had not seriously considered what he ought to demand.

He was, however, prepared for the case that France should not be accommodating. He determined to enter on separate negotiations with Austria. As he could not do this directly, he let it be known at Vienna by way of St. Petersburg that he was willing to negotiate terms of peace. At Brunn, where he was living, he opened up a new channel of intercourse. An Austrian nobleman, who was well disposed towards Prussia, undertook an unofficial mission, and announced to the Emperor the terms on which Prussia would make peace. They were extraordinarily lenient, namely, that, with the exception of Venetia, the territory of Austria should remain intact, that no war indemnity should be expected, that the Main should form the boundary of Prussian ambition, that South Germany should be left free, and might enter into close connection with Austria if it chose; the only condition was that no intervention or mediation of France should be allowed. If the negotiations with France were successful, then the French and Prussian armies united would bid defiance to the world. If those with France failed, then he hoped to bring about an understanding with Austria; the two great Powers would divide Germany between them, but present a united front to all outsiders. If both negotiations broke down, he would be reduced to a third and more terrible alternative: against a union of France and of Austria he would put himself at the head of the German national movement; he would adopt the programme of 1849; he would appeal to the Revolution; he would stir up rebellion in Hungary; he would encourage the Italians to deliver a thrust into the very heart of the Austrian Monarchy; and, while Austria was destroyed by internal dissensions, he would meet the French invasion at the head of a united army of the other German States.

After all, however, Napoleon withdrew his opposition. It was represented to him that he had not the military force to carry out his new programme; Italy refused to desert Prussia or even to receive Venetia from the hands of France; Prince Napoleon warned his cousin against undoing the work of his lifetime. The Emperor himself, broken in health and racked by pain, confessed that his action of July 5th had been a mistake; he apologised to Goltz for his proclamation; he asked only that Prussia should be moderate in her demands; the one thing was that the unity of Germany should be avoided, if only in appearance. This, we have seen, was Bismarck's own view. Napoleon accepted the terms which Goltz proposed, but asked only that the Kingdom of Saxony should be spared; if this was done, he would not only adopt, he would recommend them. An agreement was quickly come to. Benedetti went on to Vienna; he and Gramont had little difficulty in persuading the Emperor to agree to terms of peace by which the whole loss of the war would fall not upon him, not even upon his only active and faithful ally, the King of Saxony, but on those other States who had refused to join themselves to either party. What a triumph was it of Bismarck's skill that the addition of 4,000,000 subjects to the Prussian Crown and complete dominion over Northern Germany should appear, not as the demand which, as a ruthless conqueror, he enforced on his helpless enemies, but as the solution of all difficulties which was recommended to him in reward for his moderation by the ruler of France!

On the 23d of July an armistice was agreed on, and a conference was held at Nikolsburg to arrange the preliminaries of peace. There was no delay. In olden days Bismarck had shewn how he was able to prolong negotiations year after year when it was convenient to him that they should come to no conclusion; now he hurried through in three days the discussion by which the whole future of Germany and Europe were to be determined. When all were agreed on the main points, difficulties on details were easily overcome. It remained only to procure the assent of the King. Here again, as so often before, Bismarck met with most serious resistance. He drew up a careful memorandum which he presented to the monarch, pressing on him in the very strongest terms the acceptance of these conditions, Up to the last moment, however, there seems to have been a great reluctance; Sybel represents the difficulties as rising from the immoderate demands of the military party at Court; they were not prepared, after so great a victory, to leave Austria with undiminished territory; they wished at least to have part of Austrian Silesia. This account seems misleading. It was not that the King wanted more than Bismarck had desired; he wanted his acquisition of territory to come in a different way. He was not reconciled to the dethronement of the King of Hanover; he wished to take part of Hanover, part of Saxony, part of Bavaria, and something from Darmstadt; to his simple and honest mind it seemed unjust that those who had been his bitterest enemies should be treated with the greatest consideration. It was the old difficulty which Bismarck had met with in dealing with Schleswig-Holstein: the King had much regard for the rights of other Princes. This time, however, Bismarck, we are surprised to learn, had the influential support of the Crown Prince; the scruples which he had felt as regards Schleswig-Holstein did not apply to Hanover. He was sent in to his father; the interview lasted two hours; what passed we do not know; he came out exhausted and wearied with the long struggle, but the King had given in, and the policy of Bismarck triumphed. The preliminaries of Nikolsburg were signed, and two days afterwards were ratified, for Bismarck pressed on the arrangements with feverish impetuosity.

He had good reason to do so; he had just received intelligence that the Emperor of Russia was making an official demand for a congress and fresh news had come from France. On the 25th Benedetti had again come to him and had sounded him with regard to the recompense which France might receive. On the 26th, just as Bismarck was going to the final sitting of the Conference, the French Ambassador again called on him, this time to lay before him a despatch in which Drouyn de Lhuys stated that he had not wished to impede the negotiations with Austria, but would now observe that the French sanction to the Prussian annexations presupposed a fair indemnification to France, and that the Emperor would confer with Prussia concerning this as soon as his rôle of mediator was at an end. What madness this was! As soon as the rôle of mediator was at an end, as soon as peace was arranged with Austria, the one means which France had for compelling the acquiescence of Prussia was lost.

What had happened was this: Napoleon had, in conversation with Goltz, refused to consider the question of compensation: it was not worth while, he said; the gain of a few square miles of territory would not be of any use. He therefore, when he still might have procured them, made no conditions. Drouyn de Lhuys, however, who had disapproved of the whole of the Emperor's policy, still remained in office; he still wished, as he well might wish, to strengthen France in view of the great increase of Prussian power. He, therefore, on the 21st again approached Napoleon and laid before him a despatch in which he brought up the question of compensation. He was encouraged to this course by the reports which Benedetti had sent of his conversations with Bismarck; it was clear that Bismarck expected some demand; he had almost asked that it should be made. "We wish to avoid any injury to the balance of power," Goltz had said; "we will either moderate our demands or discuss those of France." It appeared absurd not to accept this offer. Napoleon was still reluctant to do so, but he was in a paroxysm of pain. "Leave me in peace," was his only answer to his Minister's request, and the Minister took it as an assent.

Bismarck, when Benedetti informed him of the demand that was to be made, at once answered that he was quite ready to consider the proposal. Benedetti then suggested that it would probably concern certain strips of territory on the left bank of the Rhine; on this, Bismarck stopped him: "Do not make any official announcements of that kind to me to-day." He went away, the Conference was concluded, the preliminaries were signed and ratified. France had been too late, and when the demand was renewed Bismarck was able to adopt a very different tone.

Let us complete the history of these celebrated negotiations.

The discussion which had been broken off so suddenly at Nikolsburg was continued at Berlin; during the interval the matter had been further discussed in Paris, and it had been determined firmly to demand compensation. Benedetti had warned the Government that Bismarck would not surrender any German territory; it was no good even asking for this, unless the demand was supported by urgent and threatening language. The result of the considerations was that he was instructed categorically to require the surrender to France of the Palatinate and Mayence. Benedetti undertook the task with some reluctance; in order to avoid being present at the explosion of anger which he might expect, he addressed the demand to Bismarck on August 5th, by letter. Two days he waited for an answer, but received none; on the evening of the 7th, he himself called on the Count, and a long discussion took place. Bismarck adopted a tone of indignation: "The whole affair makes us doubt Napoleon and threatens to destroy our confidence." The pith of it was contained in the last words: "Do you ask this from us under threat of war?" said Bismarck. "Yes," said Benedetti. "Then it will be war." Benedetti asked to have an interview with the King; it was granted, and he received the same answer. This was the result he had anticipated, and the next evening he returned to Paris to consider with the Government what was to be done. Bismarck meanwhile had taken care that some information as to these secret negotiations should become known; with characteristic cleverness he caused it to be published in a French paper, Le Siècle, that France had asked for the Rhine country and been refused. Of course, the German Press took up the matter; with patriotic fervour they supported the King and Minister. Napoleon found himself confronted by the danger of a union of all Germany in opposition to French usurpation, and his own diplomatic defeat had become known in a most inconvenient form; he at once travelled to Paris, consulted Benedetti, returned to his former policy, and asked that the demand of August 5th might be forgotten; it was withdrawn, and things were to be as if it had never been made.

Were they, however, still to give up all hope of some increase of French territory? The demand for German soil had been refused; it was not at all clear that Bismarck would not support the acquisition of at least part of Belgium. In conversation with Benedetti, on August 7th, he had said: "Perhaps we will find other means of satisfying you." Goltz was still very sympathetic; he regarded the French desire as quite legitimate in principle. It was determined, therefore, now to act on these hints and suggestions which had been repeated so often during the last twelve months; Benedetti was instructed to return with a draft treaty; the French demands were put in three forms; first of all he was to ask for the Saar Valley, Landau, Luxemburg, and Belgium; if this was too much, he was to be content with Belgium and Luxemburg, and if it seemed desirable he should offer that Antwerp be made a free city; by this perhaps the extreme hostility of England would be averted. With this demand, on August 20th, he again appeared before Bismarck. Of course, the Minister, as soon as Saarbrück and Landau were mentioned, drew himself up to his full height, adopted an angry air, and reminded Benedetti of his repeated declaration that they were not going to give up a single German village. Benedetti, therefore, in accordance with his instructions, withdrew this clause. The rest of the treaty he and Bismarck discussed together carefully; they took it line by line and clause by clause, Bismarck dealing with the matter in a serious and practical manner. After this had been finished a revised draft was written out by Benedetti, Bismarck dictating to him the alterations which had been made. This revised draft consisted of five articles: (1) The Emperor recognised the recent acquisitions of Prussia; (2) the King of Prussia should bind himself to assist France in acquiring Luxemburg from the King of Holland by purchase or exchange; (3) the Emperor bound himself not to oppose a union of the North German Federation with the South German States and the establishment of a common Parliament; (4) if the Emperor at any time wished to acquire Belgium, the King of Prussia was to support him and give him military assistance against the interference of any other Power; (5) a general treaty of alliance.

It will be seen that this treaty consists of two parts. The first refers to what has already taken place,—the Emperor of the French in return for past assistance is to have Luxemburg; this part would naturally come into operation immediately. The next two clauses referred to the future; the union of all Germany would in the natural course of events not be long delayed; this would seriously alter the balance of power and weaken France. Napoleon would naturally in the future use all his efforts to prevent it, as he had done during this year, and by an alliance with Austria he would probably be able to do so. He would, however, withdraw his opposition if he was allowed to gain a similar increase of territory for France. After all, the acquisition of at least part of Belgium by France might be justified by the same arguments by which the dethronement of the King of Hanover was defended. Many of the Belgians were French; there was no natural division between Belgium and France; probably the people would offer no opposition.

Bismarck had to remember that he could not complete the union of Germany without considering Napoleon; there were only two ways of doing the work, (1) by war with France, (2) by an alliance. Need we be surprised that he at least considered whether the latter would not be the safer, the cheaper, and the more humane? Was it not better to complete the work by the sacrifice of Belgian independence rather than by the loss of 300,000 lives?

Benedetti sent the revised draft to Paris; it was submitted to the Emperor, accepted in principle, and returned with some small alterations and suggestions. Benedetti sent in the revision to Bismarck and said he would be ready at any time to meet the Minister and finish the negotiations. He himself left Berlin for Carlsbad and there awaited the summons. It never came. Week after week went by, Bismarck retired to his Pomeranian estate; he did not return to Berlin till December and he never renewed the negotiations. The revised draft in Benedetti's handwriting was in his hands; four years later, when war had been declared against France, he published it in order to destroy whatever sympathy for Napoleon there might be in England.

Bismarck did not continue the negotiations, for he had found a better way. Till August 23d his relations to Austria were still doubtful; he always had to fear that there was some secret understanding between France and Austria, that a coalition of the two States had been completed, and that Prussia might suddenly find herself attacked on both sides. He had, therefore, not wished to offend France. Moreover his relations to Russia were not quite satisfactory. The Czar took a very serious view of the annexations in North Germany: "I do not like it," he said; "I do not like this dethronement of dynasties." It was necessary to send General Manteuffel on a special mission to St. Petersburg; the Czar did not alter his opinion, but Bismarck found it possible at least to quiet him. We do not know all that passed, but he seems to have used a threat and a promise. If the Czar attempted to interfere in Germany, Bismarck hinted, as he had already done, that he might have to put himself at the head of the Revolution, and proclaim the Constitution of 1849; then what would happen to the monarchical principles? He even suggested that a Revolution which began in Germany might spread to Poland. The Czar explained that he was discontented with many clauses in the Treaty of Paris. There was an understanding, if there was no formal compact, that Prussia would lend her support, when the time came for the Czar to declare that he was no longer willing to observe this treaty.

By the end of August Bismarck had therefore removed the chief dangers which threatened him. Russia was quieted, France was expectant, Austria was pacified. He had, however, done more than this: he had already laid the foundation for the union of the whole of Germany which Napoleon thought he had prevented.

The four southern States had joined in the war against Prussia. In a brilliant and interesting campaign a small Prussian army had defeated the Federal forces and occupied the whole of South Germany. The conquest of

Germany by Prussia was complete. These States had applied at Nikolsburg to be allowed to join in the negotiations. The request was refused, and Bismarck at this time treated them with a deliberate and obtrusive brutality. Baron von der Pfortden, the Bavarian Minister, had himself travelled to Nikolsburg to ask for peace. He was greeted by Bismarck with the words: "What are you doing here? You have no safe-conduct. I should be justified in treating you as a prisoner of war." He had to return without achieving anything. Frankfort had been occupied by the Prussian army; the citizens were required to pay a war indemnity of a million pounds; Manteuffel, who was in command, threatened to plunder the town, and the full force of Prussian displeasure was felt by the city where Bismarck had passed so many years. It was arranged with Austria and France that the southern States should participate in the suspension of hostilities; that they should preserve their independence and should be allowed to enter into any kind of Federal alliance with one another. The result of this would have been that South Germany would be a weak, disunited confederation, which would be under the control partly of France and partly of Austria. This would have meant the perpetuation in its worst form of French influence over South Germany. When this clause was agreed on, the terms of peace between these States and Prussia had not yet been arranged. The King of Prussia wished that they should surrender to him some parts of their territory. Bismarck, however, opposed this. He was guided by the same principles which had influenced him all along. Some States should be entirely absorbed in Prussia, the others treated so leniently that the events of this year should leave no feeling of hostility. If Bavaria had to surrender Bayreuth and Anspach, he knew that the Bavarians would naturally take part in the first coalition against Prussia. With much trouble he persuaded the King to adopt this point of view. The wisdom of it was soon shewn. At the beginning of August he still maintained a very imperious attitude, and talked to the Bavarians of large annexations. Pfortden in despair had cried, "Do not drive us too far; we shall have to go for help to France." Then was Bismarck's turn. He told the Bavarian Minister of Napoleon's suggestion, shewed him that it was Prussia alone who had prevented Napoleon from annexing a large part of Bavaria, and then appealed to him through his German patriotism: Would not Bavaria join Prussia in an alliance? Pfortden was much moved, the Count and the Baron embraced one another, and by the end of August Bismarck had arranged with all the four southern States a secret offensive and defensive alliance. By this they bound themselves to support Prussia if she was attacked. Prussia guaranteed to them their territory; in case of war they would put their army under the command of the King of Prussia. He was now sure, therefore, of an alliance of all Germany against France. He no longer required French assistance. The unity of Germany, when it was made, would be achieved by the unaided forces of the united German States. The draft treaty with Napoleon might now be put aside.

These negotiations mark indeed a most important change in Bismarck's own attitude. Hitherto he had thought and acted as a Prussian; he had deliberately refused on all occasions to support or adopt the German programme. He had done this because he did not wish Germany to be made strong until the ascendancy of Prussia was secured. The battle of Königgrätz had done that; North Germany was now Prussian; the time had come when he could begin to think and act as a German, for the power of Prussia was founded on a rock of bronze.

This change was not the only one which dates from the great victory. The constitutional conflict had still to be settled. The Parliament had been dissolved just before the war; the new elections had taken place on the 3d of July, after the news of the first victory was known. The result was shewn in a great gain of seats to the Government and to the Moderate Liberal party. The great question, however, was, How would Bismarck use his victory over the House? for a victory it was. It was the cannon of Königgrätz which decided the Parliamentary conflict. The House had refused the money to reorganise the army, and it was this reorganised army which had achieved so unexampled a triumph. Would the Government now press their victory and use the enthusiasm of the moment permanently to cripple the Constitution? This is what the Conservative party, what Roon and the army wished to do. It was not Bismarck's intention. He required the support of the patriotic Liberals for the work he had to do; he proposed, therefore, that the Government should come before the House and ask for an indemnity. They did not confess that they had acted wrongly, they did not express regret, but they recognised that in spending the money without a vote of the House there had been an offence against the Constitution; this could now only be made good if a Bill was brought in approving of what had happened. He carried his opinion, not without difficulty; the Bill of indemnity was introduced and passed. He immediately had his reward. The Liberal party, which had hitherto opposed him, broke into two portions. The extreme Radicals and Progressives still continued their opposition; the majority of the party formed themselves into a new organisation, to which they gave the name of National Liberals. They pledged themselves to support the National and German policy of the Government, while they undertook, so far as they were able, to maintain and strengthen the constitutional rights of Parliament. By this Bismarck had a Parliamentary majority, and he more and more depended upon them rather than his old friends, the Conservatives. He required their support because henceforward he would have to deal not with one Parliament, but two. The North German Confederation was to have its Parliament elected by universal suffrage. Bismarck foresaw that the principles he had upheld in the past could not be applied in the same form to the whole of the Confederation. The Prussian Conservative party was purely Prussian, it was Particularist; had he continued to depend upon it, then all the members sent to the new Reichstag, not only from Saxony, but also from the annexed States, would have been thrown into opposition; the Liberal party had always been not Prussian but German; now that he had to govern so large a portion of Germany, that which had in the past been the great cause of difference would be the strongest bond of union. The National Liberal party was alone able to join him in the work of creating enthusiasm for the new institutions and new loyalty. How often had he in the old days complained of the Liberals that they thought not as Prussians, that they were ashamed of Prussia, that they were not really loyal to Prussia. Now he knew that just for this reason they would be most loyal to the North German Confederation.

Bismarck's moderation in the hour of victory must not obscure the importance of his triumph.

The question had been tried which should rule—the Crown or the Parliament; the Crown had won not only a physical but a moral victory. Bismarck had maintained that the House of Representatives could not govern Prussia; the foreign affairs of the State, he had always said, must be carried on by a Minister who was responsible, not to the

House, but to the King. No one could doubt that had the House been able to control him he would not have won these great successes. From that time the confidence of the German people in Parliamentary government was broken. Moreover, it was the first time in the history of Europe in which one of these struggles had conclusively ended in the defeat of Parliament. The result of it was to be shewn in the history of every country in Europe during the next thirty years. It is the most serious blow which the principle of representative government has yet received.

By the end of August most of the labour was completed; there remained only the arrangement of peace with Saxony; this he left to his subordinates and retired to Pomerania for the long period of rest which he so much required.

During his absence a motion was brought before Parliament for conferring a donation on the victorious generals. At the instance of one of his most consistent opponents Bismarck's name was included in the list on account of his great services to his country; a protest was raised by Virchow on the ground that no Minister while in office should receive a present, and that of all men Bismarck least deserved one, but scarcely fifty members could be found to oppose the vote. The donation of 40,000 thalers he used in purchasing the estate of Varzin, in Pomerania which was to be his home for the next twenty years.

CHAPTER XII.

THE FORMATION OF THE NORTH GERMAN CONFEDERATION.

1866-1867.

We have hitherto seen Bismarck in the character of party leader, Parliamentary debater, a keen and accomplished diplomatist; now he comes before us in a new rôle, that of creative statesman; he adopts it with the same ease and complete mastery with which he had borne himself in the earlier stages of his career. The Constitution of the North German Confederation was his work, and it shews the same intellectual resource, the originality, and practical sense which mark all he did.

By a treaty of August 18, 1866, all the North German States which had survived entered into a treaty with one another and with Prussia; they mutually guaranteed each other's possessions, engaged to place their forces under the command of the King of Prussia, and promised to enter into a new federation; for this purpose they were to send envoys to Berlin who should agree on a Constitution, and they were to allow elections to take place by universal suffrage for a North German Parliament before which was to be laid the draft Constitution agreed upon by the envoys of the States. These treaties did not actually create the new federation; they only bound the separate States to enter into negotiations, and, as they expired on August 30, 1867, it was necessary that the new Constitution should be completed and ratified by that date. The time was short, for in it had to be compressed both the negotiations between the States and the debates in the assembly; but all past experience had shewn that the shorter the time allowed for making a Constitution the more probable was it that the work would be completed. Bismarck did not intend to allow the precious months, when enthusiasm was still high and new party factions had not seized hold of men's minds, to be lost.

He had spent the autumn in Pomerania and did not return to Berlin till the 21st of December; not a week remained before the representatives of the North German States would assemble in the capital of Prussia. To the astonishment and almost dismay of his friends, he had taken no steps for preparing a draft. As soon as he arrived two drafts were laid before him; he put them aside and the next day dictated the outlines of the new Constitution.

This document has not been published, but it was the basis of the discussion with the envoys; Bismarck allowed no prolonged debates; they were kept for some weeks in Berlin, but only three formal meetings took place. They made suggestions and criticisms, some of which were accepted, but they were of course obliged to assent to everything on which Bismarck insisted. The scheme as finally agreed upon by the conference was then laid before the assembly which met in Berlin on February 24th.

A full analysis of this Constitution, for which we have no space here, would be very instructive; it must not be compared with those elaborate constitutions drawn up by political theorists of which so many have been introduced during this century. Bismarck's work was like that of Augustus; he found most of the institutions of government to his hand, but they were badly co-ordinated; what he had to do was to bring them into better relations with each other, and to add to them where necessary. Many men would have swept away everything which existed, made a clear field, and begun to build up a new State from the foundations. Bismarck was much too wise to attempt this, for he knew that the foundations of political life cannot be securely laid by one man or in one generation. He built on the foundations which others had laid, and for this reason it is probable that his work will be as permanent as that of the founder of the Roman Empire.

We find in the new State old and new mixed together in an inseparable union, and we find a complete indifference to theory or symmetry; each point is decided purely by reference to the political situation at the moment. Take, for instance, the question of diplomatic representation; Bismarck wished to give the real power to the King of Prussia, but at the same time to preserve the external dignity and respect due to the Allied Princes. He arranged that the King of Prussia as President of the Confederation appointed envoys and ambassadors to foreign States; from this time there ceased to be a Prussian diplomatic service, and, in this matter, Prussia is entirely absorbed in Germany. It would have been only natural that the smaller Allied States should also surrender their right to enter into direct diplomatic relations with foreign Powers. This Bismarck did not require. Saxony, for instance, continued to have its own envoys; England and France, as in the old days, kept a Minister in Dresden. Bismarck was much criticised for this, but he knew that nothing would so much reconcile the King of Saxony to his new position, and it was indeed no small thing that the Princes thus preserved in a formal way a right which shewed to all the world that they were not subjects but sovereign allies. When it was represented to Bismarck that this right might be the source of intrigues with foreign States, he answered characteristically that if Saxony wished to intrigue nothing could prevent her doing so; it was not necessary to have a formal embassy for this purpose. His confidence was absolutely justified. A few months later Napoleon sent to the King of Saxony a special invitation to a European congress; the King at once sent on the invitation to Berlin and let it be known that he did not wish to be represented apart from the North German Confederation. The same leniency was shewn in 1870. Nothing is a better proof of Bismarck's immense superiority both in practical wisdom and in judgment of character. The Liberal Press in Germany had never ceased to revile the German dynasties; Bismarck knew that their apparent disloyalty to Germany arose not from their wishes but was a necessary result of the faults of the old Constitution. He made their interests coincide with the interests of Germany, and from this time they have been the most loyal supporters, first of the Confederation, and afterwards of the Empire. This he was himself the first to acknowledge; both before and after the foundation of the Empire he has on many occasions expressed his sense of the great services rendered to Germany by the dynasties. "They," he said once, "were the true guardians of German unity, not the Reichstag and its parties."

The most important provisions of the Constitution were those by which the military supremacy of Prussia was secured; in this chapter every detail is arranged and provided for; the armies of all the various States were henceforth to form one army, under the command of the King of Prussia, with common organisation and similar uniform in every State; in every State the Prussian military system was to be introduced, and all the details of Prussian military law.

Now let us compare with this the navy: the army represented the old Germany, the navy the new; the army was arranged and organised as Prussian, Saxon, Mecklenburg; the navy, on the other hand, was German and organised by the new Federal officials. There was a Federal Minister of Marine, but no Federal Minister of War; the army continued the living sign of Prussian supremacy among a group of sovereign States, the navy was the first fruit of the united German institutions which were to be built up by the united efforts of the whole people—a curious resemblance to the manner in which Augustus also added an Imperial navy to the older Republican army.

The very form in which the Constitution was presented is characteristic; in the Parliamentary debates men complained that there was no preamble, no introduction, no explanation. Bismarck answered that this was omitted for two reasons: first, there had not been time to draw it up, and secondly, it would be far more difficult to agree on the principles which the Constitution was to represent than on the details themselves. There is no attempt at laying down general principles, no definitions, and no enumeration of fundamental rights; all these rocks, on which so often in Germany, as in France, precious months had been wasted, were entirely omitted.

And now let us turn to that which after the organisation of the army was of most importance,—the arrangement of the administration and legislation. Here it is that we see the greatest originality. German writers have often explained that it is impossible to classify the new State in any known category, and in following their attempts to find the technical definition for the authority on which it rests, one is led almost to doubt whether it really exists at all.

There are two agents of government, the Federal Council, or Bundesrath, and the Parliament, or Reichstag. Here again we see the blending of the old and new, for while the Parliament was now created for the first time, the Council was really nothing but the old Federal Diet. Even the old system of voting was retained; not that this was better than any other system, but, as Bismarck explained, it was easier to preserve the old than to agree on a new. Any system must have been purely arbitrary, for had each State received a number of votes proportionate to its population even the appearance of a federation would have been lost, and Bismarck was very anxious not to establish an absolute unity under Prussia.

It will be asked, Why was Bismarck now so careful in his treatment of the smaller States? The answer will be found in words which he had written many years ago:

"I do not wish to see Germany substituted for Prussia on our banner until we have brought about a closer and more practical union with our fellow-countrymen."

Now the time had come, and now he was to be the first and most patriotic of Germans as in old days he had been the strictest of Prussians. Do not let us in welcoming the change condemn his earlier policy. It was only his loyalty to Prussia which had made Germany possible; for it is indeed true that he could never have ruled Germany had he not first conquered it. The real and indisputable supremacy of Prussia was still preserved; and Prussia was now so strong that she could afford to be generous. It was wise to be generous, for the work was only half completed; the southern States were still outside the union; he wished to bring them into the fold, but to do so not by force of arms but of their own free will; and they certainly would be more easily attracted if they saw that the North German States were treated with good faith and kindness.

Side by side with the Council we have the Reichstag; this was, in accordance with the proposal made in the spring of 1866, to be elected by universal suffrage. And now we see that this proposal, which a few months ago had appeared merely as a despairing bid for popularity by a statesman who had sacrificed every other means of securing his policy, had become a device convincing in its simplicity; at once all possibility of discussion or opposition was prevented; not indeed that there were not many warning voices raised, but as Bismarck, in defending this measure, asked,—what was the alternative? Any other system would have been purely arbitrary, and any arbitrary system would at once have opened the gate to a prolonged discussion and political struggle on questions of the franchise. In a modern European State, when all men can read and write, and all men must serve in the army, there is no means of limiting the franchise in a way which will command universal consent. In Germany there was not any old historical practice to which men could appeal or which could naturally be applied to the new Parliament; universal suffrage at least gave something clear, comprehensible, final. Men more easily believed in the permanence of the new State when every German received for the first time the full privilege of citizenship. We must notice, however, that Bismarck had always intended that voting should be open; the Parliament in revising the Constitution introduced the ballot. He gave his consent with much reluctance; voting seemed to him to be a public duty, and to perform it in secret was to undermine the roots of political life. He was a man who was constitutionally unable to understand fear. We have then the Council and the Parliament, and we must now enquire as to their duties. In nearly every modern State the popular representative assembly holds the real power; before it, everything else is humbled; the chief occupation of lawgivers is to find some ingenious device by which it may at least be controlled and moderated in the exercise of its power. It was not likely that Bismarck would allow Germany to be governed by a democratic assembly; he was not satisfied with creating an artificial Upper House which might, perhaps, be able for one year or two to check the extravagances of a popular House, or with allowing to the King a veto which could only be exercised with fear and trembling. Generally the Lower House is the predominant partner; it governs; the Upper House can only amend, criticise, moderate. Bismarck completely reversed the situation: the true government, the full authority in the State was given to the Council; the Parliament had to content itself with a limited opportunity for criticism, with the power to amend or veto Bills, and to refuse its assent to new taxes. In England the government rests in the House of Commons; in Germany it is in the Federal Council, and for the same reason—that the Council has both executive and legislative power. Constitutions have generally been made by men whose chief object was to weaken the power of the Government, who believed that those rulers do least harm who have least power, with whom suspicion is the first of political virtues, and who would condemn to permanent inefficiency the institutions they have invented. It was not likely Bismarck would do this. The ordinary device is to separate the legislative and executive power; to set up two rival and equal authorities which may check and neutralise each other. Bismarck, deserting all the principles of the books, united all the powers of government in the Council. The whole administration was subjected to it; all laws were introduced in it. The debates were secret; it was an assembly of the ablest statesmen in Germany; the decisions at which it arrived were laid in their complete form before the Reichstag. It was a substitute for a Second Chamber, but it was also a Council of State; it united the duties of the Privy Council and the House of Lords; it reminds us in its composition of the American Senate, but it would be a Senate in which the President of the Republic presided.

Bismarck never ceased to maintain the importance of the Federal Council; he always looked on it as the key to the whole new Constitution. Shortly after the war with France, when the Liberals made an attempt to overthrow its authority, he warned them not to do so.

"I believe," he said, "that the Federal Council has a great future. Great as Prussia is, we have been able to learn much from the small, even from the smallest member of it; they on their side have learnt much from us. From my own experience I can say that I have made considerable advance in my political education by taking part in the sittings of the Council and by the life which comes from the friction of five and twenty German centres with one another. I beg you do not interfere with the Council. I consider it a kind of Palladium for our future, a great guarantee for the future of Germany in its present form."

Now, from the peculiar character of the Council arose a very noticeable omission; just as there was no Upper House (though the Prussian Conservatives strongly desired to see one), so, also, there was no Federal Ministry. In every modern State there is a Council formed of the heads of different administrative departments; this was so universal that it was supposed to be essential to a constitution. In the German Empire we search for it in vain; there is only one responsible Minister, and he is the Chancellor, the representative of Prussia and Chairman of the Council. The

Liberals could not reconcile themselves to this strange device; they passed it with reluctance in the stress of the moment, but they have never ceased to protest against it. Again and again, both in public and in private, we hear the same demand: till we have a responsible Ministry the Constitution will never work. Two years later a motion was introduced and passed through the Reichstag demanding the formation of a Federal Ministry; Bismarck opposed the motion and refused to carry it out.

He had several reasons for omitting what was apparently almost a necessary institution. The first was respect for the rights of the Federal States. If a Ministry, responsible to Parliament, had existed, the executive power would have been taken away from the Bundesrath, and the Princes of the smaller States would really have been subjected to the new organ; the Ministers must have been appointed by the President; they would have looked to him and to the Reichstag for support, and would soon have begun to carry out their policy, not by agreement with the Governments arrived at by technical discussions across the table of the Council-room, but by orders and decrees based on the will of the Parliament. This would inevitably have aroused just what Bismarck wished to avoid. It would have produced a struggle between the central and local authorities; it would again have thrown the smaller Governments into opposition to national unity; it would have frightened the southern States.

His other reasons for opposing the introduction of a Ministry were that he did not wish to give more power to the Parliament, and above all he disliked the system of collegiate responsibility.

"You wish," he said, "to make the Government responsible, and do it by introducing a board. I say the responsibility will disappear as soon as you do so; responsibility is only there when there is a single man who can be brought to task for any mistakes.... I consider that in and for itself a Constitution which introduces joint ministerial responsibility is a political blunder from which every State ought to free itself as soon as it can. Anyone who has ever been a Minister and at the head of a Ministry, and has been obliged to take resolutions upon his own responsibility, ceases at last to fear this responsibility, but he does shrink from the necessity of convincing seven people that that which he wishes is really right. That is a very different work from governing a State."

These reasons are very characteristic of him; the feeling became more confirmed as he grew older. In 1875 he says:

"Under no circumstances could I any longer submit to the thankless rôle of Minister-President of Prussia in a Ministry with joint responsibility, if I were not accustomed, from my old affection, to submit to the wishes of my King and Master. So thankless, so powerless, and so little responsible is that position; one can only be responsible for that which one does of one's own will; a board is responsible for nothing."

He always said himself that he would be satisfied with the position of an English Prime Minister. He was thinking, of course, of the constitutional right which the Prime Minister has, to appoint and dismiss his colleagues, which if he has strength of character will, of course, give him the real control of affairs, and also of the right which he enjoys of being the sole means by which the views of the Ministers are represented to the sovereign. In Prussia the Minister-

President had not acquired by habit these privileges, and the power of the different Ministers was much morc equal. In the new Federation he intended to have a single will directing the whole machine.

The matter is of some interest because of the light it throws on one side of his character. He was not a man with whom others found it easy to work; he did not easily brook opposition, and he disliked having to explain and justify his policy to anyone besides the King. He was not able to keep a single one of his colleagues throughout his official career. Even Roon found it often difficult to continue working with him; he complained of the Hermit of Varzin, "who wishes to do everything himself, and nevertheless issues the strictest prohibition that he is never to be disturbed." What suited him best was the position of almost absolute ruler, and he looked on his colleagues rather as subordinates than as equals.

But, it will be objected, if there was to be a single will governing the whole, the government could not be left to the Council; a board comprising the representatives of twenty States could not really administer, and in truth the Council was but the veil; behind it is the all-pervading power of the King of Prussia—and his Minister. The ruler of Germany was the Chancellor of the Federation; it was he alone that united and inspired the whole. Let us enumerate his duties. He was sole Minister to the President of the Confederation (after 1870 to the Emperor). The President (who was King of Prussia) could declare peace and war, sign treaties, and appointed all officials, but all his acts required the signature of the Chancellor, who was thereby Foreign Minister of the Confederation and had the whole of the patronage. More than this, he was at the head of the whole internal administration; from time to time different departments of State were created,—marine, post-office, finance,—but the men who stood at the head of each department were not co-ordinate with the Chancellor; they were not his colleagues, but were subordinates to whom he delegated the work. They were not immediately responsible to the Emperor, Council, or Reichstag, but to him; he, whenever he wished, could undertake the immediate control of each department, he could defend its actions, and was technically responsible to the Council for any failure. Of course, as a matter of fact, the different departments generally were left to work alone, but if at any time it seemed desirable, the Chancellor could always interfere and issue orders which must be obeyed; if the head of the department did not agree, then he had nothing to do but resign, and the Chancellor would appoint his successor.

The Chancellor was, then, the working head of the Government; but it will be said that his power would be so limited by the interference of the Emperor, the Council, the Parliament, that he would have no freedom. The contrary is the truth. There were five different sources of authority with which he had to deal: the President of the Federation (the Emperor), who was King of Prussia, the Council, the Prussian Parliament, the German Parliament, and the Prussian Ministry. Now in the Council he presided, and also represented the will of Prussia, which was almost irresistible, for if the Constitution was to work well there must be harmony of intention between Prussia and the Federal Government; here therefore he could generally carry out his policy: but in the Prussian Ministry he spoke as sole Minister of the Federation and the immense authority he thus enjoyed raised him at once to a position of superiority to all his colleagues. More than this, he was now free from the danger of Parliamentary control; it was easier to deal with one Parliament than two; they had no locus standi for constitutional opposition to his policy. The double position he held enabled him to elude all control. Policy was decided in the Council; when he voted there he acted as representative of the King of Prussia and was bound by the instructions he received from the Prussian Minister of Foreign Affairs; the Reichstag had nothing to do with Prussian policy and had no right to criticise the action of the Prussian Minister. It did not matter that Bismarck himself was not only Chancellor of the Diet, but also Minister-President of Prussia and Foreign Minister, and was really acting in accordance with the instructions he had given to himself [8] ; the principle remained,—each envoy to the Diet was responsible, not to the Reichstag, but to the Government he represented. When, however, he appeared in the Reichstag to explain and defend the policy adopted by the Council, then he stood before them as representative not necessarily of his own policy, but of that which had been decided on by a board in which he had possibly been outvoted. The Reichstag could reject the proposal if it were a law or a tax; they could criticise and debate, but there was no ground on which they could constitutionally demand the dismissal of the Minister.

Of course Bismarck did not attempt to evade the full moral responsibility for the policy which he advocated, but he knew that so long as he had the confidence of the King of Prussia and the majority of the Allied States, all the power of Parliament could not injure him.

What probably not even he foresaw was that the new Constitution so greatly added to the power of the Minister that even the authority of the King began to pale before it. As before, there was only one department of State where his authority ceased,—the army.

It will be easily understood that this Constitution, when it was laid before the assembly, was not accepted without much discussion and many objections. There were some—the representatives of conquered districts, Poles, Hanoverians, and the deputies from Schleswig-Holstein—who wished to overthrow the new Federation which was built up on the destruction of the States to which they had belonged. Theirs was an enmity which was open, honourable, and easy to meet. More insidious and dangerous was the criticism of those men who, while they professed to desire the ends which Bismarck had attained, refused to approve of the Constitution because they would have to renounce some of the principles of the parties to which they belonged.

There were some to whom it seemed that he gave too much freedom to the individual States; they wished for a more complete unity, but now Bismarck, for the first time, was strong enough to shew the essential moderation of his character; he knew what the Liberals were ready to forget, that moderation, while foolish in the moment of conflict, is the proper adornment of the conqueror. When they asked him to take away many of the privileges reserved to the smaller States, he reminded them that, though Mecklenburg and the Saxon duchies were helpless before the increased power of the Prussian Crown, they were protected by Prussian promises, and that a King of Prussia, though he might strike down his enemies, must always fulfil in spirit and in letter his obligations to his friends. The basis of the new alliance must be the mutual confidence of the allies; he had taught them to fear Prussia, now they must learn to trust her.

The Prussian Conservatives feared that the power of the Prussian King and the independence of the Prussian State would be affected; but Bismarck's influence with them was sufficient to prevent any open opposition. More dangerous were the Progressives, who apprehended that the new Constitution would limit the influence of the Prussian Parliament. On many points they refused to accept the proposals of the Government; they feared for liberty. For them Bismarck had no sympathy and no words but contempt, and he put curtly before them the question, did they wish to sacrifice all he had attained to their principles of Parliamentary government? They demanded, for instance, that, as the Constitution of Prussia could not be altered without the consent of the Prussian Parliament, the new Federal Constitution must be laid before the Prussian Parliament for discussion and ratification. It is curious to notice that this is exactly the same claim which Bismarck in 1852 had supported as against Radowitz; he had, however, learned much since then; he pointed out that the same claim which was made by the Prussian Parliament might be made by the Parliament of each of the twenty-two States. It was now his duty to defend the unification of Germany against this new Particularism; in old days Particularism found its support in the dynasties, "now it is," he said, "in the Parliaments."

"Do you really believe," he said, "that the great movement which last year led the peoples to battle from the Belt to the Sicilian Sea, from the Rhine to the Pruth and the Dniester, in the throw of the iron dice when we played for the crowns of kings and emperors, that the millions of German warriors who fought against one another and bled on the battle-fields from the Rhine to the Carpathians, that the thousands and ten thousands who were left dead on the battle-field and struck down by pestilence, who by their death have sealed the national decision,--that all this can be pigeon-holed by a resolution of Parliament? Gentlemen, in this case you really do not stand on the height of the situation.... I should like to see the gentlemen who consider this possibility answer an invalid from Königgrätz when he asks for the result of this mighty effort. You would say to him: 'Yes, indeed, for the German unity nothing is achieved, the occasion for that will probably come, that we can have easily, we can come to an understanding any day, but we have saved the Budget-right of the Chamber of Deputies, we have saved the right of the Prussian Parliament every year to put the existence of the Prussian army in question,' ... and therewith the invalid must console himself for the loss of his limbs and the widow as she buries her husband."

It is interesting to compare this speech with the similar speech he made after Olmütz: how great is the similarity in thought and expression, how changed is the position of the speaker! He had no sympathy with these doubts and hesitations; why so much distrust of one another? His Constitution might not be the best, it might not be perfect, but at least let it be completed. "Gentlemen," he said, "let us work quickly, let us put Germany in the saddle; it will soon learn to ride." He was annoyed and irritated by the opposition he met.

"If one has struggled hard for five years to achieve that which now lies before us, if one has spent one's time, the best years of one's life, and sacrificed one's health for it, if one remembers the trouble it has cost to decide quite a small paragraph, even a question of punctuation, with two and twenty Governments, if at last we have agreed on that as it here lies before us, then gentlemen who have experienced little of all these struggles, and know nothing of the official proceedings which have gone before, come forward in a manner which I can only compare to that of a man who throws a stone at my window without knowing where I stand. He knows not where he hits me, he knows not what business he impedes."

He compared himself with Hotspur when after the battle he met the courtier who came to demand his prisoners, and when wounded and tired from the fight had to hear a long lecture over instruments of slaughter and internal wounds.

The debates were continued for two months with much spirit and ability; again and again a majority of the Parliament voted amendments against which Bismarck had spoken. When they had completed the revision of the Constitution, these had again to be referred to the separate Governments. Forty were adopted; on two only Bismarck informed the Parliament that their proposals could not be accepted. One of these was the arrangements for the army Budget; so soon did a fresh conflict on this matter threaten. A compromise was agreed upon; in consideration of the immediate danger (it was just the time when a war with France regarding Luxemburg appeared imminent), the House voted the money required for the army for the next four years; in 1871 a new arrangement would have to be made, but for this time the Government was able to maintain the army at the strength which they wished for. The other matter was of less immediate importance: the majority of the House had voted that members of the Parliament should receive payment for their services. Bismarck had spoken strongly against this; now he made it a question of confidence, and warned them that the Governments would not accept it. The House had no alternative except to withdraw their vote.

The Constitution as finally agreed on exists to this day as that of the German Empire. Notwithstanding the evil forebodings made at the time, it has worked well for over thirty years.

From the moment that the new State had been created and the new Constitution adopted, a great change took place in Bismarck's public position. He was no longer merely the first and ablest servant of the Prussian King; he was no longer one in the distinguished series of Prussian Ministers. His position was—let us recognise it clearly—greater than that of the King and Emperor, for he was truly the Father of the State: it was his will which had created and his brain which had devised it; he watched over it with the affection of a father for his son; none quite understood it but himself; he alone could authoritatively expound the laws of the Constitution. A criticism of it was an attack upon himself; opposition to him was scarcely to be distinguished from treason to the State. Is it not inevitable that as years went on we should find an increasing intolerance of all rivals, who wished to alter what he had made, or to take his place as captain of his ship, and at the same time a most careful and strict regard for the loyal fulfilment of the law and spirit of the Constitution? From this time all other interests are laid aside, his whole life is absorbed in the prosperity of Germany.

Of course Germany did not at once settle down to political rest; there were many difficulties to be overcome on which we cannot enter here. The most serious arose from the regulation of the affairs in the conquered provinces, and especially in the Kingdom of Hanover. The annexation to Prussia was very unpopular among all classes except the tradesmen and middle classes of the towns. The Hanoverian deputies to both the Prussian Parliament and the Parliament of the North German Confederation on principle opposed all measures of the Government. The

King himself, though in exile, kept up a close connection with his former subjects. There were long negotiations regarding his private property. At last it was agreed that this should be paid over to him. The King, however, used the money for organising a Legion to be used when the time came against Prussia; it was therefore necessary to cease paying him funds which could be used for this purpose. This is the origin of the notorious Welfenfond. The money was to be appropriated for secret service and especially for purposes of the Press. The party of the Guelphs, of course, maintained a bitter feud against the Government in their papers. Bismarck, who had had ample experience of this kind of warfare, met them on their own ground.

He defended this proposal by drawing attention to one of the weaknesses of Germany. What other country, he asked, was there where a defeated party would look forward to the help of foreign armies? "There are unfortunately," he said, "many Coriolani in Germany, only the Volsci are wanting; if they found their Volsci they would soon be unmasked." Everyone knew that the Volsci from over the Rhine would not be slow to come when the occasion offered.

"It was," he said, "a melancholy result of the centuries of disunion. There were traitors in the country; they did not hide themselves; they carried their heads erect; they found public defenders even in the walls of Parliament."

Then he continued:

"Everywhere where corruption is found there a form of life begins which no one can touch with clean kid gloves. In view of these facts you speak to me of espionage. In my nature I am not born to be a spy, but I believe we deserve your thanks if we condescend to follow malignant reptiles into their cave to observe their actions."

This is the origin of the expression "the reptile Press," for the name was given by the people not to those against whom the efforts of the Government were directed, but to the paid organs to which, if report is true, so large a portion of the Guelph fund was given.

But we must pass on to the events by which the work of 1866 was to be completed.

CHAPTER XIII.

THE OUTBREAK OF WAR WITH FRANCE.

1867-1870.

Ever since the conclusion of peace, the danger of a conflict between France and Germany had been apparent. It was not only the growing discontent and suspicion of the French nation and the French army, who truly felt that the supremacy of France had been shaken by the growth of this new power; it was not only that the deep-rooted hatred of France which prevailed in Germany had been stirred by Napoleon's action, and that the Germans had received confidence from the consciousness of their own strength. Had there been nothing more than this, year after year might have gone by and, as has happened since and had happened before, a war always anticipated might have been always deferred. We may be sure that Bismarck would not have gone to war unless he believed it to be necessary and desirable, and he would not have thought this unless there was something to be gained. He has often shewn, before and since, that he was quite as well able to use his powers in the maintenance of peace as in creating causes for war. There was, however, one reason which made war almost inevitable. The unity of Germany was only half completed; the southern States still existed in a curious state of semi-isolation. This could not long continue; their position must be regulated. War arises from that state of uncertainty which is always present when a political community has not found a stable and permanent constitution. In Germany men were looking forward to the time when the southern States should join the north. The work was progressing; the treaties of offensive and defensive alliance had been followed by the creation of a new Customs' Union, and it was a further step when at Bismarck's proposal a Parliament consisting of members elected throughout the whole of Germany was summoned at Berlin for the management of matters connected with the tariff. Further than this, however, he was not able to go; the new Constitution was working well; they could risk welcoming the States of the south into it; but this could not be done without a war with France. Bismarck had rejected the French proposal for an alliance. He knew, and everyone else knew, that France would oppose by the sword any attempt to complete the unity of Germany; and, which was more serious, unless great caution was used, that she would be supported by Austria and perhaps by the anti-Prussian party in Bavaria. There were some who wished to press it forward at once. Bismarck was very strongly pressed by the National Liberals to hasten the union with the south; at the beginning of 1870 the Grand Duke of Baden, himself a son-in-law of the King of Prussia and always the chief supporter of Prussian influence in the south, formally applied to be admitted into the Federation. The request had to be refused, but Bismarck had some difficulty in defending his position against his enthusiastic friends. He had to warn them not to hurry; they must not press the development too quickly. If they did so, they would stir the resentment of the anti-Prussian party; they would play into the hands of Napoleon and Austria. But if there was danger in haste, there was equal danger in delay; the prestige of Prussia would suffer.

It is clear that there was one way in which the union might be brought about almost without resistance, and that was, if France were to make an unprovoked attack upon Germany, an attack so completely without reason and excuse that the strong national passion it provoked might in the enthusiasm of war sweep away all minor differences and party feelings.

There was another element which we must not omit. These years witnessed the growth in determination and in power of the Ultramontane party. We can find their influence in every country in Europe; their chief aim was the preservation of the temporal power of the Pope and the destruction of the newly created Kingdom of Italy. They were also opposed to the unity of Germany under Prussia. They were very active and powerful in South Germany, and at the elections in 1869 had gained a majority. Their real object must be to win over the Emperor of the French to a complete agreement with themselves, to persuade him to forsake his earlier policy and to destroy what he had done so much to create. They had a strong support in the person of the Empress, and they joined with the injured vanity of the French to press the Emperor towards war.

In 1867, war had almost broken out on the question of Luxemburg. Napoleon had attempted to get at least this small extension of territory; relying on the support of Prussia he entered into negotiations with the King of Holland; the King agreed to surrender the Grand Duchy to France, making, however, a condition that Napoleon should secure the assent of Prussia to this arrangement. At the very last moment, when the treaty was almost signed, Bismarck made it clear that the national feeling in Germany was so strong that if the transaction took place he would have to declare war against France. At the same time, he published the secret treaties with the southern States. These events destroyed the last hope of maintaining the old friendly relations with Napoleon; "I have been duped," said the Emperor, who at once began reorganising and rearming his forces. For some weeks there was great danger of war concerning the right of garrisoning Luxemburg; this had hitherto belonged to Prussia, but of course with the dissolution of the German Confederation the right had lapsed. The German nation, which was much excited and thought little of the precise terms of treaties, wished to defend the right; Bismarck knew that in this matter the Prussian claim could not be supported; moreover, even if he had wished to go to war with France he was not ready; for some time must elapse before the army of the North German Confederation could be reorganised on the Prussian model. He therefore preserved the peace and the matter was settled by a European Congress. In the summer of 1867, he visited Paris with the King; externally the good relations between the two States were restored, but it was in reality only an armed peace.

It is difficult to decipher Napoleon's wishes; he seems to have believed that war was inevitable; there is no proof that he desired it. He made preparations; the army was reorganised, the numbers increased, and a new weapon introduced. At the same time he looked about for allies. Negotiations were carried on with Austria; in 1868 a meeting was arranged between the two Emperors; Beust, who was now Chancellor of the Austrian Empire, was anxious to make an attempt to overthrow the power of Prussia in Germany. In 1870, negotiations were entered into for a military alliance; a special envoy, General Lebrun, was sent to Vienna to discuss the military arrangements in case of war. No treaty was signed, but it was an almost understood thing that sooner or later an alliance between the two Emperors should be formed against Prussia.

It will be seen then that at the beginning of 1870 everything was tending towards war, and that under certain circumstances war was desirable, both for France and for Germany; much seemed to depend on the occasion of the outbreak. If Prussia took the offensive, if she attempted by force to win the southern States, she would be faced by a coalition of France and Austria, supported only too probably by Bavaria, and this was a coalition which would find much sympathy among the discontented in North Germany. On the other hand, it was for the advantage of Prussia not to delay the conflict: the King was growing old; Bismarck could never be sure how long he would remain in office; moreover, the whole forces of North Germany had now been completely reorganised and were ready for war, but with the year 1871 it was to be foreseen that a fresh attempt would be made to reduce their numbers; it was desirable to avoid a fresh conflict on the military budget;

everything shews that 1870 was the year in which it would be most convenient for Prussia to fight.

Prussia, at this time, had no active allies on whom she could depend; Bismarck indeed had secured the neutrality of Russia, but he did not know that the Czar would come actively to his help; we may feel sure that he would prefer not to have to call upon Russia for assistance, for, as we have seen in older days, a war between France and Russia, in which Germany joined, would be very harmful to Germany. It was in these circumstances that an opportunity shewed itself of gaining another ally who would be more subservient than Russia. One of the many revolutions which had harassed Spain during this century had broken out. Queen Isabella had lost the throne, and General Prim found himself obliged to look about for a new sovereign. He applied in vain to all the Catholic Courts; nobody was anxious to accept an honour coupled with such danger as ruling over the Spanish people. Among others he applied to Leopold, hereditary Prince of Hohenzollern, eldest son of that Prince of Hohenzollern who a few years before had been President of the Prussian Ministry. The choice seemed a good one: the Prince was an amiable, courageous man; he was a Catholic; he was, moreover, connected with the Napoleonic family. His brother had, three years before, been appointed King of Roumania with Napoleon's good-will.

The proposal was probably made in all good faith; under ordinary circumstances, the Prince, had he been willing to accept, would have been a very proper candidate. It was, however, known from the first that Napoleon would not give his consent, and, according to the comity of Europe, he had a right to be consulted. Nor can we say that Napoleon was not justified in opposing the appointment. It has indeed been said that the Prince was not a member of the Prussian Royal House and that his connection with Napoleon was really closer than that with the King of Prussia. This is true, but to lay stress on it is to ignore the very remarkable voluntary connection which united the two branches of the House of Hohenzollern. The Prince's father had done what no sovereign prince in Germany has ever done before or since: out of loyalty to Prussia he had surrendered his position as sovereign ruler and presented his dominions to the King of Prussia; he had on this occasion been adopted into the Royal Family; he had formally recognised the King as Head of the House, and subjected himself to his authority. More than this, he had even condescended to accept the position of Prussian Minister. Was not Napoleon justified if he feared that the son of a man who had shewn so great an affection to Prussia would not be an agreeable neighbour on the throne of Spain?

It was in the early spring of 1869 that the first proposals were made to the Prince; our information as to this is very defective, but it seems that they were at once rejected. Benedetti's suspicions were, however, aroused. He heard that a Spanish diplomatist, who had formerly been Ambassador at Berlin, had again visited the city and had had two interviews with Bismarck. He feared that perhaps he had some mission with regard to the Hohenzollern candidature, and, in accordance with instructions from his Government, enquired first of Thiele and, after a visit to Paris, saw Bismarck himself. The Count was quite ready to discuss the matter; with great frankness he explained all the reasons why, if the throne were offered to the Prince, the King would doubtless advise him not to accept it. Benedetti was still suspicious, but for the time the matter dropped. From what happened later, though we have no proof, we must, I think, share his suspicion that Bismarck was already considering the proposal and was prepared to lend it his support.

In September of the same year, the affair began to advance. Prim sent Salazar, a Spanish gentleman, to Germany with a semi-official commission to invite the Prince to become a candidate, and gave him a letter to a German acquaintance who would procure him an introduction to the Prince. This German acquaintance was no other than Herr von Werther, Prussian Ambassador at Vienna. If we remember the very strict discipline which Bismarck maintained in the Diplomatic Service we must feel convinced that Werther was acting according to instructions.[9] He brought the envoy to the Prince of Hohenzollern; the very greatest caution was taken to preserve secrecy; the Spaniard did not go directly to the castle of Weinburg, but left the train at another station, waited in the town till it was dark, and only approached the castle when hidden from observation by night and a thick mist. He first of all asked Prince Charles himself to accept the throne, and when he refused, offered it to Prince Leopold, who also, though he did not refuse point-blank, left no doubt that he was disinclined to the proposal; he could only accept, he said, if the Spanish Government procured the assent of the Emperor Napoleon and the King of Prussia. Notwithstanding the reluctance of the family to take the proffered dignity, Herr von Werther (and we must look on him as Bismarck's agent [9]) a fortnight later travelled from Munich in order to press on the Prince of Roumania that he should use his influence not to allow the House of Hohenzollern to refuse the throne. For the time, however, the subject seems to have dropped. A few months later, for the third time, the offer was repeated, and now Bismarck uses the whole of his influence in its favour. At the end of February, Salazar came on an official mission to Berlin; he had three letters, one to the King, one to Bismarck, one to the Prince. The King refused to receive him; Prince Leopold did not waver in his refusal and was supported by his father; their attitude was that they should not consider the matter seriously unless higher reasons of State required it. With Prince Bismarck, however, the envoy was more successful; he had several interviews with the Minister, and then left the city in order that suspicions might not be aroused or the attention of the French Government directed to the negotiations. Bismarck pleaded with great warmth for the acceptance of the offer; in a memoir to the King, he dwelt on the great importance which the summons of a Hohenzollern prince to the Spanish throne would have for Germany; it would be politically invaluable to have a friendly land in the rear of France; it would be of the greatest economic advantage for Germany and Spain if this thoroughly monarchical country developed its resources under a king of German descent. In consequence of this, a conference was held at Berlin, at which there were present, besides the King, the Crown Prince, Prince Carl Anton, and Prince Leopold, Bismarck, Roon, Moltke, Schleinitz, Thiele, and Delbrück. By summoning the advice of these men, the matter was taken out of the range of a private and family matter; it is true that it was not officially brought before the Prussian Ministry, but those consulted were the men by whom the policy of the State was directed. The unanimous decision of the councillors was for acceptance on the ground that it was the fulfilment of a patriotic duty to Prussia. The Crown Prince saw great difficulties in the way, and warned his cousin, if he accepted, not to rely on Prussian help in the future, even if, for the attainment of a definite end, the Prussian Government furthered the project for the moment. The King did not agree with his Ministers; he had many serious objections, and refused to give any definite order to the Prince that he should accept the offer; he left the final decision to him. He eventually refused.

Bismarck, however, was not to be beaten; he insisted that the Hohenzollerns should not let the matter drop; and, as he could not persuade the King to use his authority, acted directly upon the family with such success that Prince Carl Anton telegraphed to his third son, Frederick, to ask if he would not accept instead of his brother. Bismarck had now declared that the acceptance by one of the Princes was a political necessity; this he said repeatedly and with the greatest emphasis. At the same time, he despatched a Prussian officer of the general staff and his private secretary, Lothar Bucher, to Spain in order that they might study the situation. It was important that as far as possible the official representative of Prussia should have no share in the arrangement of this matter.

Prince Frederick came to Berlin, but, like his brother, he refused, unless the King gave a command. At the end of April, the negotiations seemed again to have broken down. Bismarck, who was in ill health, left Berlin for Varzin, where he remained for six weeks.

We are, however, not surprised, since we know that Bismarck's interest was so strongly engaged, that he was able after all to carry the matter through. He seems to have persuaded Prince Carl Anton; he then wrote to Prim telling him not to despair; the candidature was an excellent thing which was not to be lost sight of; he must, however, negotiate not with the Prussian Government, but with the Prince himself. When he wrote this he knew that he had at last succeeded in breaking down the reluctance of the Prince, and that the King, though he still was unwilling to undertake any responsibility, would not refuse his consent if the Prince voluntarily accepted. Prince Leopold was influenced not only by his interest in the Spanish race, but also by a letter from Bismarck, in which he said that he ought to put aside all scruples and accept in the interests of Prussia. The envoys had also returned from Spain and brought back a favourable report; they received an extraordinarily hearty welcome; we may perhaps suspect with the King that they had allowed their report to receive too rosy a colour; no doubt, however, they were acting in accordance with what they knew were the wishes of the man who had sent them out. In the beginning of June the decision was made; Prince Leopold wrote to the King that he accepted the crown which had been offered to him, since he thereby hoped to do a great service to his Fatherland. King William immediately answered that he approved of the decision.

Bismarck then at last was successful. A few days later Don Salazar again travelled to Germany; this time he brought a formal offer, which was formally-accepted. The Cortes were then in session; it was arranged that they should remain at Madrid till his return; the election would then be at once completed, for a majority was assured. The secrecy had been strictly maintained; there were rumours indeed, but no one knew of all the secret interviews; men might suspect, but they could not prove that it was an intrigue of Bismarck. If the election had once been made the solemn act of the whole nation, Napoleon would have been confronted with a fait accompli. To have objected would have been most injurious; he would have had to do, not with Prussia, which apparently was not concerned, but with the Spanish nation. The feeling of France would not allow him to acquiesce in the election, but it would have deeply offended the dignity and pride of Spain had he claimed that the King who had been formally accepted should, at his demand, be rejected. He could scarcely have done so without bringing about a war; a war with Spain would have crippled French resources and diverted their attention from Prussia; even if a war did not ensue, permanent ill feeling would be created. It is not difficult to understand the motives by which Bismarck had been influenced. At the last moment the plan failed. A cipher telegram from Berlin was misinterpreted in Madrid; and in consequence the Cortes, instead of remaining in session, were prorogued till the autumn. All had depended on the election being carried out before the secret was disclosed; a delay of some weeks must take place, and some indiscreet words of Salazar disclosed the truth. General Prim had no course left him but to send to the French Ambassador, to give him official information as to what had been done and try to calm his uneasiness.

What were Bismarck's motives in this affair? It is improbable that he intended to use it as a means of bringing about a war with France. He could not possibly have foreseen the very remarkable series of events which were to follow, and but for them a war arising out of this would have been very unwise, for German public opinion and the sympathy of all the neutral Powers would have been opposed to Prussia, had it appeared that the Government was disturbing the peace of Europe simply in order to put a Prussian prince on the throne of Spain contrary to the wishes of France. He could not ignore German public opinion now as he had done in old days; he did not want to conquer South Germany, he wished to attract it. It seems much more probable that he had no very clear conception of the results which would follow; he did not wish to lose what might be the means of gaining an ally to Germany and weakening France. It would be quite invaluable if, supposing there were to be war (arising from this or other causes), Spain could be persuaded to join in the attack on France and act the part which Italy had played in 1866. What he probably hoped for more than anything else was that France would declare war against Spain; then Napoleon would waste his strength in a new Mexico; he would no longer be a danger to Germany, and whether Germany joined in the war or not, she would gain a free hand. by the preoccupation of France. If none of these events happened, it would be an advantage that some commercial gain might be secured for Germany.

On the whole, the affair is not one which shews his strongest points as a diplomatist; it was too subtle and too hazardous.

The news aroused the sleeping jealousy of Prussia among the French people; the suspicion and irritation of the Government was extreme, and this feeling was not ill-founded. They assumed that the whole matter was an intrigue of Bismarck's, though, owing to the caution with which the negotiations had been conducted, they had no proofs. They might argue that a Prussian prince could not accept such an offer without the permission of his sovereign, and they had a great cause of complaint that this permission had been given without any communication with Napoleon, whom the matter so nearly concerned. The arrangement itself was not alone the cause of alarm. The secrecy with which it had been surrounded was interpreted as a sign of malevolence.

Of course they must interfere to prevent the election being completed. Where, however, were they to address themselves? With a just instinct they directed their remonstrance, not to Madrid, but to Berlin; they would thereby appear not to be interfering with the independence of the Spaniards, but to be acting in self-defence against the insidious advance of German power.

They could not, however, approach Bismarck; he had retired to Varzin, to recruit his health; the other Ministers also were absent; the King was at Ems. It was convenient that at this sudden crisis they should be away, for it was imperative that the Prussian Government should deny all complicity. Bismarck must not let it appear that he had any interest in, or knowledge of, the matter; he therefore remained in the seclusion of Pomerania.

Benedetti also was absent in the Black Forest. On the 4th of July, therefore, the French Chargé d'Affaires, M. de Sourds, called at the Foreign Office and saw Herr von Thiele. "Visibly embarrassed," he writes, "he told me that the Prussian Government was absolutely ignorant of the matter and that it did not exist for them." This was the only answer to be got; in a despatch sent on the 11th to the Prussian agents in Germany, Bismarck repeated the assertion. "The matter has nothing to do with Prussia. The Prussian Government has always considered and treated this affair as one in which Spain and the selected candidate are alone concerned." This was literally true, for it had never been brought before the Prussian Ministry, and no doubt the records of the office would contain no allusion to it; the majority of the Ministers were absolutely ignorant of it.

Of course M. de Sourds did not believe Herr von Thiele's statement, and his Government was not satisfied with the explanation; the excitement in Paris was increasing; it was fomented by the agents of the Ministry, and in answer to an interpolation in the Chamber, the Duc de Grammont on the 6th declared that the election of the Prince was inadmissible; he trusted to the wisdom of the Prussian and the friendship of the Spanish people not to proceed in it, but if his hope were frustrated they would know how to do their duty. They were not obliged to endure that a foreign Power by setting one of its Princes on the throne of Charles V. should destroy the balance of power and endanger the interests and honour of France. He hoped this would not happen; they relied on the wisdom of the German and the friendship of the Spanish people to avoid it; but if it were necessary, then, strong in the support of the nation and the Chamber, they knew how to fulfil their duty without hesitation or weakness.

The French Ministry hereby publicly declared that they held the Prussian Government responsible for the election, and they persisted in demanding the withdrawal, not from Spain, but from Prussia; Prim had suggested that as the Foreign Office refused to discuss the matter, Grammont should approach the King personally. Benedetti received instructions to go to the King at Ems and request him to order or advise the Prince to withdraw. At first Grammont wished him also to see the Prince himself; on second thoughts he forbade this, for, as he said, it was of the first importance that the messages should be conveyed by the King; he was determined to use the opportunity for the humiliation of Germany.

If it was the desire of the French in this way to establish the complicity of Prussia, it was imperative that the Prussian Government should not allow them to do so. They were indeed in a disagreeable situation; they could not take up the French challenge and allow war to break out; not only would the feeling of the neutral Powers, of England and of Russia, be against them, but that of Germany itself would be divided. With what force would the anti-Prussian party in Bavaria and Wurtemberg be able to oppose a war undertaken apparently for the dynastic interests of the Hohenzollern! If, however, the Prince now withdrew, the French would be able to proclaim that he had done so in consequence of the open threats of France; supposing they were able to connect the King in any way with him, then they might assert that they had checked the ambition of Prussia; Prussian prestige would be seriously injured at home, and distrust of Prussian good faith would be aroused abroad.

The King therefore had a difficult task when Benedetti asked for an interview. He had been brought into this situation against his own will, and his former scruples seemed fully justified. He complained of the violence of the French Press and the Ministry; he repeated the assertion that the Prussian Government had been unconnected with the negotiations and had been ignorant of them; he had avoided associating himself with them, and had only given an opinion when Prince Leopold, having decided to accept, asked his consent. He had then acted, not in his sovereign capacity as King of Prussia, but as head of the family. He had neither collected nor summoned his council of Ministers, though he had informed Count Bismarck privately. He refused to use his authority to order the Prince to withdraw, and said that he would leave him full freedom as he had done before.

These statements were of course verbally true; probably the King did not know to what extent Bismarck was responsible for the acceptance by the Prince. They did not make the confidence of the French any greater; it was now apparent that the King had been asked, and had given his consent without considering the effect on France; they could not acquiesce in this distinction between his acts as sovereign and his acts as head of the family, for, as

Benedetti pointed out, he was only head of the family because he was sovereign.

All this time Bismarck was still at Varzin; while Paris was full of excitement, while there were hourly conferences of the Ministers and the city was already talking of war, the Prussian Ministers ostentatiously continued to enjoy their holidays. There was no danger in doing so; the army was so well prepared that they could afford quietly to await what the French would do. What Bismarck's plans and hopes were we do not know; during these days he preserved silence; the violence of the French gave him a further reason for refusing to enter into any discussion. When, however, he heard of Benedetti's visit to Ems he became uneasy; he feared that the King would compromise himself; he feared that the French would succeed in their endeavour to inflict a diplomatic defeat on Prussia. He proposed to go to Ems to support the King, and on the 12th left Varzin; that night he arrived in Berlin. There he received the news that the Prince of Hohenzollern, on behalf of his son, had announced his withdrawal.

The retirement was probably the spontaneous act of the Prince and his father; the decisive influence was the fear lest the enmity of Napoleon might endanger the position of the Prince of Roumania. Everyone was delighted; the cloud of war was dispelled; two men only were dissatisfied—Bismarck and Grammont. It was the severest check which Bismarck's policy had yet received; he had persuaded the Prince to accept against his will; he had persuaded the King reluctantly to keep the negotiations secret from Napoleon; however others might disguise the truth, he knew that they had had to retreat from an untenable position, and retreat before the noisy insults of the French Press and the open menace of the French Government; his anger was increased by the fact that neither the King nor the Prince had in this crisis acted as he would have wished.

We have no authoritative statement as to the course he himself would have pursued; he had, according to his own statement, advised the King not to receive the French Ambassador; probably he wished that the Prince should declare that as the Spaniards had offered him the crown and he had accepted it, he could not now withdraw unless he were asked to do so by Spain; the attempt of Grammont to fasten a quarrel on Prussia would have been deprived of any responsible pretext; he would have been compelled to bring pressure to bear on the Spaniards, with all the dangers that that course would involve. We may suspect that he had advised this course and that his advice had been rejected. However this may be, Bismarck felt the reverse so keenly that it seemed to him impossible he could any longer remain Minister, unless he could obtain redress for the insults and menaces of France. What prospect was there now of this? It was no use now going on to Ems; he proposed to return next day to Varzin, and he expected that when he did so he would be once more a private man.

He was to be saved by the folly of the French. Grammont, vain, careless, and inaccurate, carried away by his hatred of Prussia, hot-headed and blustering, did not even see how great an advantage he had gained. When Guizot, now a very old man, living in retirement, heard that the Prince had withdrawn, he exclaimed: "What good fortune these people have! This is the finest diplomatic victory which has been won in my lifetime." This is indeed the truth; how easy it would have been to declare that France had spoken and her wishes had been fulfilled! the Government need have said no more, but every Frenchman would have always told the story how Bismarck had tried to put a Hohenzollern on the throne of Spain, had been foiled by the word of the Emperor, and had been driven from office. Grammont prepared to complete the humiliation of Prussia, and in doing so he lost all and more than all he had won.

He had at first declared that the withdrawal of the Prince was worthless when it was officially communicated to him by Prussia; now he extended his demands. He suggested to the Prussian Ambassador at Paris that the King should write to the Emperor a letter, in which he should express his regret for what had happened and his assurance that he had had no intention of injuring France. To Benedetti he telegraphed imperative orders that he was to request from the King a guarantee for the future, and a promise that he would never again allow the Prince to return to the candidature. It was to give himself over to an implacable foe. As soon as Bismarck heard from Werther of the first suggestion, he telegraphed to him a stern reprimand for having listened to demands so prejudicial to the honour of his master, and ordered him, under the pretext of ill health, to depart from Paris and leave a post for which he had shewn himself so ill-suited.

That same morning he saw Lord Augustus Loftus, and he explained that the incident was not yet closed; Germany, he said, did not wish for war, but they did not fear it. They were not called on to endure humiliations from France; after what had happened they must have some security for the future; the Duc de Grammont must recall or explain the language he had used; France had begun to prepare for war and that would not be allowed.

"It is clear," writes the English Ambassador, "that Count Bismarck and the Prussian Ministry regret the attitude which the King has shewn to Count Benedetti, and feel, in regard to public opinion, the necessity of guarding the honour of the nation."

To the Crown Prince, who had come to Berlin, Bismarck was more open; he declared that war was necessary.

This very day there were taking place at Ems events which were to give him the opportunity for which he longed. On Benedetti had fallen the task of presenting the new demands to the King; it was one of the most ungrateful of the many unpleasant duties which had been entrusted to him during the last few years. In the early morning, he went out in the hope that he might see someone of the Court; he met the King, himself who was taking the waters. The King at once beckoned to him, entered into conversation, and shewed him a copy of the Cologne Gazette containing the statement of the Prince's withdrawal. Benedetti then, as in duty bound, asked permission to inform his Government that the King would undertake that the candidature should not be resumed at any time. The King, of course, refused, and, when Benedetti pressed the request, repeated the refusal with some emphasis, and then, beckoning to his adjutant, who had withdrawn a few paces, broke off the conversation. When a few hours later the King received a letter from the Prince of Hohenzollern confirming the public statement, he sent a message to Benedetti by his aide-decamp, Count Radziwill, and added to it that there would now be nothing further to say, as the incident was closed. Benedetti twice asked for another interview, but it was refused.

He had done his duty, he had made his request, as he expected, in vain, but between him and the King there had been no departure by word or gesture from the ordinary courtesy which we should expect from these two accomplished gentlemen. All the proceedings indeed had been unusual, for it was not the habit of the King, as it was of Napoleon, to receive foreign envoys except on the advice of his Ministers, and the last conversation had taken place on the public promenade of the fashionable watering-place; but the exception had been explained and justified by the theory that the King's interest in the affair was domestic and not political. Both were anxious to avoid war, and the King to the last treated Benedetti with marked graciousness; he had while at Ems invited him to the royal table, and even now, the next morning before leaving Ems, granted him an audience, at the station to take leave. Nevertheless, he had been seriously annoyed by this fresh demand; he was pained and surprised by the continuance of the French menaces; he could not but fear that there was a deliberate intention to force a quarrel on him. He determined, therefore, to return to Berlin, and ordered Abeken, Secretary to the Foreign Office, who was with him, to telegraph to Bismarck an account of what had taken place, with a suggestion that the facts should be published.

It happened that Bismarck, when the telegram arrived, was dining with Roon and Moltke, who had both been summoned to Berlin. The three men were gloomy and depressed; they felt that their country had been humiliated, and they saw no prospect of revenge. This feeling was increased when Bismarck read aloud the telegram to his two colleagues. These repeated and impatient demands, this intrusion on the King's privacy, this ungenerous playing with his kindly and pacific disposition, stirred their deepest indignation; to them it seemed that Benedetti had been treated with a consideration he did not deserve; the man who came with these proposals should have been repulsed with more marked indignation. But in the suggestion that the facts should be published, Bismarck saw the opportunity he had wished. He went into the next room and drafted a statement; he kept to the very words of the original telegram, but he left out much, and arranged it so that it should convey to the reader the impression, not of what had really occurred, but of what he would have wished should happen. With this he returned, and as he read it to them, Roon and Moltke brightened; here at last was an answer to the French insults; before, it sounded like a "Chamade" (a retreat), now it is a "Fanfare," said Moltke. "That is better," said Roon. Bismarck asked a few questions about the army. Roon assured him that all was prepared; Moltke, that, though no one could ever foretell with certainty the result of a great war, he looked to it with confidence; they all knew that with the publication of this statement the last prospect of peace would be gone. It was published late that night in a special edition of the North German Gazette, and at the same time a copy was sent from the Foreign Office to all German embassies and legations.

It is not altogether correct to call this (as has often been done) a falsification of the telegram. Under no circumstances could Bismarck have published in its original form the confidential message to him from his sovereign; all he had to do was to communicate to the newspapers the facts of which he had been informed, or so much of the facts as it seemed to him desirable that the public should know. He, of course, made the selection in such a form as to produce upon public opinion the particular effect which for the purposes of his policy he wished. What to some extent justifies the charge is that the altered version was published under the heading, "Ems." The official statement was supplemented by another notice in the North German Gazette, which was printed in large type, and stated that Benedetti had so far forgotten all diplomatic etiquette that he had allowed himself to disturb the King in his holidays, to intercept him on the promenade, and to attempt to force demands upon him. This was untrue, but on this point the telegram to Bismarck had been itself incorrect. Besides this, Bismarck doubtless saw to it that the right instructions should be given to the writers for the Press.

But, indeed, this was hardly necessary; the statement itself was a call to arms. During all these days the German people had been left almost without instruction or guidance from the Government; they had heard with astonishment the sudden outbreak of Gallic wrath; they were told, and were inclined to believe it, that the Prussian Government was innocent of the hostile designs attributed to it; and the calm of the Government had communicated itself to them. They remained quiet, but they were still uneasy, they knew not what to think; now all doubt was removed. It was then true that with unexampled eagerness the French had fastened an alien quarrel upon them, had without excuse or justification advanced from insult to insult and menace to menace; and now, to crown their unparalleled acts, they had sent this foreigner to intrude on the reserve of the aged King, and to insult him publicly in his own country. Then false reports came from Ems; it was said that the King had publicly turned his back on Benedetti on the promenade, that the Ambassador had followed the King to his house, and had at last been shewn the door, but that even then he had not scrupled again to intrude on the King at the railway station. [10] From one end of Germany to another a storm of indignation arose; they had had enough of this French annoyance; if the French wished for war then war should they have; now there could no longer be talk of Prussian ambition; all differences of North and South were swept away; wherever the German tongue was spoken men felt that they had been insulted in the person of the King, that it was theirs to protect his honour, and from that day he reigned in their hearts as uncrowned Emperor.

The telegram was as successful in France as in Germany. There the question of peace and war was still in debate; there was a majority for peace, and indeed there was no longer an excuse for war which would satisfy even a Frenchman. Then there came in quick succession the recall and disavowment of the Prussian Ambassador, news of the serious language Bismarck had used to Lord A. Loftus, and then despatches from other Courts that an official message had been sent from Berlin carrying the record of an insult offered to the King by the French Ambassador; add to this the changed tone of the German Press, the enthusiasm with which the French challenge had been taken up; they could have no doubt that they had gone too far; they would now be not the accuser but the accused; had they wished, they did not dare retreat with the fear of the Paris mob before them, and so they decided on war, and on the 15th the official statement was made and approved in the Chamber.

It was on this same day that the King travelled from Ems to Berlin. When he left Ems he still refused to believe in the serious danger of war, but as he travelled north and saw the excited crowd that thronged to meet him at every station his own belief was almost overthrown. To his surprise, when he reached Brandenburg he found Bismarck and the Crown Prince awaiting him; the news that they had come to meet the King was itself looked on almost as a declaration of war; all through the return journey Bismarck unsuccessfully tried to persuade his master to give the order for mobilisation. When they reached Berlin they found the station again surrounded by a tumultuous throng; through it pressed one of the secretaries of the Foreign Office; he brought the news that the order for mobilisation had been given in France. Then, at last, the reluctance of the King was broken down; he gave the order, and at once the Crown Prince, who was standing near, proclaimed the news to all within earshot. The North German Parliament was summoned, and five days later Bismarck was able to announce to them that he had received the Declaration of War from France, adding as he did so that this was the first official communication which throughout the whole affair he had received from the French Government, a circumstance for which there was no precedent in history.

What a contrast is there between the two countries! On the one hand, a King and a Minister who by seven years of loyal co-operation have learnt to trust and depend upon one another, who together have faced danger, who have not shrunk from extreme unpopularity, and who, just for this reason, can now depend on the absolute loyalty of the people. On the other side, the Emperor broken in health, his will shattered by prolonged pain and sickness, trying by the introduction of liberal institutions to free himself from the burden of government and weight of responsibility which he had voluntarily taken upon his shoulders. At Berlin, Bismarck's severity and love of power had brought it about that the divergent policy and uncertainty of early years had ceased; there was one mind and one will directing this State; the unauthorised interference and amateur criticism of courtiers were no longer permitted. In France, all the evils from which Prussia had been freed by Bismarck were increasing; here there was no single will; the Ministry were divided, there was no authority over them; no one could foresee by whom the decision of the Emperor would be determined; the deliberate results of long and painful negotiations might be overthrown in ten minutes by the interference of the Empress or the advice of Prince Napoleon. The Emperor would pursue half a dozen inconsistent policies in as many hours. And then, below all, there was this fatal fact, that Napoleon could not venture to be unpopular. He knew the folly of the course into which he was being driven, but he did not dare to face the mob of Paris, or to defy the Chamber of Deputies. He owed his throne to universal suffrage, and he knew that the people who had set him up could quickly overthrow him. No man can ever govern who fears unpopularity. Bismarck did not, Napoleon did.

Before the campaign began, two events took place which we must record. The first was the publication in the Times of the text of the treaty with France regarding Belgium. We need not add anything further to what we have said regarding it; published at this moment it had a great effect on English public opinion. The other arose out of the opposition which the exiled King of Hanover had continued to maintain. He had used the very large sums of money which he possessed to keep together a Hanoverian Legion, recruited from former officers and soldiers of the Hanoverian army. He had hoped that war would break out before this and would be accompanied by a rising in Hanover. His means had now come to an end, and the unfortunate men were living in Paris almost without support. They were now exposed to a terrible alternative. They could not return to Germany; they did not wish to take part in a war on the French side. Their only hope was emigration to America. Bismarck heard of their position; he offered to pardon them all and to pay to them from the Prussian funds the full pension which they would have received had they continued to serve in the Hanoverian army. It was a timely act of generosity, and it had the effect that the last element of hostility in Germany was stilled and the whole nation could unite as one man in this foreign war.

NOTE.—In this chapter, besides the ordinary authorities, I have depended largely on the memoirs of the King of Roumania. Bismarck, in his own memoirs, states that the writer was not accurately informed; but even if there are some errors in detail, the remarkable statements contained in this work must command belief until they are fully contradicted and disproved. There has, I believe, been no attempt to do this.

CHAPTER XIV.

THE WAR WITH FRANCE AND FOUNDATION OF THE EMPIRE.

1870-1871.

On July 31, 1870, Bismarck left Berlin with the King for the seat of war, for, as in 1866, he was to accompany the army in the field. For the next few months indeed Germany was to be governed from the soil of France, and it was necessary for the Minister to be constantly with the King. Bismarck never forgot that he was a soldier; he was more proud of his general's uniform than of his civil rank, and, though not a combatant, it was his pride and pleasure that he should share something of the hardships and dangers of war. He was as a matter of fact never so well as during the campaign: the early hours, the moderate and at times meagre food, the long hours in the saddle and the open air, restored the nerves and health which had been injured by the annoyances of office, late hours, and prolonged sedentary work. He was accompanied by part of the staff of the Foreign Office, and many of the distinguished strangers who followed the army were often guests at his table; he especially shewed his old friendliness for Americans: General Sheridan and many others of his countrymen found a hearty welcome from the Chancellor.

It was not till the 17th of August that the headquarters came up with the fighting front of the army; but the next day, during the decisive battle of Gravelotte, Bismarck watched the combat by the side of the King, and, as at Königgrätz, they more than once came under fire. At one period, Bismarck was in considerable danger of being taken prisoner. His two sons were serving in the army; they were dragoons in the Cuirassiers of the Guards, serving in the ranks in the same regiment whose uniform their father was entitled to wear. They both took part in the terrible cavalry charge at Mars-la-Tour, in which their regiment suffered so severely; the eldest, Count Herbert, was wounded and had to be invalided home. Bismarck could justly boast that there was no nepotism in the Prussian Government when his two sons were serving as privates. It was not till the war had gone on some weeks and they had taken part in many engagements, that they received their commissions. This would have happened in no other country or army. This was the true equality, so different from the exaggerated democracy of France,—an equality not of privilege but of obligation; every Pomeranian peasant who sent his son to fight and die in France knew that the sons of the most powerful man in the country and in Europe were fighting with them not as officers but as comrades. Bismarck was more fortunate than his friends in that neither of his sons—nor any of his near relatives—lost his life; Roon's second son fell at Sedan, and the bloody days of Mars-la-Tour and

Gravelotte placed in mourning nearly every noble family in Prussia.

From Gravelotte to Sedan he accompanied the army, and he was by the King's side on that fatal day when the white flag was hoisted on the citadel of Sedan, and the French general came out of the town with the message that Napoleon, having in vain sought death at the head of his troops, placed his sword in the hands of the King of Prussia.

The surrender of Sedan was a military event, and the conditions had to be arranged between Moltke and Wimpffen, who had succeeded MacMahon in command, but Bismarck was present at the conference, which was held in his quarters, in case political questions arose. As they rode down together to Doncheroy he and Moltke had agreed that no terms could be offered except the unconditional surrender of the whole army, the officers alone being allowed to retain their swords. Against these conditions Wimpffen and his companions struggled long, but in vain. Moltke coldly assured them that they could not escape, and that it would be madness to begin the fight again; they were surrounded; if the surrender were not complete by four o'clock the next morning the bombardment of the town would begin. Wimpffen suggested that it would be more politic of the Germans to show generosity; they would thereby earn the gratitude of France, and this might be made the beginning of a lasting peace; otherwise what had they to look forward to but a long series of wars? Now was the time for Bismarck to interfere; it was impossible, he declared, to reckon on the gratitude of nations; at times men might indeed build with confidence on that of a sovereign and his family; "but I repeat, nothing can be expected from the gratitude of a nation." Above all was this true of France. "The

Governments there have so little power, the changes are so quick and so unforeseen, that there is nothing on which one can rely." Besides, it would be absurd to imagine that France would ever forgive us our successes. "You are an irritable and jealous people, envious and jealous to the last degree. You have not forgiven us Sadowa, and would you forgive us Sedan? Never."

They could not therefore modify the terms in order to win the gratitude and friendship of France; they might have done so had there been prospects of immediate peace. One of the officers, General Castelnau, announced that he had a special message from Napoleon, who had sent his sword to the King and surrendered in the hope that the King would appreciate the sacrifice and grant a more honourable capitulation. "Whose sword is it that the Emperor Napoleon has surrendered?" asked Bismarck; "is it the sword of France or his own? If it is the sword of France the conditions can be greatly softened; your message would have an extraordinary importance." He thought and he hoped that the Emperor wished to sue for peace, but it was not so. "It is only the sword of the Emperor," answered the General. "All then remains as it was," said Moltke; he insisted on his demands; Wimpffen asked at least that time might be allowed him to return to Sedan and consult his colleagues. He had only come from Algeria two days before; he could not begin his command by signing so terrible a surrender. Even this Moltke refused. Then Wimpffen declared the conference ended; rather than this they would continue the battle; he asked that his horses might be brought. A terrible silence fell on the room; Moltke, with Bismarck by his side, stood cold and impenetrable, facing the three French officers; their faces were lighted by two candles on the table; behind stood the stalwart forms of the German officers of the staff, and from the walls of the room looked down the picture of Napoleon I. Then again Bismarck interfered; he begged Wimpffen not in a moment of pique to take a step which must have such horrible consequences; he whispered a few words to Moltke, and procured from him a concession; hostilities should not be renewed till nine o'clock the next morning. Wimpffen might return to Sedan and report to the Emperor and his colleagues.

It was past midnight when the conference broke up; before daybreak Bismarck was aroused by a messenger who announced that the Emperor had left Sedan and wished to see him. He hastily sprang up, and as he was, unwashed, without breakfast, in his undress uniform, his old cap, and his high boots, shewing all the marks of his long day in the saddle, he mounted his horse and rode down to the spot near the highroad where the Emperor in his carriage, accompanied by three officers and attended by three more on horseback, awaited him. Bismarck rode quickly up to him, dismounted, and as he approached saluted and removed his cap, though this was contrary to etiquette, but it was not a time when he wished even to appear to be wanting in courtesy. Napoleon had come to plead for the army; he wished to see the King, for he hoped that in a personal interview he might extract from him more favourable terms. Bismarck was determined just for this reason that the sovereigns should not meet until the capitulation was signed; he answered, therefore, that it was impossible, as the King was ten miles away. He then accompanied the Emperor to a neighbouring cottage; there in a small room, ten feet square, containing a wooden table and two rush chairs, they sat for some time talking; afterwards they came down and sat smoking in front of the cottage.

"A wonderful contrast to our last meeting in the Tuileries," wrote Bismarck to his wife. "Our conversation was difficult, if I was to avoid matters which would be painful to the man who had been struck down by the mighty hand of God. He first lamented this unhappy war, which he said he had not desired; he had been forced into it by the pressure of public opinion. I answered that with us also no one, least of all the King, had wished for the war. We had looked on the Spanish affair as Spanish and not as German."

The Emperor asked for more favourable terms of surrender, but Bismarck refused to discuss this with him; it was a military question which must be settled between Moltke and Wimpffen. On the other hand, when Bismarck enquired if he were inclined for negotiations for peace, Napoleon answered that he could not discuss this; he was a prisoner of war and could not treat; he referred Bismarck to the Government in Paris.

This meeting had therefore no effect on the situation. Bismarck suggested that the Emperor should go to the neighbouring Château of Belle Vue, which was not occupied by wounded; there he would be able to rest. Thither Bismarck, now in full uniform (for he had hurried back to his own quarters), accompanied him, and in the same house the negotiations of the previous evening were continued; Bismarck did not wish to be present at them, for, as he said, the military men could be harsher; and so gave orders that after a few minutes he should be summoned out of the room by a message that the King wished to see him. After the capitulation was signed, he rode up with Moltke to present it to the King, who received it on the heights whence he had watched the battle, surrounded by the headquarters staff and all the princes who were making the campaign. Then, followed by a brilliant cavalcade, he rode down to visit the captive sovereign.

Bismarck would at this time willingly have made peace, but there was no opportunity of opening negotiations and it is doubtful whether even his influence would have been able successfully to combat the desire of the army to march on Paris. On September 4th, the march, which had been interrupted ten days before, was begun.

Immediately afterwards news came which stopped all hopes of a speedy peace. How soon was his warning as to the instability of French Governments to be fulfilled! A revolution had broken out in Paris, the dethronement of the Emperor had been proclaimed, and a Provisional Government instituted. They at once declared that they were a government of national defence, they would not rest till the invaders were driven from the land, they appealed to the memories of 1792. They were indeed ready to make peace, for the war, they said, had been undertaken not against France but against the Emperor; the Emperor had fallen, a free France had arisen; they would make peace, but they would not yield an inch of their country or a stone of their fortresses. With great energy they prepared the defence of Paris and the organisation of new armies; M. Thiers was instructed to visit the neutral Courts and to beg for the support of Europe.

Under these circumstances it was Bismarck's duty to explain the German view; he did so in two circular notes of September 13th and September 16th. He began by expounding those principles he had already expressed to Wimpffen, principles which had already been communicated by his secretaries to the German Press and been repeated in almost every paper of the country. The war had not been caused by the Emperor; it was the nation which was responsible for it. It had arisen from the intolerance of the French character, which looked on the prosperity of other nations as an insult to themselves. They must expect the same feeling to continue:

"We cannot seek guarantees for the future in French feeling. We must not deceive ourselves; we must soon expect a new attack; we cannot look forward to a lasting peace, and this is quite independent of the conditions we might impose on France. It is their defeat which the French nation will never forgive. If now we were to withdraw from France without any accession of territory, without any contribution, without any advantage but the glory of our arms, there would remain in the French nation the same hatred, the same spirit of revenge, for the injury done to their vanity and to their love of power."

Against this they must demand security; the demand was addressed not to any single Government but to the nation as a whole; South Germany must be protected from the danger of French attack; they would never be safe so long as Strasburg and Metz were in French hands; Strasburg was the gate of Germany; restored to Germany, these cities would regain their defensive character. Twenty times had France made war on Germany, but from Germany no danger of disturbance to the peace of Europe was to be feared.

For the first time he hereby officially stated that Germany would not make peace without some accession of territory; that this would be the case, everyone had known since the beginning of the war. At a council of war directly after Gravelotte it was determined to require Alsace; after Sedan the terms naturally rose. The demand for at least some territory was indeed inevitable. The suggestion that from confidence in the peaceful and friendly character of the French nation they should renounce all the advantages gained by their unparalleled victories scarcely deserved serious consideration. Had the French been successful they would have taken all the left bank of the Rhine; this was actually specified in the draft treaty which General Le Brun had presented to the Emperor of Austria. What claim had France to be treated with a leniency which she has never shewn to any conquered enemy? Bismarck had to meet the assumption that France was a privileged and special land; that she had freedom to conquer, pillage, and divide the land of her neighbours, but that every proposal to win back from her what she had taken from others was a crime against humanity.

So long as the Provisional Government adopted the attitude that they would not even consider peace on the basis of some surrender of territory, there was no prospect of any useful negotiations. The armies must advance, and beneath the walls of Paris the struggle be fought out to its bitter end. Bismarck meanwhile treated the Government with great reserve. They had no legal status; as he often pointed out, the Emperor was still the only legal authority in France, and he would be quite prepared to enter into negotiations with him. When by the medium of the English Ambassador they asked to be allowed to open negotiations for an armistice and discuss the terms of peace, he answered by the question, what guarantee was there that France or the armies in Metz and Strasburg would recognise the arrangements made by the present Government in Paris, or any that might succeed it? It was a quite fair question; for as events were to shew, the commander of the army in Metz refused to recognise them, and wished to restore the Emperor to the throne; and the Government themselves had declared that they would at once be driven from power if they withdrew from their determination not to accept the principle of a cession of territory. They would be driven from power by the same authority to which they owed their existence,—the mob of Paris; it was the mob of Paris which, from the beginning, was really responsible for the war. What use was there in a negotiation in which the two parties had no common ground? None the less Bismarck consented to receive M. Jules Favre, who held the portfolio of Foreign Affairs, and who at the advice of Lord Lyons came out from Paris, even at the risk of a rebuff, to see if by a personal interview he might not be able to influence the German Chancellor. "It is well at least to see what sort of man he is," was the explanation which Bismarck gave; but as the interview was not strictly official he did not, by granting it, bind himself to recognise Favre's authority.

Jules Favre met Bismarck on September 18th. They had a long conversation that evening, and it was continued the next day at Ferneres, Baron Rothschild's house, in which the King was at that time quartered. The French envoy did not make a favourable impression; a lawyer by profession, he had no experience in diplomatic negotiations; vain, verbose, rhetorical, and sentimental, his own report of the interview which he presented to his colleagues in Paris is sufficient evidence of his incapacity for the task he had taken upon himself. "He spoke to me as if I were a public meeting," said Bismarck afterwards, using an expression which in his mouth was peculiarly contemptuous, for he had a platonic dislike of long speeches. But let us hear Favre himself:

"Although fifty-eight years of, age Count Bismarck appeared to be in full vigour. His tall figure, his powerful head, his strongly marked features gave him an aspect both imposing and severe, tempered, however, by a natural simplicity amounting to good-nature. His manners were courteous and grave, and quite free from stiffness or affectation. As soon as the conversation commenced he displayed a communicativeness and good-will which he preserved while it lasted. He certainly regarded me as a negotiator unworthy of him and he had the politeness not to let this be seen, and appeared interested by my sincerity. I was struck with the clearness of his ideas, his vigorous good sense, and his originality of mind. His freedom from all pretensions was no less remarkable."

It is interesting to compare with this the account given by another Frenchman of one of the later interviews between the two men [11] :

"The negotiations began seriously and quietly. The Chancellor said simply and seriously what he wanted with astonishing frankness and admirable logic. He went straight to the mark and at every turn he disconcerted Jules Favre, who was accustomed to legal quibbles and diplomatic jobbery, and did not in the least understand the perfect loyalty of his opponent or his superb fashion of treating questions, so different from the ordinary method. The Chancellor expressed himself in French with a fidelity I have never met with except among the Russians. He made use of expressions at once elegant and vigorous, finding the proper word to describe an idea or define a situation without effort or hesitation."

"I was at the outset struck by the contrast between the two negotiators. Count Bismarck wore the uniform of the White Cuirassiers, white tunic, white cap, and yellow band. He looked like a giant. In his tight uniform, with his broad chest and square shoulders and bursting with health and strength, he overwhelmed the stooping, thin, tall, miserable-looking lawyer with his frock coat, wrinkled all over, and his white hair falling over his collar. A look, alas, at the pair was sufficient to distinguish between the conqueror and the conquered, the strong and the weak."

This, however, was four months later, when Jules Favre was doubtless much broken by the anxieties of his position, and perhaps also by the want of sufficient food, and Comte d'Hérisson is not an impartial witness, for, though a patriotic Frenchman, he was an enemy of the Minister.

Bismarck in granting the interview had said that he would not discuss an armistice, but only terms of peace. For the reasons we have explained, Favre refused to listen even to the proposition of the only terms which Bismarck was empowered to bring forward. The Chancellor explained those ideas with which we are already acquainted: "Strasburg," he said, "is the key of our house and we must have it." Favre protested that he could not discuss conditions which were so dishonourable to France. On this expression we need only quote Bismarck's comment:

"I did not succeed in convincing him that conditions, the fulfilment of which France had required from Italy, and demanded from Germany without having been at war, conditions which France would undoubtedly have imposed upon us had we been defeated and which had been the result of nearly every war, even in the latest time, could not have anything dishonourable in themselves for a country which had been defeated after a brave resistance, and that the honour of France was not of a different kind to that of other countries."

It was impossible to refuse to discuss terms of an armistice; as in 1866 the military authorities objected to any kind of armistice because from a military point of view any cessation of hostilities must be an advantage to France; it would enable them to continue their preparations and get together new armies, while Germany would have the enormous expense of maintaining 500,000 men in a foreign country. Bismarck himself from a political point of view also knew the advantage of bringing the war to a rapid close, while the moral effect of the great victories had not been dissipated. However, France had no Government; a legal Government could not be created without elections, and Favre refused to consider holding elections during the progress of hostilities. After a long discussion Bismarck, other suggestions being rejected, offered an armistice on condition that the war should continue round Metz and Paris, but that Toul and Strasburg should be surrendered and the garrison of Strasburg made prisoners of war. "The towns would anyhow fall into our hands," he said; "it is only a question of engineering." "At these words," says Favre, "I sprang into the air from pain and cried out, 'You forget that you speak to a Frenchman. To sacrifice an heroic garrison which is the object of our admiration and that of the world would be a cowardice. I do not promise even to say that you have offered such a condition.'" Bismarck said that he had no wish to offend him; if the King allowed it the article might be modified; he left the room, and after a quarter of an hour returned, saying that the King would accept no alteration on this point. "My powers were exhausted," writes Favre; "I feared for a moment that I should fall down; I turned away to overcome the tears which choked me, and, while I excused myself for this involuntary weakness, I took leave with a few simple words." He asked Bismarck not to betray his weakness. The Count, who seems really to have been touched by the display of emotion, attempted in some sort of way to console him, but a few days later his sympathy was changed into amusement when he found that the tears which he had been asked to pass over in silence were paraded before the people of Paris to prove the patriotism of the man. "He may have meant it," said Bismarck, "but people ought not to bring sentiment into politics."

The terms which Bismarck had offered were as a matter of fact not at all harsh; a week later the garrison of Strasburg had become prisoners of war; had the French accepted the armistice and begun negotiations for peace they would probably, though they could not have saved Strasburg and Alsace, have received far better terms than those to which they had to assent four months later.

Bismarck in refusing to recognise the Provisional Government always reminded them that the Emperor was still the only legitimate Government in France. He professed that he was willing to negotiate with the Emperor, and often talked of releasing him from his confinement in Germany, coming to terms with Bazaine, and allowing the Emperor at the head of the army at Metz to regain his authority in France. We do not quite know to what extent he was serious in using this language, for he often threatened more than he intended to perform. It is at least possible that he only used it as a means for compelling the Provisional Government quickly to come to terms and thereby to bring the war to an end. It is, however, certain that negotiations went on between him and the Empress and also with Bazaine. They came to nothing because the

Empress absolutely refused to negotiate if she was to be required to surrender any French territory. In this she adopted the language of the Provisional Government in Paris, and was supported by the Emperor.

The negotiations with the Provisional Government were more than once renewed; soon after the investiture of Paris had begun, General Burnside and another American passed as unofficial messengers between the French and German Governments, and at the beginning of November, Thiers came as the official agent of the Government in Tours; these attempts were, however, always without result; the French would not accept an armistice on the only conditions which Bismarck was authorised by the King and the military authorities to offer. During the rest of the year there was little direct communication with the French authorities. Bismarck, however, was not idle. In his quarters at Versailles he had with him many of the Foreign Office staff; he had not only to conduct important diplomatic negotiations, but also to maintain control over the nation, to keep in touch with the Press, to communicate to the newspapers both events and comments on them. At this crisis he could not leave public opinion without proper direction; he had to combat the misstatements of the French, who had so long had the ear of Europe, and were still carrying their grievances to the Courts of the neutral Powers, and found often eager advocates in the Press of the neutral countries. He had to check the proposal of the neutral Powers to interfere between the two combatants, to inform the German public of the demands that were to be made on France and the proposals for the unity of the country, and to justify the policy of the Government; all this was done not only by official notes, but by articles written at his dictation or under his instruction, and by information or suggestions conveyed by his secretaries to his newspapers. In old days the Prussian Government had been inarticulate, it had never been able to defend itself against the attacks of foreign critics; it had suffered much by misrepresentation; it had lost popularity at home and prestige abroad. In the former struggles with France the voice of Germany had scarcely been heard; Europe, which was accustomed to listen to every whisper from Paris, ignored the feelings and the just grievances of Germany. Bismarck changed all this; now he saw to it that the policy of the Government should be explained and defended in Germany itself; for though he despised public opinion when it claimed to be the canon by which the Government should be directed, he never neglected this, as he never neglected any means by which the Government might be strengthened. Speaking now from Versailles, he could be confident that Europe would listen to what Germany said, and it was no small benefit to his nation that it had as its spokesman a man whose character and abilities ensured that no word that he uttered would be neglected.

The neutral Powers really gave him little concern. There was no intention of supporting France either in England, Russia, or Austria. He shewed great activity, however, in defending the Germans from the charges so freely made against them by the French Press, of conducting the war in a cruel manner; charges which were untrue, for, according to the unanimous testimony of foreign observers who accompanied the army, the moderation of the German soldiers was as remarkable as their successes. Bismarck was not content with rebutting unjust accusations,—he carried on the war into the enemy's camp. He was especially indignant at the misuse made by the French of irregular troops; he often maintained that the German soldiers ought never to imprison the franc-tireurs, but shoot them at once. He feared that if civilians were encouraged to take part in the war it would necessarily assume a very cruel character. At Meaux he came upon a number of franc-tireurs who had been taken prisoners. "You are assassins, gentlemen," he said to them; "you will all be hung." And, indeed, these men who fired secretly on the German troops from behind hedges and in forests, and had no kind of uniform, could not claim to be treated as prisoners of war. When the bombardment of Paris began he took great pains to defend a measure which was much attacked in other countries; he had used all his influence that the bombardment should not be delayed, and often spoke with great annoyance of the reluctance of the military authorities to begin. He wished every measure to be taken which would bring the war to an end as soon as possible. The long delay before Paris seems to have affected his nerves and spirits; there were many anxious hours, and it was always difficult for him to wait patiently the result of what others were doing. The military authorities were, as always, very jealous of all attempts by him to interfere in their department, and he was not always satisfied with their decisions. Like all the Germans he was surprised and angry at the unexpected resistance of Paris, and the success of Gambetta's appeal to the nation. He was especially indignant at the help which Garibaldi gave: "This," he said, "is the gratitude of the Italians"; he declared that he would have the General taken prisoner and paraded through the streets of Berlin.

During the long weeks at Versailles, Bismarck was much occupied with German affairs. The victory of Sedan was the foundation of German unity; Bismarck's moderation and reserve now earned its reward; he had always refused to press the southern States into the Federation; now the offer to join came from them. Baden asked, as she had already done at the beginning of the year, to be received into the Union; the settlement with Wurtemberg, and above all with Bavaria, was less simple. At the request of the Bavarian Government Delbrück was sent to Munich for an interchange of opinion, and the negotiations which were begun there were afterwards continued at Versailles and Berlin. There were many difficulties to be overcome: the Bavarians were very jealous of their independence and were not prepared to put themselves into the position which, for instance, Saxony occupied. But the difficulties on the Prussian side were equally great: the Liberal party wished that the Constitution should be revised and those points in it which they had always disliked altered; they would have made the government of the Federal authorities more direct, have created a Federal Ministry and a Federal Upper House, and so really changed the Federation into a simple State, thereby taking away all the independence of the dynasties. It was quite certain that Bavaria would not accept this, and there was some considerable danger that their exaggerated demands might lead to a reaction in South Germany. Probably under any circumstances the unification of Germany would have been completed, but it required all Bismarck's tact to prevent the outbreak of a regular party struggle. The most extreme line was taken by the Crown Prince of Prussia; he desired the immediate creation of an emperor who should have sovereign authority over the whole of Germany, and he even went so far as to suggest that, if the Bavarians would not accept this voluntarily, they might be compelled to do so. He had repeated conversations with Bismarck on this, and on one occasion at least it ended in an angry scene. The Crown Prince wished to threaten the South Germans. "There is no danger," he said; "let us take a firm and commanding attitude. You will see I was right in maintaining that you are not nearly sufficiently conscious of your own power." It is almost incredible that he should have used such language, but the evidence is conclusive; he was at this time commanding the Bavarian troops against the French; Bavaria had with great loyalty supported Prussia through the war and performed very valuable services, and now he proposed to reward their friendship by compelling them to accept terms by which the independence of the King and the very existence of the State would be endangered. The last request which the King of Bavaria had sent to the Crown Prince as he left Munich to take command of the Bavarian army was that nothing might be done to interfere with Bavarian independence. Of course Bismarck refused to listen to these suggestions; had he done so, the probable result would have been that the Bavarian army would have been withdrawn from France and then all the result of the victories would have been lost.

What Bismarck did was in accordance with his usual practice to make no greater alteration in existing institutions than was absolutely necessary; he did not therefore undertake any reform of the Federal Constitution, but simply proposed treaties by which the southern States, each separately, entered into the existing alliance. Certain special conditions were allowed: the King of Bavaria was to maintain the command over his troops in time of peace; a Voice was given to Bavaria in the management of foreign affairs; she retained her own post and telegraph, and there were certain special privileges with regard to finance to meet the system of taxation on beer; and then the Prussian military code was not to apply to Bavaria, and Bavaria was to retain her own special laws with regard to marriage and citizenship. These concessions were undoubtedly very considerable, but Bismarck granted them, for, as he said to the Bavarian envoys, "we do not want a discontented Bavaria; we want one which will join us freely." The Liberal Publicists in Germany with characteristic intolerance complained that when they had hoped to see the Constitution made simpler and the central government stronger it had really become more federal; they did not see that this federalism was merely the expression of existing facts which could not be ignored. They prophesied all kinds of difficulties which have not been fulfilled, for they forgot that harmonious working, in an alliance voluntarily made, would be a firmer bond of union than the most stringent articles of treaties which were looked on as an unjust burden. Bismarck's own words, spoken the evening after the agreements were signed, give the true account of the matter:

"The newspapers will not be satisfied, the historian may very likely condemn our Conventions; he may say, 'The stupid fellow might easily have asked for more, he would have got it, they would have had to give it him; his might was his right.' I was more anxious that these people should go away heartily satisfied. What is the use of treaties which men are forced to sign? I know that they went away satisfied. I do not wish to press them or to take full advantage of the situation. The Convention has its defects, but it is all the stronger on account of them."

He could afford now to be generous because in 1866 he had been so stern; he had refused to take in Bavaria when it would have weakened the association of the North; now that the nucleus had been formed he could allow the Catholic South greater freedom. He was right; the concessions granted to Bavaria have not been in any way a danger to the Empire.

As soon as he had signed the Convention he looked into the room where his secretaries were and said: "The work is done; the unity of Germany is completed and with it Kaiser and Reich." Up to this time he had taken no open steps towards the proclamation of the Empire; but it was unanimously demanded by almost the whole nation and especially by the South Germans. But here he kept himself in the background; he refused to make it appear as though he were to make the Emperor or found the Empire. He allowed the natural wish of the people to work itself out spontaneously. There was indeed some reluctance to assume the title at the Prussian Court; the King himself was not anxious for a new dignity which would obscure that title which he and his ancestors had made so honourable. This feeling was shared by many of the nobility and the officers; we find it strongest in Roon, who in this represents the genuine feeling of the older Prussian nobility. They disliked a change which must mean that the Prussia to which they were so devotedly attached was to become merged in a greater Germany. There was also some apprehension that with the new title the old traditions of the Prussian Court, traditions of economy, almost of parsimony, might be forgotten, and that a new career might begin in which they would attempt to imitate the extravagance and pomp of less prudent sovereigns. With this perhaps Bismarck himself had some sympathy.

The King would, of course, only assume the new title if it was offered to him by his fellow-princes; there was some danger lest the Reichstag, which had been summoned to ratify the treaties, might ask him to assume it before the princes did; had they done so, he would probably have refused. The Crown Prince, who was very eager for the new title, and the Grand Duke of Baden used all their influence with their fellow-princes. The initiative must come from the King of Bavaria; he was in difficulty as to the form in which the offer should be made. Bismarck, who throughout the whole negotiations worked behind the scenes, smoothing away difficulties, thereupon drafted a letter which he sent by special messenger to the King of Bavaria. The King at once adopted it, copied it out and signed it, and at the same time wrote another letter to the other princes, asking them to join in the request which he had made to the King of Prussia, to assume the title of Emperor which had been in abeyance for over sixty years. So it came about that the letter by which the offer to the King was made had really emanated from his own Chancellor. It shews to what good purpose Bismarck used the confidence which, by his conduct in the previous negotiations, the King of Bavaria had been led to place in him.

On the 18th of January, 1871, in the Palace of Versailles, the King publicly assumed the new title; a few days later Bismarck was raised to the rank of Prince.

A few days later Paris fell; the prolonged siege was over and the power of resistance exhausted; then again, as three months before, Favre asked for an audience, this time to negotiate the capitulation of the city; we need not here dwell on the terms of the capitulation—we need only quote what Favre himself says of Bismarck's attitude:

"I should be unfaithful to truth if I did not recognise that in these mournful discussions I always found the Chancellor eager to soften in form the cruelty of his requirements. He applied himself as much as was possible to temper the military harshness of the general staff, and on many points he consented to make himself the advocate of our demands."

A few weeks were allowed for elections to be held and an assembly to meet at Bordeaux, and then once more M.

Thiers appeared, to negotiate the terms of peace. He knew that the demands would be very heavy; he anticipated that they would be asked to surrender Alsace, including Belfort, and of Lorraine at least the department of the Moselle, with Metz; he expected a large war indemnity—five thousand million francs. The terms Bismarck had to offer were almost identical with these, except that the indemnity was placed at six thousand million francs. The part Thiers had to play was a very difficult one; he knew that if Germany insisted on her full demands he must accept; he was too experienced a politician to be misled by any of the illusions under which Favre had laboured. He, as all other Frenchmen, had during the last three months learned a bitter lesson. "Had we made peace," he said, "before the fall of Metz, we might at least have saved Lorraine." He hoped against hope that he might still be able to do so. With all the resources of his intellect and his eloquence he tried to break down the opposition of the Count. When Metz was refused to him then he pleaded for Belfort. Let us hear what Favre, who was present at the decisive interview, tells us; we may use his authority with more confidence that he was a silent and passive auditor.

"One must have been present at this pathetic scene to have an idea of the superhuman resources which the illustrious statesman displayed. I still see him, pale, agitated, now sitting, now springing to his feet; I hear his voice broken by grief, his words cut short, his tones in turn suppliant and proud; I know nothing grander than the sublime passion of this noble heart bursting out in petitions, menaces, prayers, now caressing, now terrible, growing by degrees more angry in face of this cruel refusal, ready for the last extremities, impervious to the counsels of reason, so violent and sacred were the sentiments by which he was governed."

Bismarck remained obdurate; he would surrender neither Metz nor Belfort. Then Thiers cried out:

"Well, let it be as you will; these negotiations are a pretence. We appear to deliberate, we have only to pass under your yoke. We ask for a city absolutely French, you refuse it to us; it is to avow that you have resolved to wage against us a war of extremity. Do it! Ravish our provinces, burn our houses, cut the throats of their unoffending inhabitants, in a word, complete your work. We will fight to the last breath; we shall succumb at last, but we will not be dishonoured."

It was a burst of passion, all the more admirable that Thiers knew his threats were vain; but it was not ineffective. Bismarck was troubled; he said he understood what they suffered; he would be glad to make a concession, "but," he added, "I can promise nothing; the King has commanded me to maintain the conditions, he alone has the right to modify them; I will take his orders; I must consult with Mons. de Moltke." He left the room; it was nearly an hour before he could find Moltke; then he returned to give the answer to the Frenchmen. "You had refused that we should enter Paris; if you will agree that the German troops occupy Paris, then Belfort shall be restored to you." There could be no doubt as to the answer, and some hours later the assent of the King was given to this alteration in the conditions. Before this the indemnity had been reduced to five thousand million francs; below that all the efforts of the French were not able to bring it. There were many other exciting scenes during the progress of the negotiations; on one occasion Thiers threatened Bismarck with interposition of the neutral Powers; "If you speak to me of Europe, I will speak of the Emperor," was Bismarck's answer. He threatened to open negotiations with him and to send him back to France at the head of Bazaine's army. On another occasion—it was during the discussion of finance—another scene took place which Favre describes:

"As the discussion continued, he grew animated, he interrupted Thiers at every word, accused him of wishing to spoil everything; he said that he was ill, at the end of his powers, he was incapable of going further, in a work that we were pleased to make of no use. Then, allowing his feelings to break out, walking up and down the little room in which we were deliberating with great strides, he cried, 'It is very kind of me to take the trouble to which you condemn me; our conditions are ultimatums--you must accept or reject them. I will not take part in it any longer; bring an interpreter to-morrow, henceforward I will not speak French any longer.'"

And he began forthwith to talk German at a great rate, a language which of course neither of the Frenchmen understood.

It is interesting to compare with this Bismarck's own account of the same scene:

"When I addressed a definite demand to Thiers, although he generally could command himself, he sprang up and cried, 'Mais c'est un indignité.' I took no notice but began to talk German. For a time he listened, but obviously did not know what to think of it. Then in a plaintive voice he said, 'But, Count, you know that I do not understand German.' I answered him now in French. 'When just now you spoke of indignité, I found that I did not understand French enough and preferred to speak German, here I know what I say and hear.' He understood what I meant and at once agreed to that which he had just refused as an indignité."

Bismarck's part in these negotiations was not altogether an easy one, for it is probable that, in part at least, he secretly sympathised with the arguments and protests of the French. He was far too loyal to his master and his country not to defend and adopt the policy which had been accepted; but there is much reason to believe that, had he been completely master, Germany would not have insisted on having Metz, but would have made the demand only to withdraw it. The arguments for the annexation of Alsace were indeed unanswerable, and again and again Bismarck had pointed out that Germany could never be safe so long as France held Strasburg, and a French army supported on the strong basis of the Vosges could use Strasburg as a gate whence to sally forth into Germany. No one indeed who has ever stood on the slopes of the Black Forest and looked across the magnificent valley, sheltered by the hills on either side, through which the Rhine flows, can doubt that this is all one country, and that the frontier must be sought, not in the river, which is not a separation, but the chief means of communication, but on the top of the hills on the further side. Every argument, however, which is used to support German claims to Strasburg may be used with equal force to support French claims to Metz. If Strasburg in French hands is the gate of Germany, Metz in German hands is, and always will remain, a military post on the soil of France. No one who reads Bismarck's arguments on this point can fail to notice how they are all nearly conclusive as to Strasburg, but that he scarcely takes the trouble to make it even appear as though they applied to Metz. Even in the speech before the Reichstag in which he explains and justifies the terms of peace, he speaks again and again of Strasburg but hardly a word of Metz. He told how fourteen years before, the old King of Würtemberg had said to him, at the time of the Crimean troubles, that Prussia might count on his voice in the Diet as against the Western Powers, but only till war broke out.

"Then the matter takes another form. I am determined as well as any other to maintain the engagements I have entered into. But do not judge me unjustly; give us Strasburg and we shall be ready for all eventualities, but so long as Strasburg is a sally-port for a Power which is always armed, I must fear that my country will be overrun by foreign troops before my confederates can come to my help."

The King was right; Germany would never be secure so long as Strasburg was French; but can France ever be secure so long as Metz is German?

The demand for Metz was based purely on military considerations; it was supported on the theory, which we have already learnt, that Germany could never take the offensive in a war with France, and that the possession of Metz would make it impossible, as indeed is the case, for France to attack Germany. It was not, however, Bismarck's practice to subordinate political considerations to military. It may be said that France would never acquiesce in the loss of either province, but while we can imagine a generation of Frenchmen arising who would learn to recognise the watershed of the Vosges as a permanent boundary between the two nations, it is difficult to believe that the time will ever come when a single Frenchman will regard with contentment the presence of the Germans on the Upper Moselle.

Even after the preliminaries of peace were settled fresh difficulties arose; the outbreak of the Commune in Paris made it impossible for the French to fulfil all the arrangements; Bismarck, who did not trust the French, treated them with much severity, and more than once he threatened again to begin hostilities. At last Favre asked for a fresh interview; the two statesmen met at Frankfort, and then the final treaty of peace was signed.

CHAPTER XV.

THE NEW EMPIRE.

1871-1878.

WITH the peace of Frankfort, Bismarck's work was completed. Not nine years had passed since he had become Minister; in that short time he completed the work which so many statesmen before him had in vain attempted. Nine years ago he had found the King ready to retire from the throne; now he had made him the most powerful ruler in Europe. Prussia, which then had been divided in itself and without influence in the councils of Europe, was the undisputed leader in a United Germany.

Fate, which always was so kind to Bismarck, was not to snatch him away, as it did Cavour, in the hour of his triumph; twenty years longer he was to preside over the State which he had created and to guide the course of the ship which he had built. A weaker or more timid man would quickly have retired from public life; he would have considered that nothing that he could do could add to his fame, and that he was always risking the loss of some of the reputation he had attained. Bismarck was not influenced by such motives. The exercise of power had become to him a pleasure; he was prepared if his King required it to continue in office to the end of his days, and he never feared to hazard fame and popularity if he could thereby add to the prosperity of the State.

These latter years of Bismarck's life we cannot narrate in detail; space alone would forbid it. It would be to write the history of the German Empire, and though events are not so dramatic they are no less numerous than in the earlier period. Moreover, we have not the material for a complete biographical narrative; there is indeed a great abundance of public records; but as to the secret reasons of State by which in the last resource the policy of the Government was determined, we have little knowledge. From time to time indeed some illicit disclosure, the publication of some confidential document, throws an unexpected light on a situation which is obscure; but these disclosures, so hazardous to the good repute of the men who are responsible and the country in which they are possible, must be treated with great reserve. Prompted by motives of private revenge or public ambition, they disclose only half the truth, and a portion of the truth is often more misleading than complete ignorance.

In foreign policy he was henceforward sole, undisputed master; in Parliament and in the Press scarcely a voice was raised to challenge his pre-eminence; he enjoyed the complete confidence of the allied sovereigns and the enthusiastic affection of the nation; even those parties which often opposed and criticised his internal policy supported him always on foreign affairs. Those only opposed him who were hostile to the Empire itself, those whose ideals or interests were injured by this great military monarchy—Poles and Ultramontanes, Guelphs and Socialists; in opposing Bismarck they seemed to be traitors to their country, and he and his supporters were not slow to divide the nation into the loyal and the Reichsfeindlich.

He deserved the confidence which was placed in him. He succeeded in preserving to the newly founded Empire all the prestige it had gained; he was enabled to soothe the jealousy of the neutral Powers. He did so by his policy of peace. Now he pursued peace with the same decision with which but two years before he had brought about a war. He was guided by the same motive; as war had then been for the benefit of Germany, so now was peace. He had never loved war for the sake of war; he was too good a diplomatist for this; war is the negation of diplomacy, and the statesman who has recourse to it must for the time give over the control to other hands. It is always a clumsy method. The love of war for the sake of war will be found more commonly among autocratic sovereigns who are their own generals than among skilled and practised ministers, and generally war is the last resource by which a weak diplomatist attempts to conceal his blunders and to regain what he has lost.

There had been much anxiety in Europe how the new Empire would deport itself; would it use this power which had been so irresistible for fresh conflicts? The excuse might easily have been found; Bismarck might have put on his banner, "The Union of All Germans in One State"; he might have recalled and reawakened the enthusiasm of fifty years ago; he might have reminded the people that there were still in Holland and in Switzerland, in Austria and in Russia, Germans who were separated from their country, and languishing under a foreign rule. Had he been an idealist he would have done so, and raised in Germany a cry like that of the Italian Irredentists. Or he might have claimed for his country its natural boundaries; after freeing the upper waters of the Rhine from foreign dominion he might have claimed that the great river should flow to the sea, German. This is what Frenchmen had done under similar circumstances, but he was not the man to repeat the crimes and blunders of Louis and Napoleon.

He knew that Germany desired peace; a new generation must grow up in the new order of things; the old wounds must be healed by time, the old divisions forgotten; long years of common work must cement the alliances that he had made, till the jealousy of the defeated was appeased and the new Empire had become as firm and indissoluble as any other State in Europe.

The chief danger came from France; in that unhappy country the cry for revenge seemed the only link with the pride which had been so rudely overthrown. The defeat and the disgrace could not be forgotten; the recovery of the lost provinces was the desire of the nation, and the programme of every party. As we have seen, the German statesmen had foreseen the danger and deliberately defied it. They cared not for the hostility of France, now that they need not fear her power. Oderint dum metuant. Against French demands for restitution they presented a firm and unchangeable negative; it was kinder so and juster, to allow no opening for hope, no loophole for negotiation, no intervention by other Powers. Alsace-Lorraine were German by the right of the hundred thousand German soldiers who had perished to conquer them. Any appearance of weakness would have led to hopes which could never be realised, discussions which could have had no result. The answer to all suggestions was to be found in the strength of Germany; the only diplomacy was to make the army so strong that no French statesman, not even the mob of Paris, could dream of undertaking single-handed a war of revenge.

This was not enough; it was necessary besides to isolate France. There were many men in Europe who would have wished to bring about a new coalition of the armies by whose defeat Germany had been built up—France and Austria, Denmark and the Poles; then it was always to be expected that Russia, who had done so much for Germany in the past, would cease to regard with complacency the success of her protégé; after all, the influence of the Czar in Europe had depended upon the divisions of Germany as much as had that of France. How soon would the Russian nation wake up, as the French had done, to the fact that the sympathies of their Emperor had created a great barrier to Russian ambition and Russian diplomacy? It was especially the Clerical party who wished to bring about some coalition; for them the chief object was the overthrow of Italy, and the world still seemed to centre in Rome; they could not gain the assistance of Germany in this work, and they therefore looked on the great Protestant Empire as an enemy. They would have liked by monarchical reaction to gain control of France; by the success of the Carlist movement to obtain that of Spain, and then, assisted by Austria, to overthrow the new order in Europe. Against this Bismarck's chief energies were directed; we shall see how he fought the Ultramontanes at home. With regard to France, he was inclined to support the Republic, and refused all attempts which were made by some German statesmen, and especially by Count Arnim, the Ambassador at Paris, to win German sympathy and support to the monarchical party. In Spain his support and sympathy were given to the Government, which with difficulty maintained itself against the Carlists; a visit of Victor Emmanuel to

Berlin confirmed the friendship with Italy, over which the action of Garibaldi in 1870 had thrown a cloud. The greatest triumph of Bismarck's policy was, however, the reconciliation with Austria. One of the most intimate of his councillors, when asked which of Bismarck's actions he admired most, specified this. It was peculiarly his own; he had long worked for it; even while the war of 1866 was still being waged, he had foreseen that a day would come when Germany and Austria, now that they were separated, might become, as they never had been when joined by an unnatural union, honest allies. It was probably to a great extent brought about by the strong regard and confidence which the Austrian Emperor reposed in the German Chancellor. The beginnings of an approximation were laid by the dismissal of Beust, who himself now was to become a personal friend of the statesman against whom he had for so long and with such ingenuity waged an unequal conflict. The union was sealed when, in December, 1872, the Czar of Russia and Francis Joseph came to Berlin as guests of the Emperor. There was no signed contract, no written alliance, but the old union of the Eastern monarchies under which a generation before Europe had groaned, was now restored, and on the Continent there was no place to which France could look for help or sympathy.

The years that followed were those in which foreign affairs gave Bismarck least anxiety or occupation. He even began to complain that he was dull; after all these years of conflict and intrigue he found the security which he now enjoyed uninteresting. Now and again the shadow of war passed over Europe, but it was soon dispelled. The most serious was in 1875.

It appears that the French reforms of the army and some movements of French troops had caused alarm at Berlin; I say alarm, though it is difficult to believe that any serious concern could have been felt. There was, however, a party who believed that war must come sooner or later, and it was better, they said, not to wait till France was again powerful and had won allies; surely the wisest thing was while she was still weak and friendless to take some excuse (and how easy would it be to find the excuse!), fall upon her, and crush her—crush and destroy, so that she could never again raise her head; treat her as she had in old days treated Germany. How far this plan was deliberately adopted we do not know, but in the spring of this year the signs became so alarming that both the Russian and the English Governments were seriously disturbed, and interfered. So sober a statesman as Lord Derby believed that the danger was real. The Czar, who visited Berlin at the beginning of April, dealt with the matter personally; the Queen of England wrote a letter to the German Emperor, in which she said that the information she had could leave no doubt that an aggressive war on France was meditated, and used her personal influence with the sovereign to prevent it. The Emperor himself had not sympathised with the idea of war, and it is said did not even know of the approaching danger. It did not require the intervention of other sovereigns to induce him to refuse his assent to a wanton war, but this advice from foreign Powers of course caused great indignation in Bismarck; it was just the kind of thing which always angered him beyond everything. He maintained that he had had no warlike intentions, that the reports were untrue. The whole story had its origin, he said, in the intrigues of the Ultramontanes and the vanity of Gortschakoff; the object was to make it appear that France owed her security and preservation to the friendly interference of Russia, and thereby prepare the way for an alliance between the two Powers. It is almost impossible to believe that Bismarck had seriously intended to bring about a war; he must have known that the other Powers of Europe would not allow a second and unprovoked attack on France; he would not be likely to risk all he had achieved and bring about a European coalition against him. On the other hand his explanation is probably not the whole truth; even German writers confess that the plan of attacking France was meditated, and it was a plan of a nature to recommend itself to the military party in Prussia.

Yet this may have been the beginning of a divergence with Russia. The union had depended more on the personal feelings of the Czar than on the wishes of the people or their real interests. The rising Pan-Slavonic party was anti-German; their leader was General Ignatieff, but Gortschakoff, partly perhaps from personal hostility to Bismarck, partly from a just consideration of Russian interests, sympathised with their anti-Teutonic policy. The outbreak of disturbances in the East roused that national feeling which had slept for twenty years; in truth the strong patriotism of modern Germany naturally created a similar feeling in the neighbouring countries; just as the Germans were proud to free themselves from the dominant culture of France, so the Russians began to look with jealousy on the Teutonic influence which since the days of Peter the Great had been so powerful among them.

In internal matters the situation was very different; here Bismarck could not rule in the same undisputed manner; he had rivals, critics, and colleagues. The power of the Prussian Parliament and the Reichstag was indeed limited, but without their assent no new law could be passed; each year their assent must be obtained to the Budget. Though they had waived all claim to control the foreign policy, the parties still criticised and often rejected the laws proposed by the Government. Then in Prussian affairs he could not act without the good-will of his colleagues; in finance, in legal reform, the management of Church and schools, the initiative belonged to the Ministers responsible for each department. Some of the difficulties of government would have been met had Bismarck identified himself with a single party, formed a party Ministry and carried out their programme. This he always refused to do; he did not wish in his old age to become a Parliamentary Minister, for had he depended for his support on a party, then if he lost their confidence, or they lost the confidence of the country, he would have had to retire from office. The whole work of his earlier years would have been undone. What he wished to secure was a Government party, a Bismarck party sans phrase, who would always support all his measures in internal as well as external policy. In this, however, he did not succeed. He was therefore reduced to another course: in order to get the measures of the Government passed, he executed a series of alliances, now with one, now with another party. In these, however, he had to give as well as to receive, and it is curious to see how easily his pride was offended and his anger roused by any attempt of the party with which at the time he was allied to control and influence his policy. No one of the alliances lasted long, and he seems to have taken peculiar pleasure in breaking away from each of them in turn when the time came.

The alliance with the Conservatives which he had inherited from the older days had begun to break directly after 1866. Many of them had been disappointed by his policy in that year. The grant of universal suffrage had alarmed them; they had wished that he would use his power to check and punish the Parliament for its opposition; instead of that he asked for an indemnity. They felt that they had borne with him the struggle for the integrity of the Prussian Monarchy; no sooner was the victory won than he held out his hand to the Liberals and it was to them that the prize went. They were hurt and disappointed, and this personal feeling was increased by Bismarck's want of consideration, his brusqueness of manner, his refusal to consider complaints and remonstrances. Even the success of 1870 had not altogether reconciled them; these Prussian nobles, the men to whom in earlier days he himself had belonged, saw with regret the name of King of Prussia hidden behind the newer glory of the German Emperor; it is curious to read how even Roon speaks with something of contempt and disgust of this new title: "I hope," he writes, "Bismarck will be in a better temper now that the Kaiser egg has been safely hatched." It was, however, the struggle with the Catholic Church which achieved the separation; the complete subjection of the Church to the State, the new laws for school inspection, the introduction of compulsory civil marriage, were all opposed to the strongest and the healthiest feelings of the Prussian Conservatives. These did not seem to be matters in which the safety of the Empire was concerned; Bismarck had simply gone over to, and adopted the programme of, the Liberals; he was supporting that all-pervading power of the Prussian bureaucracy which he, in his earlier days, had so bitterly attacked. Then came a proposal for change in the local government which would diminish the influence of the landed proprietors. The Conservatives refused to support these measures; the Conservative majority in the House of Lords threw them out. Bismarck's own brother, all his old friends and comrades, were now ranged against him. He accepted opposition from them as little as from anyone else; the consent of the King was obtained to the creation of new peers, and by this means the obnoxious measures were forced through the unwilling House. Bismarck by his speeches intensified the bitterness; he came down himself to make an attack on the Conservatives. "The Government is disappointed," he said; "we had looked for confidence from the Conservative party; confidence is a delicate plant; if it is once destroyed it does not grow again. We shall have to look elsewhere for support."

A crisis in his relations to the party came at the end of 1872; up to this time Roon had still remained in the Government; now, in consequence of the manner in which the creation of peers had been decided upon, he requested permission to resign. The King, who could not bear to part with him, and who really in many matters of internal policy had more sympathy with him than with Bismarck, refused to accept the resignation. The crisis which arose had an unexpected ending: Bismarck himself resigned the office of Minister-President of Prussia, which was transferred to Roon, keeping only that of Foreign Minister and Chancellor of the Empire.

A letter to Roon shews the deep depression under which he laboured at this time, chiefly the result of ill-health. "It was," he said, "an unheard-of anomaly that the Foreign Minister of a great Empire should be responsible also for internal affairs." And yet he himself had arranged that it should be so. The desertion of the Conservative party had, he said, deprived him of his footing; he was dispirited by the loss of his old friends and the illness of his wife; he spoke of his advancing years and his conviction that he had not much longer to live; "the King scarcely knows how he is riding a good horse to death." He would continue to do what he could in foreign affairs, but he would no longer be responsible for colleagues over whom he had no influence except by requests, and for the wishes of the Emperor which he did not share. The arrangement lasted for a year, and then Roon had again to request, and this time received, permission to retire into private life; his health would no longer allow him to endure the constant anxiety of office. His retirement occasioned genuine grief to the King; and of all the severances which he had to undergo, this was probably that which affected Bismarck most. For none of his colleagues could he ever have the same affection he had had for Roon; he it was who had brought him into the Ministry, and had gone through with him all the days of storm and trouble. "It will be lonely for me," he writes, "in my work; ever more so, the old friends become enemies and one makes no new ones. As God will." In 1873 he again assumed the Presidency. The resignation of Roon was followed by a complete breach with the party of the Kreuz Zeitung; the more moderate of the Conservatives split off from it and continued to support the Government; the remainder entered on a campaign of factious opposition.

The quarrel was inevitable, for quite apart from the question of religion it would indeed have been impossible to govern Germany according to their principles. We may, however, regret that the quarrel was not conducted with more amenity. These Prussian nobles were of the same race as Bismarck himself; they resembled him in character if not in ability; they believed that they had been betrayed, and they did not easily forgive. They were not scrupulous in the weapons they adopted; the Press was used for anonymous attacks on his person and his character; they accused him of using his public position for making money by speculation, and of sacrificing to that the alliance with Russia. More than once he had recourse to the law of libel to defend himself against these unworthy insults. When he publicly in the Reichstag protested against the language of the Kreuz Zeitung, the dishonourable attacks and the scandalous lies it spread abroad, a large number of the leading men among the Prussian nobility signed a declaration formally defending the management of the paper, as true adherents of the monarchical and Conservative banner. These Declaranten, as they were called, were henceforward enemies whom he could never forgive. At the bottom of the list we read, not without emotion, the words, "Signed with deep regret, A. von Thadden"; so far apart were now the two knight-errants of the Christian Monarchy. It was in reality the end of the old Conservative party; it had done its work; Bismarck was now thrown on the support of the National Liberals.

Since 1866 they had grown in numbers and in weight. They represented at this time the general sense of the German people; it was with their help that during the years down to 1878 the new institutions for the Empire were built up. In the elections of 1871 they numbered 120; in 1874 their numbers rose to 152; they had not an absolute majority, but in all questions regarding the defence of the Empire, foreign policy, and the army they were supported by the moderate Conservatives; in the conflict with the Catholics and internal matters they could generally depend on the support of the Progressives; so that as long as they maintained their authority they gave the Government the required majority in both the Prussian and the German Parliament. There were differences in the party which afterwards were to lead to a secession, but during this time, which they looked upon as the golden era of the Empire, they succeeded in maintaining their unity. They numbered many of the ablest leaders, the lawyers and men of learning who had opposed Bismarck at the time of the conflict. Their leader was Bennigsen; himself a Hanoverian, he had brought no feelings of hostility from the older days of conflict. Moderate, tactful, restrained, patriotic, he was the only man who, when difficulties arose, was always able to approach the Chancellor, sure of finding some tenable compromise. Different was it with Lasker, the ablest of Parliamentary orators, whose subordination to the decisions of the party was often doubtful, and whose criticism, friendly as it often was, always aroused Bismarck's anger.

As a matter of fact the alliance was, however, never complete; it was always felt that at any moment some question might arise on which it would be wrecked. This was shewn by Bismarck's language as early as 1871; in a debate on the army he explained that what he demanded was full support; members, he said, were expressly elected to support him; they had no right to make conditions or withdraw their support; if they did so he would resign. The party, which was very loyal to him, constantly gave up its own views when he made it a question of confidence, but the strain was there and was always felt. The great question now as before was that of the organisation of the army. It will be remembered that, under the North German Confederation, a provisional arrangement was made by which the numbers of the army in peace were to be fixed at one per cent. of the population. This terminated at the end of 1871; the Government, however, did not then consider it safe to alter the arrangement, and with some misgiving the Reichstag accepted the proposal that this system should be applied to the whole Empire for three years. If, however, the numbers of the army were absolutely fixed in this way, the Reichstag would cease to have any control over the expenses; all other important taxes and expenses came before the individual States. In 1874, the Government had to make their proposal for the future. This was that the system which had hitherto been provisionally accepted should become permanent, and that the army should henceforward in time of peace always consist of the same number of men. To agree to this would be permanently to give up all possibility of exercising any control over the finance. It was impossible for the National Liberal party to accept the proposal without giving up at the same time all hope of constitutional development; Bismarck was ill and could take no part in defending the law; they voted against it, it was thrown out, and it seemed as though a new conflict was going to arise.

When the Reichstag adjourned in April for the Easter holidays the agitation spread over the country, but the country was determined not again to have a conflict on the Budget. "There was a regular fanaticism for unconditional acceptance of the law; those even on the Left refused to hear anything of constitutional considerations," writes one member of the National Liberty party after meeting his constituents. If the Reichstag persisted in their refusal and a dissolution took place, there was no doubt that there would be a great majority for the Government. It was the first time since 1870 that the question of constitutional privileges was raised, and now it was found, as ever afterwards was the case, that, for the German people, whatever might be the opinion of their elected representatives, the name of Bismarck alone outweighed all else. Bennigsen arranged a compromise and the required number of men was agreed to, not indeed permanently, but for seven years. For four years more the alliance was continued.

At this time all other questions were thrown into the shade by the great conflict with the Roman Catholic Church on which the Government had embarked. Looking back now, it is still difficult to judge or even to understand the causes which brought it about. Both sides claim that they were acting in self-defence. Bismarck has often explained his motives, but we cannot be sure that those he puts forward were the only considerations by which he was moved. He, however, insisted that the struggle was not religious but political; he was not moved by Protestant animosity to the Catholic Church, but by his alarm lest in the organisation of the Roman hierarchy a power might arise within the Empire which would be hostile to the State. But even if the Chancellor himself was at first free from Protestant hatred to Catholicism,—and this is not quite clear,—he was forced into alliance with a large party who appealed at once to the memories of the Reformation, who stirred up all that latent hatred of Rome which is as strong a force in North Germany as in England; and with others who saw in this an opportunity for more completely subduing all, Protestant and Catholic alike, to the triumphant power of the State, and making one more step towards the dissociation of the State from any religious body.

The immediate cause of the struggle was the proclamation of the infallibility of the Pope. It might be thought that this change or development in the Constitution of the Roman Church was one which concerned chiefly Roman Catholics. This is the view which Bismarck seems to have taken during the meetings of the Vatican Council. The opposition to the decrees was strongest among the German Bishops, and Prince Hohenlohe, the Prime Minister of Bavaria, supported by his brother the Cardinal, was anxious to persuade the Governments of Europe to interfere, and, as they could have done, to prevent the Council from coming to any conclusion. Bismarck refused on behalf of the Prussian Government to take any steps in this direction. The conclusion of the Council and the proclamation of the decrees took place just at the time of the outbreak of war with France. For some months Bismarck, occupied as he was with other matters, was unable to consider the changes which might be caused; it was moreover very important for him during the negotiations with Bavaria, which lasted all through the autumn, not to do anything which would arouse the fears of the Ultramontanes or intensify their reluctance to enter the Empire.

In the winter of 1870 the first sign of the dangers ahead was to be seen. They arose from the occupation of Rome by the Italians. The inevitable result of this was that the Roman Catholics of all countries in Europe were at once given a common cause of political endeavour; they were bound each of them in his own State to use his full influence to procure interference either by diplomacy or by arms, and to work for the rescue of the prisoner of the Vatican. The German Catholics felt this as strongly as their co-religionists, and, while he was still at Versailles, a cardinal and bishop of the Church addressed a memorial to the King of Prussia on this matter. This attempt to influence the foreign policy of the new Empire, and to use it for a purpose alien to the direct interest of Germany, was very repugnant to Bismarck and was quite sufficient to arouse feelings of hostility towards the Roman Catholics. These were increased when he heard that the Roman Catholic leaders were combining to form a new political party; in the elections for the first Reichstag this movement was very successful and fifty members were returned whose sole bond of union was religion. This he looked upon as "a mobilisation of the Church against the State"; the formation of a political party founded simply on unity of confession was, he said, an unheard-of innovation in political life. His distrust increased when he found that their leader was Windthorst, a former Minister of the King of Hanover, and, as a patriotic Hanoverian, one of the chief opponents of a powerful and centralised Government. The influence the Church had in the Polish provinces was a further cause of hostility, and seemed to justify him in condemning them as anti-German. During the first session the new party prominently appeared on two occasions. In the debate on the address to the Crown they asked for the interference of Germany on behalf of the Pope; in this they stood alone and on a division found no supporters. Then they demanded that in the Constitution of the Empire certain clauses from the Prussian Constitution should be introduced which would ensure freedom to all religious denominations. Here they gained considerable support from some other parties.

An impartial observer will find it difficult to justify from these acts the charge of disloyalty to the Empire, but a storm of indignation arose in the Press, especially in the organs of the National Liberal party, and it was supported by those of the Government.

The desire for conflict was awakened; meetings were held in the autumn of 1871 to defend the Protestant faith, which hardly seemed to have been attacked, and a clearer cause for dispute soon occurred. It was required by the authorities of the Church that all bishops and priests should declare their assent to the new Vatican decrees; the majority did so, but a certain number refused; they were of course excommunicated; a secession from the Roman Catholic Church took place, and a new communion formed to which the name of Old Catholics was given. The bishops required that all the priests and religious teachers at the universities and schools who had refused to obey the orders of the Pope should be dismissed from their office; the Prussian Government refused their assent. The legal question involved was a difficult one. The Government held that as the Roman Catholic Church had changed its teachings, those who maintained the old doctrine must be supported in the offices conferred on them. The Church authorities denied there had been any essential change. On the whole we may say that they were right; a priest of the Catholic Church held his position not only in virtue of his assent to the actual doctrines taught, but was also bound by his vow of obedience to accept any fresh teaching which, in accordance with the Constitution of the Church and by the recognised organ of Government, should in the future also be declared to be of faith. The duty of every man to obey the laws applies not only to the laws existing at any moment, but to any future laws which may be passed by the proper agent of legislation. Even though the doctrine of infallibility were a new doctrine, which is very doubtful, it had been passed at a Council; and the proceedings of the Council, even if, in some details, they were irregular, were not more so than those of any other Council in the past.

The action of the Government in supporting the Old Catholics may, however, be attributed to another motive. The Catholics maintained that Bismarck desired to take this opportunity of creating a national German Church, and reunite Protestants and Catholics. To have done so, had it been possible, would have been indeed to confer on the country the greatest of all blessings. We cannot doubt that the thought had often come into Bismarck's mind; it would be the proper and fitting conclusion to the work of creating a nation. It was, however, impossible; under no circumstances could it have been done by a Protestant statesman; the impulse must have come from Bavaria, and the opposition of the Bavarian bishops to the Vatican decrees had been easily overcome. Twice an opportunity had presented itself of making a national German Church: once at the Reformation, once after the Revolution. On both occasions it was lost and it will never recur.

The result, however, was that a bitter feeling of opposition was created between Church and State. The secessionist priests were maintained in their positions by the Government, they were excommunicated by the bishops;

students were forbidden to attend their lectures and the people to worship in the churches where they ministered. It spread even to the army, when the Minister of War required the army chaplain at Cologne to celebrate Mass in a church which was used also by the Old Catholics. He was forbidden to do so by his bishop, and the bishop was in consequence deprived of his salary and threatened with arrest.

The conflict having once begun soon spread; a new Minister of Culture was appointed; in the Reichstag a law was proposed expelling the Jesuits from Germany; and a number of important laws, the so-called May laws, were introduced into the Prussian Parliament, giving to the State great powers with regard to the education and appointment of priests; it was, for instance, ordered that no one should be appointed to a cure of souls who was not a German, and had not been brought up and educated in the State schools and universities of Prussia. Then other laws were introduced, to which we have already referred, making civil marriage compulsory, so as to cripple the very strong power which the Roman Catholic priests could exercise, not only by refusing their consent to mixed marriages, but also by refusing to marry Old Catholics; a law was introduced taking the inspection of elementary schools out of the hands of the clergy, and finally a change was made in those articles of the Prussian Constitution which ensured to each denomination the management of its own affairs. Bismarck was probably not responsible for the drafting of all these laws; he only occasionally took part in the discussion and was often away from Berlin.

The contrast between these proposals and the principles he had maintained in his earlier years was very marked; his old friend Kleist recalled the eloquent speech which in former years he had made against civil marriage. Bismarck did not attempt to defend himself against the charge of inconsistency; he did not even avow that he had changed his personal opinions; he had, however, he said, learnt to submit his personal convictions to the requirements of the State; he had only done so unwillingly and by a great struggle. This was to be the end of the doctrine of the Christian State. With Gneist, Lasker, Virchow, he was subduing the Church to this new idol of the State; he was doing that against which in the old days he had struggled with the greatest resolution and spoken with the greatest eloquence. Not many years were to go by before he began to repent of what he had done, for, as he saw the new danger from Social Democracy, he like many other Germans believed that the true means of defeating it was to be found in increased intensity of religious conviction. It was, however, then too late.

He, however, especially in the Prussian Upper House, threw all the weight of his authority into the conflict. It was, he said, not a religious conflict but a political one; they were not actuated by hatred of Catholicism, but they were protecting the rights of the State.

"The question at issue," he said, "is not a struggle of an Evangelical dynasty against the Catholic Church; it is the old struggle ... a struggle for power as old as the human race ... between king and priest ... a struggle which is much older than the appearance of our Redeemer in this world.... a struggle which has filled German history of the Middle Ages till the destruction of the German Empire, and which found its conclusion when the last representative of the glorious Swabian dynasty died on the scaffold, under the axe of a French conqueror who stood in alliance with the

Pope. [12] We are not far from an analogous solution of the situation, always translated into the customs of our time."

He assured the House that now, as always, he would defend the Empire against internal and external enemies. "Rest assured we will not go to Canossa," he said.

In undertaking this struggle with the Church he had two enemies to contend with—the Pope and the government of the Church on the one side, on the other the Catholic population of Germany. He tried to come to some agreement with the Pope and to separate the two; it seemed in fact as if the real enemy to be contended against was not the foreign priesthood, but the Catholic Democracy in Germany. All Bismarck's efforts to separate the two and to procure the assistance of the Pope against the party of the Centre were to be unavailing; for some years all official communication between the German Government and the Papal See was broken off. It was not till the death of Pius IX. and the accession of a more liberal-minded Pope that communication was restored; then we are surprised to find Bismarck appealing to the Pope to use his influence on the Centre in order to persuade them to vote for a proposed increase in the German army. This is a curious comment on the boast, "We will not go to Canossa."

The truth is that in undertaking the conflict and associating himself with the anti-Clerical party Bismarck had stirred up an enemy whom he was not able to overcome. He soon found that the priests and the Catholics were men of a different calibre to the Liberals. They dared to do what none of the Progressives had ventured on—they disobeyed the law. With them it was not likely that the conflict would be confined to Parliamentary debates. The Government attempted to meet this resistance, but in vain. The priests were deprived of their cures, bishops were thrown into prison, nearly half the Catholic parishes in Prussia were deprived of their spiritual shepherds, the churches were closed, there was no one to celebrate baptisms or weddings. Against this resistance what could the Government do? The people supported the leaders of the party, and a united body of one hundred members under Windhorst, ablest of Parliamentary leaders, was committed to absolute opposition to every Government measure so long as the conflict continued. Can we be surprised that as the years went on Bismarck looked with some concern on the result of the struggle he had brought about?

He attempted to conceal the failure: "The result will be," he said, "that we shall have two great parties—one which supports and maintains the State, and another which attacks it. The former will be the great majority and it will be formed in the school of conflict." These words are the strongest condemnation of his policy. It could not be wise for any statesman to arrange that party conflict should take the form of loyalty and disloyalty to the Empire.

There can be little doubt that his sense of failure helped to bring about a feeling of enmity towards the National Liberals. Suddenly in the spring of 1877 he sent in his resignation. There were, however, other reasons for doing this. He had become aware that the financial policy of the Empire had not been successful; on every side it seemed that new blood and new methods were required. In financial matters he had little experience or authority; he had to depend on his colleagues and he complained of their unfruitfulness. Influenced perhaps by his perception of this, under the pretext—a genuine pretext—of ill-health, he asked the Emperor to relieve him of his offices. The Emperor refused. "Never," he wrote on the side of the minute. Instead he granted to Bismarck unlimited leave of absence. In the month of April the Chancellor retired to Varzin; for ten months he was absent from Berlin, and when he returned, recruited in health, in February, 1878, it was soon apparent that a new period in his career and in the history of the Empire was to begin.

CHAPTER XVI.

THE TRIPLE ALLIANCE AND ECONOMIC REFORM.

1878-1887.

The year 1878 forms a turning-point both in internal and in external politics. Up to this year Prussia has been allied with the two Eastern monarchies; the Empire has been governed by the help of the National Liberal party; the chief enemy has been the Clericals. The traditions of the time before the war are still maintained. After this year the understanding with Russia breaks down; instead of it the peace of Europe is preserved by the Triple Alliance with Austria and Italy. In internal affairs the change is even more marked; the rising power of the Socialists is the enemy to be fought against; for this conflict, peace has to be made with the Catholics—the May laws are modified or repealed. The alliance with Liberalism breaks down, and the efforts of the Government are devoted to a far-reaching scheme of financial reform and social legislation.

When, in April, 1877, the Emperor refused to accept Bismarck's resignation, the whole country applauded the decision. In the Reichstag a great demonstration was made of confidence in the Chancellor. Everyone felt that he could not be spared at a time when the complications in the East were bringing new dangers upon Europe, and in the seclusion of Varzin he did not cease during the next months to direct the foreign policy of the Empire. He was able with the other Governments of Europe to prevent the spread of hostilities from Turkey to the rest of Europe, and when the next year the English Government refused its assent to the provisional peace of San Stefano, it was the unanimous desire of all the other States that the settlement of Turkey should be submitted to a Congress at Berlin over which he should preside. It was the culmination of his public career; it was the recognition by Europe in the most impressive way of his primacy among living statesmen. In his management of the Congress he answered to the expectations formed of him. "We do not wish to go," he had said, "the way of Napoleon; we do not desire to be the arbitrators or schoolmasters of Europe. We do not wish to force our policy on other States by appealing to the strength of our army. I look on our task as a more useful though a humbler one; it is enough if we can be an honest broker." He succeeded in the task he had set before himself, and in reconciling the apparently incompatible desires of England and Russia. Again and again when the Congress seemed about to break up without result he made himself the spokesman of Russian wishes, and conveyed them to Lord Beaconsfield, the English plenipotentiary.

None the less the friendship of Russia, which had before wavered, now broke down. A bitter attack on Germany and Bismarck was begun in the Russian Press; the new German fiscal policy led to misunderstandings; the Czar in private letters to the Emperor demanded in the negotiations that were still going on the absolute and unconditional support of Germany to all Russian demands as the condition of Russian friendship. In the autumn of the next year matters came near to war; it was in these circumstances that Bismarck brought about that alliance which ever since then has governed European politics. He hastily arranged a meeting with Count Andrassy, the Austrian Minister, and in a few days the two statesmen agreed on a defensive alliance between the two Empires. Many years later, in 1886, the instrument of alliance was published. It was agreed that if either of the German States was attacked by Russia the other would join to defend it; if either was attacked by France the other would observe neutrality; but if the French were supported by Russia then the first clause would come into force. The Emperor of Austria willingly gave his assent; it was only after a prolonged struggle that Bismarck was able to gain the assent of his own sovereign. This alliance, which in the next year was joined by Italy, again gave Germany the ruling position in Europe.

During this crisis in foreign affairs Bismarck was occupied by another, which threatened to be equally serious, in home politics. In the spring of 1878 an attempt was made on the life of the Emperor; a young man, named Hobel, a shoemaker's apprentice, shot at him in the streets of Berlin, fortunately without result. The attempt naturally created intense indignation throughout the country. This was increased when it became known that he had been to some extent connected with the Socialist party, and it seemed as though the motives of the crime were supplied by the violent speeches made at Socialist gatherings. Bismarck had long regarded the growth of Socialism with concern. He determined to use this opportunity to crush it. He at once brought into the Bundesrath a very severe law, forbidding all Socialist agitation and propaganda. He succeeded in passing it through the Council, but it was thrown out in the Reichstag by a very large majority. No one voted for it except the Conservatives. The law indeed was so drawn up that one does not see how anyone could have voted for it; the first clause began, "Printed writings and unions which follow the aims of Social Democracy may be forbidden by the Federal Council," but, as was pointed out, among the aims of Social Democracy were many which were good in themselves, and many others which, though they might be considered harmful by other parties, were at least legitimate. Directly afterwards the Reichstag was prorogued. Ten days later, another attempt was made on the Emperor's life; this time a man of the name of Nobeling (an educated man who had studied at the University) shot at him while driving in the Unter den Linden, and wounded him severely in the head and arms with large shot. The Emperor was driven home to his palace almost unconscious, and for some time his life was in danger. This second attempt in so short a time on the life of a man almost eighty years of age, so universally loved and respected, who had conferred such benefits on his country, naturally aroused a storm of indignation. When Bismarck received the news his first words were, "Now the Reichstag must be dissolved." This was done; the general elections took place while the excitement was still hot, and of course resulted in a great loss to those parties—especially the National Liberals—who had voted against the Socialist law; the Centre alone retained its numbers. Before this new Parliament a fresh law was laid, drafted with much more skill. It absolutely forbade all speeches or writing in favour of plans for overthrowing the order of society, or directed against marriage and property. It enabled the Government to proclaim in all large towns a state of siege, and to expel from them by the mere decree of the police anyone suspected of Socialist agitation. The law, which was easily carried, was enforced with great severity; a state of siege was proclaimed in Berlin and many other places. Socialist papers, and even books, for instance the writings of Lassalle, were forbidden; they might not even be read in public libraries; and for the next twelve years the Socialist party had to carry on their propaganda by secret means.

This Socialist law is very disappointing; we find the Government again having recourse to the same means for checking and guiding opinion which Metternich had used fifty years before. Not indeed that the Socialists themselves had any ground for complaint; their avowed end was the overthrow of government and society; they professed to be at war with all established institutions; if they confined their efforts to legal measures and did not use violence, it was only because the time had not yet come. The men who avowed admiration for the Paris Commune, who were openly preparing for a revolution more complete than any which Europe had hitherto seen, could not complain if the Government, while there was yet time, used every means for crushing them. The mistake was in supposing that this measure would be successful. Bismarck would, indeed, had he been able, have made it far more severe; his own idea was that anyone who had been legally convicted of holding Socialist opinions should be deprived of the franchise and excluded from the Parliament. What a misunderstanding does this shew of the whole object and nature of representative institutions! It had been decided that in Germany Parliament was not to govern; what then was its function except to display the opinions of the people? If, as was the case, so large a proportion of the German nation belonged to a party of discontent, then it was above all desirable that their wishes and desires should have open expression, and be discussed where they could be overthrown. The Government had enormous means of influencing opinion. In the old days the men of letters had been on principle in opposition; now Germany was flooded by papers, books, and pamphlets; all devoted to the most extravagant praise of the new institutions. The excuse which was made for these laws was not a sufficient one. It is seldom necessary to meet political assassination by repressive measures, for they must always create a danger which they intend to avert. There was not the slightest ground for supposing that either Hobel or Nobeling had any confederates; there was no plot; it was but the wild and wicked action of an individual. It was as absurd to put a large party under police control for this reason as it was to punish Liberals for the action of Sand. And it was ineffective, as the events of the next years shewed; for the Socialist law did not spare Germany from the infection of outrage which in these years overran Europe.

The Socialist laws were soon followed by other proposals of a more useful kind, and now we come to one of the most remarkable episodes in Bismarck's career. He was over sixty years of age; his health was uncertain; he had long complained of the extreme toil and the constant annoyance which his public duties brought upon him. It might appear that he had finished his work, and, if he could not retire altogether, would give over the management of all internal affairs to others. That he would now take upon himself a whole new department of public duties, that he would after his prolonged absence appear again as leader and innovator in Parliamentary strife—this no one anticipated.

Up to the year 1876 he had taken little active part in finance; his energies had been entirely absorbed by foreign affairs and he had been content to adopt and support the measures recommended by his technical advisers. When he had interfered at all it had only been on those occasions when, as with regard to commercial treaties, the policy of his colleagues had impeded his own political objects. In 1864 he had been much annoyed because difference on commercial matters had interfered with the good understanding with Austria, which at that time he was trying to maintain. Since the foundation of the Empire almost the complete control over the commercial policy of the Empire had been entrusted to Delbrück, who held the very important post of President of the Imperial Chancery, and was treated by Bismarck with a deference and consideration which no other of his fellow-workers received, except Moltke and Roon. Delbrück was a confirmed Free-Trader, and the result was that, partly by commercial treaties, and partly by the abolition of customs dues, the tariff had been reduced and simplified. The years following the war had, however, not been altogether prosperous; a great outbreak of speculation was followed in 1873 by a serious commercial crisis. And since that year there had been a permanent decrease in the Imperial receipts. This was, for political reasons, a serious inconvenience. By the arrangement made in 1866 the proceeds of the customs and of the indirect taxation (with some exceptions) were paid into the Exchequer of the Federation, and afterwards of the Empire. If the receipts from these sources were not sufficient to meet the Imperial requirements, the deficit had to be made up by contributions paid (in proportion to their population) by the separate States. During later years these contributions had annually increased, and it is needless to point out that this was sufficient to make the relations of the State Governments to the central authorities disagreeable, and to cause some discontent with the new Constitution. This meant also an increase of the amount which had to be raised by direct taxation. Now Bismarck had always much disliked direct taxes; he had again and again pointed out that they were paid with great reluctance, and often fell with peculiar hardship on that very large class which could only just, by constant and assiduous labour, make an income sufficient for their needs. Worst of all was it when they were unable to pay even the few shillings required; they then had to undergo the hardship and disgrace of distraint, and see their furniture seized and sold by the tax-collectors. He had therefore always wished that the income derived from customs and indirect taxation should be increased so as by degrees to do away with the necessity for direct taxation, and if this could be done, then, instead of the States paying an annual contribution to the Empire, they would receive from the central Government pecuniary assistance.

The dislike of direct taxation is an essential part of Bismarck's reform; he especially disapproved of the Prussian system, the barbarous system, as he called it, according to which every man had to pay a small portion, it might be even a few groschen, in direct taxes.

"I ascribe," he said, "the large part of our emigration to the fact that the emigrant wishes to escape the direct pressure of the taxes and execution, and to go to a land where the klassensteuer does not exist, and where he will also have the pleasure of knowing that the produce of his labours will be protected against foreign interference."

His opinion cannot be called exaggerated if it is true that, as he stated, there were every year over a million executions involving the seizure and sale of household goods on account of arrears of taxation. It was not only the State taxes to which he objected; the local rates for municipal expenses, and especially for education, fell very heavily on the inhabitants of large cities such as Berlin. He intended to devote part of the money which was raised by indirect taxation to relieving the rates.

His first proposals for raising the money were of a very sweeping nature. He wished to introduce a State monopoly for the sale of tobacco, brandy, and beer. He entered into calculations by which he proved that were his policy adopted all direct taxation might be repealed, and he would have a large surplus for an object which he had very much at heart—the provision of old-age pensions. It was a method of legislation copied from that which prevails in France and Italy. He pointed out with perfect justice that the revenue raised in Germany from the consumption of tobacco was much smaller than it ought to be. The total sum gained by the State was not a tenth of that which was produced in England by the taxing of tobacco, but no one could maintain that smoking was more common in England than in Germany. In fact tobacco was less heavily taxed in Germany than in any other country in Europe.

In introducing a monopoly Bismarck intended and hoped not only to relieve the pressure of direct taxation,—though this would have been a change sufficient in its magnitude and importance for most men,—but proposed to use the very large sum which the Government would have at its disposal for the direct relief of the working classes. The Socialist law was not to go alone; he intended absolutely to stamp out this obnoxious agitation, but it was not from any indifference as to the condition of the working classes. From his earliest days he had been opposed to the Liberal doctrine of laissez-faire; it will be remembered how much he had disliked the bourgeois domination of the July Monarchy; as a young man he had tried to prevent the abolition of guilds. He considered that much of the distress and discontent arose from the unrestricted influence of capital. He was only acting in accordance with the oldest and best traditions of the Prussian Monarchy when he called in the power of the State to protect the poor. His plan was a very bold one; he wished to institute a fund from which there should be paid to every working man who was incapacitated by sickness, accident, or old age, a pension from the State. In his original plan he intended the working men should not be required to make any contribution themselves towards this fund. It was not to be made to appear to them as a new burden imposed on them by the State. The tobacco monopoly, he said, he looked on as "the patrimony of the disinherited."

He did not fear the charge of Socialism which might be brought against him; he defended himself by the provisions of the Prussian law. The Code of Frederick the Great contained the words:

"It is the duty of the State to provide for the sustenance and support of those of its citizens who cannot procure sustenance themselves"; and again, "work adapted to their strength and capacity shall be supplied to those who lack means and opportunity of earning a livelihood for themselves and those dependent on them."

In the most public way the new policy was introduced by an Imperial message, on November 17, 1881, in which the Emperor expressed his conviction that the social difficulties could not be healed simply by the repression of the exaggerations of Social Democracy, but at the same time the welfare of the workmen must be advanced. This new policy had the warm approval of both the Emperor and the Crown Prince; no one greeted more heartily the change than Windthorst.

"Allow me," he once said to Bismarck, "to speak openly: you have done me much evil in my life, but, as a German patriot, I must confess to you my gratitude that after all his political deeds you have persuaded our Imperial Master to turn to this path of Social Reform."

There were, he said, difficulties to be met; he approved of the end, but not of all the details,

"and," he continued, "something of the difficulty, if I may say so, you cause yourself. You are often too stormy for us; you are always coming with something new and we cannot always follow you in it, but you must not take that amiss. We are both old men and the Emperor is much older than we are, but we should like ourselves in our lifetime to see some of these reforms established. That I wish for all of us and for our German country, and we will do our best to help in it."

Opinions may differ as to the wisdom of Bismarck's social and financial policy; nobody can deny their admiration for the energy and patriotism which he displayed. It was no small thing for him, at his age, to come out of his comparative retirement to bring forward proposals which would be sure to excite the bitterest opposition of the men with whom he had been working, to embark again on a Parliamentary conflict as keen as any of those which had so taxed his energies in his younger years. Not content with inaugurating and suggesting these plans, he himself undertook the immediate execution of them. In addition to his other offices, in 1880 he undertook that of Minister of Trade in Prussia, for he found no one whom he could entirely trust to carry out his proposals. During the next years he again took a prominent part in the Parliamentary debates; day after day he attended to answer objections and to defend his measures in some of his ablest and longest speeches. By his proposals for a duty on corn he regained the support of most of the Conservatives, but in the Reichstag which was elected in 1884 he found himself opposed by a majority consisting of the Centre, Socialists, and Progressives. Many of the laws were rejected or amended, and it was not until 1890 that, in a modified form, the whole of the social legislation had been carried through.

For the monopoly he gained no support; scarcely a voice was raised in its favour, nor can we be surprised at this. It was a proposal very characteristic of his internal policy; he had a definite aim in view and at once took the shortest, boldest, and most direct road towards it, putting aside the thought of all further consequences. In this others could not follow him; quite apart from the difficulties of organisation and the unknown effect of the law on all those who gained their livelihood by the growth, preparation, and sale of tobacco, there was a deep feeling that it was not safe to entrust the Government with so enormous a power. Men did not wish to see so many thousands enrolled in the army of officials, already too great; they did not desire a new check on the freedom of life and occupation, nor that the Government should have the uncontrolled use of so great a sum of money. And then the use he proposed to make of the proceeds: if the calculations were correct, if the results were what he foretold, if from this monopoly they would be able to pay not only the chief expenses of the Government but also assign an old-age pension to every German workman who reached the age of seventy—what would this be except to make the great majority of the nation prospective pensioners of the State? With compulsory attendance at the State schools; with the State universities as the only entrance to public life and professions; when everyone for three years had to serve in the army; when so large a proportion of the population earned their livelihood in the railways, the post-office, the customs, the administration—the State had already a power and influence which many besides the Liberals regarded with alarm. What would it be when every working man looked forward to receiving, after his working days were over, a free gift from the Government? Could not this power be used for political measures also; could not it become a means for checking the freedom of opinions and even for interfering in the liberty of voting?

He had to raise the money he wanted in another way, and, in 1879, he began the great financial change that he had been meditating for three years; he threw all his vigour into overthrowing Free Trade and introducing a general system of Protection.

In this he was only doing what a large number of his countrymen desired. The results of Free Trade had not been satisfactory. In 1876 there was a great crisis in the iron trade; owing to overproduction there was a great fall of prices in England, and Germany was being flooded with English goods sold below cost price. Many factories had to be closed, owners were ruined, and men thrown out of work; it happened that, by a law passed in 1873, the last duty on imported iron would cease on the 31st of December, 1876. Many of the manufacturers and a large party in the Reichstag petitioned that the action of the law might at any rate be suspended. Free-Traders, however, still had a majority, for the greater portion of the National Liberals belonged to that school, and the law was carried out. It was, however, apparent that not only the iron but other industries were threatened. The building of railways in Russia would bring about an increased importation of Russian corn and threatened the prosperity, not only of the large proprietors, but also of the peasants. It had always been the wise policy of the Prussian Government to maintain and protect by legislation the peasants, who were considered the most important class in the State. Then the trade in Swedish wood threatened to interfere with the profits from the German forests, an industry so useful to the health of the country and the prosperity of the Government. But if Free Trade would injure the market for the natural products of the soil, it did not bring any compensating advantages by helping industry. Germany was flooded with English manufactures, so that even the home market was endangered, and every year it became more apparent that foreign markets were being closed. The sanguine expectations of the Free-Traders had not been realised; America, France, Russia, had high tariffs; German manufactured goods were excluded from these countries. What could they look forward to in the future but a ruined peasantry and the crippling of the iron and weaving industries? "I had the impression," said Bismarck, "that under Free Trade we were gradually bleeding to death."

He was probably much influenced in his new policy by Lothar Bucher, one of his private secretaries, who was constantly with him at Varzin. Bucher, who had been an extreme Radical, had, in 1849, been compelled to fly from the country and had lived many years in England. In 1865 he had entered Bismarck's service. He had acquired a peculiar enmity to the Cobden Club, and looked on that institution as the subtle instrument of a deep-laid plot to persuade other nations to adopt a policy which was entirely for the benefit of England. He drew attention to Cobden's words—"All we desire is the prosperity and greatness of England." We may in fact look on the Cobden Club and the principles it advocated from two points of view. Either they are, as Bucher maintained, simply English and their only result will be the prosperity of England, or they are merely one expression of a general form of thought which we know as Liberalism; it was an attempt to create cosmopolitan institutions and to induce German politicians to take their economic doctrines from England, just as a few years before they had taken their political theories. In either case these doctrines would be very distasteful to Bismarck, who disliked internationalism in finance as much as he did in constitutional law or Socialist propaganda.

Bismarck in adopting Protection was influenced, not by economic theory, but by the observation of facts. "All nations," he said, "which have Protective duties enjoy a certain prosperity; what great advantages has America reached since it threatened to reduce duties twice, five times, ten times as high as ours!" England alone clung to Free Trade, and why? Because she had grown so strong under the old system of Protection that she could now as a Hercules step down into the arena and challenge everyone to come into the lists. In the arena of commerce England was the strongest. This was why she advocated Free Trade, for Free Trade was really the right of the most powerful. English interests were furthered under the veil of the magic word Freedom, and by it German enthusiasts for liberty were enticed to bring about the ruin and exploitation of their own country.

If we look at the matter purely from the economic point of view, it is indeed difficult to see what benefits Germany would gain from a policy of Free Trade. It was a poor country; if it was to maintain itself in the modern rivalry of nations, it must become rich. It could only become rich through manufactures, and manufactures had no opportunity of growing unless they had some moderate protection from foreign competition.

The effect of Bismarck's attention to finance was not limited to these great reforms; he directed the whole power of the Government to the support of all forms of commercial enterprise and to the removal of all hindrances to the prosperity of the nation. To this task he devoted himself with the same courage and determination which he had formerly shewn in his diplomatic work.

One essential element in the commercial reform was the improvement of the railways. Bismarck's attention had long been directed to the inconveniences which arose from the number of private companies, whose duty it was to regard the dividends of the shareholders rather than the interests of the public. The existence of a monopoly of this kind in private hands seemed to him indefensible. His attention was especially directed to the injury done to trade by the differential rate imposed on goods traffic; on many lines it was the custom to charge lower rates on imported than on exported goods, and this naturally had a very bad effect on German manufactures. He would have liked to remedy all these deficiencies by making all railways the property of the Empire (we see again his masterful mind, which dislikes all compromise); in this, however, he was prevented by the opposition of the other States, who would not surrender the control of their own lines. In Prussia he was able to carry out this policy of purchase of all private lines by the State; by the time he laid down the Ministry of Commerce hardly any private companies remained. The acquisition of all the lines enabled the Government greatly to improve the communication, to lower fares, and to introduce through communications; all this of course greatly added to the commercial enterprise and therefore the wealth of the country.

He was now also able to give degrees his encouragement and support to those Germans who for many years in countries beyond the sea had been attempting to lay the foundations for German commerce and even to acquire German colonies. Bismarck's attitude in this matter deserves careful attention. As early as 1874 he had been approached by German travellers to ask for the support of the Government in a plan for acquiring German colonies in South Africa. They pointed out that here was a country fitted by its climate for European occupation; the present inhabitants of a large portion of it, the Boers, were anxious to establish their independence of England and would welcome German support. It was only necessary to acquire a port, either at Santa Lucia or at Delagoa Bay, to receive a small subsidy from the Government, and then private enterprise would divert the stream of German emigration from North America to South Africa. Bismarck, though he gave a courteous hearing to this proposal, could not promise them assistance, for, as he said, the political situation was not favourable. He must foresee that an attempt to carry out this or similar plans would inevitably bring about very serious difficulties with England, and he had always been accustomed to attach much importance to his good understanding with the English Government. During the following years, however, the situation was much altered. First of all, great enterprise had been shewn by the German merchants and adventurers in different parts of the world, especially in Africa and in the Pacific. They, in those difficulties which will always occur when white traders settle in half-civilised lands, applied for support to the German Government. Bismarck, as he himself said, did not dare to refuse them this support.

"I approached the matter with some reluctance; I asked myself, how could I justify it, if I said to these enterprising men, over whose courage, enthusiasm, and vigour I have been heartily pleased: 'That is all very well, but the German Empire is not strong enough, it would attract the ill-will of other States.' I had not the courage as Chancellor to declare to them this bankruptcy of the German nation for transmarine enterprises."

It must, however, happen that wherever these German settlers went, they would be in the neighbourhood of some English colony, and however friendly were the relations of the Governments of the two Powers, disputes must occur in the outlying p arts of the earth. In the first years of the Empire Bismarck had hoped that German traders would find sufficient protection from the English authorities, and anticipated their taking advantage of the full freedom of trade allowed in the British colonies; they would get all the advantages which would arise from establishing their own colonies, while the Government would be spared any additional responsibility. He professed, however, to have learnt by experience from the difficulties which came after the annexation of the Fiji Islands by Great Britain that this hope would not be fulfilled; he acknowledged the great friendliness of the Foreign Office, but complained that the Colonial Office regarded exclusively British interests. As a complaint coming from his mouth this arouses some amusement; the Colonial Office expressed itself satisfied to have received from so high an authority a testimonial to its efficiency which it had rarely gained from Englishmen.

The real change in the policy of the Empire must, however, be attributed not to any imaginary shortcomings of the English authorities; it was an inevitable result of the abandonment of the policy of Free Trade, and of the active support which the Government was now giving to all forms of commercial enterprise. It was shewn, first of all, in the grant of subsidies to mail steamers, which enabled German trade and German travellers henceforward to be carried by German ships; before they had depended entirely on English and French lines. It was not till 1884 that the Government saw its way to undertake protection of German colonists. They were enabled to do so by the great change which had taken place in the political situation. Up to this time Germany was powerless to help or to injure England, but, on the other hand, required English support. All this was changed by the occupation of Egypt. Here England required a support on the Continent against the indignation of France and the jealousy of Russia. This could only be found in Germany, and therefore a close approximation between the two countries was natural. Bismarck let it be known that England would find no support, but rather opposition, if she, on her side, attempted, as she so easily could have done, to impede German colonial enterprise.

In his colonial policy Bismarck refused to take the initiative; he refused, also, to undertake the direct responsibility for the government of their new possessions. He imitated the older English plan, and left the government in the hands of private companies, who received a charter of incorporation; he avowedly was imitating the East India Company and the Hudson's Bay Company. The responsibilities of the German Government were limited to a protection of the companies against the attack or interference by any other Power, and a general control over their actions. In this way it was possible to avoid calling on the Reichstag for any large sum, or undertaking the responsibility of an extensive colonial establishment, for which at the time they had neither men nor experience. Another reason against the direct annexation of foreign countries lay in the Constitution of the Empire; it would have been easier to annex fresh land to Prussia; this could have been done by the authority of the King; there was, however, no provision by which the Bundesrath could undertake this responsibility, and it probably could not be done even with the assent of the Reichstag unless some change were made in the Constitution. It was, however, essential that the new acquisitions should be German and not Prussian.

All these changes were not introduced without much opposition; the Progressives especially distinguished themselves by their prolonged refusal to assent even to the subsidies for German lines of steamers. In the Parliament of 1884 they were enabled often to throw out the Government proposals. It was at this time that the conflict between Bismarck and Richter reached its height. He complained, and justly complained, that the policy of the Progressives was then, as always, negative. It is indeed strange to notice how we find reproduced in Germany that same feeling which a few years before had in England nearly led to the loss of the colonies and the destruction of the Empire.

It is too soon even now to consider fully the result of this new policy; the introduction of Protection has indeed, if we are to judge by appearances, brought about a great increase in the prosperity of the country; whether the scheme for old-age pensions will appease the discontent of the working man seems very doubtful. One thing, however, we must notice: the influence of the new policy is far greater than the immediate results of the actual laws passed. It has taught the Germans to look to the Government not only as a means of protecting them against the attacks of other States, but to see in it a thoughtful, and I think we may say kindly, guardian of their interests. They know that every attempt of each individual to gain wealth or power for his country will be supported and protected by the Government; they know that there is constant watchfulness as to the dangers to life and health which arise from the conditions of modern civilisation. In these laws, in fact, Bismarck, who deeply offended and irretrievably alienated the survivors of his own generation, won over and secured for himself and also for the Government the complete loyalty of the rising generation. It might be supposed that this powerful action on the part of the State would interfere with private enterprise; the result shews that this is not the case. A watchful and provident Government really acts as an incentive to each individual. Let us also recognise that Bismarck was acting exactly as in the old days every English Government acted, when the foreign policy was dictated by the interests of British trade and the home policy aimed at preserving, protecting, and assisting the different classes in the community.

Bismarck has often been called a reactionary, and yet we find that by the social legislation he was the first statesman deliberately to apply himself to the problem which had been created by the alteration in the structure of society. Even if the solutions which he proposed do not prove in every case to have been the best, he undoubtedly foresaw what would be the chief occupation for the statesmen of the future. In these reforms he had, however, little help from the Reichstag; the Liberals were bitterly opposed, the Socialists sceptical and suspicious, the Catholics cool and unstable allies; during these years the chronic quarrel between himself and Parliament broke out with renewed vigour. How bitterly did he deplore party spirit, the bane of German life, which seemed each year to gain ground!

"It has," he said, "transferred itself to our modern public life and the Parliaments; the Governments, indeed, stand together, but in the German Reichstag I do not find that guardian of liberty for which I had hoped. Party spirit has overrun us. This it is which I accuse before God and history, if the great work of our people achieved between 1866 and 1870 fall into decay, and in this House we destroy by the pen what has been created by the sword."

In future years it will perhaps be regarded as one of his chief claims that he refused to become a party leader. He saved Germany from a serious danger to which almost every other country in Europe which has attempted to adopt English institutions has fallen a victim—the sacrifice of national welfare to the integrity and power of a Parliamentary fraction. His desire was a strong and determined Government, zealously working for the benefit of all classes, quick to see and foresee present and future evil; he regarded not the personal wishes of individuals, but looked only in each matter he undertook to its effect on the nation as a whole. "I will accept help," he said, "wherever I may get it. I care not to what party any man belongs. I have no intention of following a party policy; I used to do so when I was a young and angry member of a party, but it is impossible for a Prussian or German Minister." Though the Constitution had been granted, he did not wish to surrender the oldest and best traditions of the Prussian Monarchy; and even if the power of the King and Emperor was limited and checked by two Parliaments it was still his duty, standing above all parties, to watch over the country as a hundred years before his ancestors had done.

His power, however, was checked by the Parliaments. Bismarck often sighed for a free hand; he longed to be able to carry out his reforms complete and rounded as they lay clear before him in his own brain; how often did he groan under all the delay, the compromise, the surrender, which was imposed upon him when, conscious as he was that he was only striving for the welfare of his country, he had to win over not only the King, not only his colleagues in the Prussian Ministry, his subordinates, who had much power to check and impede his actions, but, above all, the Parliaments. It was inevitable that his relation to them should often be one of conflict; it was their duty to submit to a searching criticism the proposals of the Government and to amend or reject them, and let us confess that it was better they were there. The modifications they introduced in the bills he proposed were often improvements; those they rejected were not always wise. The drafting of Government bills was often badly done; the first proposals for the Socialistic law, the original drafts of many of his economic reforms, were all the better when they had been once rejected and were again brought forward in a modified form. More than this, we must confess that Bismarck did not possess that temperament which would make it wise to entrust him with absolute dictatorial power in internal matters. He attempted to apply to legislation habits he had learnt in diplomacy. And it is curious to notice Bismarck's extreme caution in diplomacy, where he was a recognised master, and his rashness in legislation, where the ground was often new to him. In foreign affairs a false move may easily be withdrawn, a change of alliance quickly made; it often happens that speed is more important than wisdom. In internal affairs it is different; there, delay is in itself of value; moreover, false legislation cannot be imposed with impunity, laws cannot be imposed and repealed.

Bismarck often complained of the conduct of the Reichstag. There were in it two parties, the Socialists and the Centre, closely organised, admirably disciplined, obedient to leaders who were in opposition by principle; they looked on the Parliamentary campaign as a struggle for power, and they maintained the struggle with a persistency and success which had not been surpassed by any Parliamentary Opposition in any other country. Apart from them the attitude of all the parties was normally that of moderate criticism directed to the matter of the Government proposals. There were, of course, often angry scenes; Bismarck himself did not spare his enemies, but we find no events which shew violence beyond what is, if not legitimate, at least inevitable in all Parliamentary assemblies. The main objects of the Government were always attained; the military Budgets were always passed, though once not until after a dissolution. In the contest with the Clerical party and the Socialists the Government had the full support of a large majority. Even in the hostile Reichstag of 1884, in which the Socialists, Clericals, and Progressives together commanded a majority, a series of important laws were passed. Once, indeed, the majority in opposition to the Government went beyond the limits of reason and honour when they refused a vote of £1000 for an additional director in the Foreign Office. It was the expression of a jealousy which had no justification in facts; at the time the German Foreign Office was the best managed department in Europe; the labour imposed on the secretaries was excessive, and the nation could not help contrasting this vote with the fact that shortly before a large number of the members had voted that payments should be made to themselves. The nation could not help asking whether it would not gain more benefit from another £1000 a year expended on the Foreign Office than from £50,000 a year for payment of members. Even this unfortunate action was remedied a few months later, when the vote was passed in the same Parliament by a majority of twenty.

Notwithstanding all their internal differences and the extreme party spirit which often prevailed, the Reichstag always shewed determination in defending its own privileges. More than once Bismarck attacked them in the most tender points. At one time it was on the privileges of members and their freedom from arrest; both during the struggle with the Clericals and with the Socialists the claim was made to arrest members during the session for political utterances. When Berlin was subject to a state of siege, the President of the Police claimed the right of expelling from the capital obnoxious Socialist members. On these occasions the Government found itself confronted by the unanimous opposition of the whole House. In 1884, Bismarck proposed that the meetings of the Reichstag should be biennial and the Budget voted for two years; the proposal was supported on the reasonable grounds that thereby inconvenience and press of work would be averted, which arose from the meeting of the Prussian and German Parliaments every winter. Few votes, however, could be obtained for a suggestion which seemed to cut away the most important privileges of Parliament.

Another of the great causes of friction between Bismarck and the Parliament arose from the question as to freedom of debate. Both before 1866, and since that year, he made several attempts to introduce laws that members should be to some extent held responsible, and under certain circumstances be brought before a court of law, in consequence of what they had said from their places in Parliament. This was represented as an interference with freedom of speech, and was bitterly resented. Bismarck, however, always professed, and I think truly, that he did not wish to control the members in their opposition to the Government, but to place some check on their personal attacks on individuals. A letter to one of his colleagues, written in 1883, is interesting:

"I have," he says, "long learned the difficulties which educated people, who have been well brought up, have to overcome in order to meet the coarseness of our Parliamentary Klopfechter [pugilists] with the necessary amount of indifference, and to refuse them in one's own consciousness the undeserved honour of moral equality. The repeated and bitter struggles in which you have had to fight alone will have strengthened you in your feeling of contempt for opponents who are neither honourable enough nor deserve sufficient respect to be able to injure you."

There was indeed a serious evil arising from the want of the feeling of responsibility in a Parliamentary assembly which had no great and honourable traditions. He attempted to meet it by strengthening the authority of the House over its own members; the Chairman did not possess any power of punishing breaches of decorum. Bismarck often contrasted this with the very great powers over their own members possessed by the British Houses of Parliament. He drew attention to the procedure by which, for instance, Mr. Plimsoll could be compelled to apologise for hasty words spoken in a moment of passion. It is strange that neither the Prussian nor the German Parliament consented to adopt rules which are really the necessary complement for the privileges of Parliament.

The Germans were much disappointed by the constant quarrels and disputes which were so frequent in public life; they had hoped that with the unity of their country a new period would begin; they found that, as before, the management of public affairs was disfigured by constant personal enmities and the struggle of parties. We must not, however, look on this as a bad sign; it is rather more profitable to observe that the new institutions were not affected or weakened by this friction. It was a good sign for the future that the new State held together as firmly as any old-established monarchy, and that the most important questions of policy could be discussed and decided without even raising any point which might be a danger to the permanence of the Empire.

Bismarck himself did much to put his relations with the Parliament on a new and better footing. Acting according to his general principle, he felt that the first thing to be done was to induce mutual confidence by unrestrained personal intercourse. The fact that he himself was not a member of the Parliament deprived him of those opportunities which an English Minister enjoys. He therefore instituted, in 1868, a Parliamentary reception. During the session, generally one day each week, his house was opened to all members of the House. The invitations were largely accepted, especially by the members of the National Liberal and Conservative parties. Those who were opponents on principle, the Centre, the Progressives, and the Socialists, generally stayed away. These receptions became the most marked feature in the political life of the capital, and they enabled many members to come under the personal charm of the Chancellor. What an event was it in the life of the young and unknown Deputy from some obscure provincial town, when he found himself sitting, perhaps, at the same table as the Chancellor, drinking the beer which Bismarck had brought into honour at Berlin, and for which his house was celebrated, and listening while, with complete freedom from all arrogance or pomposity, his host talked as only he could!

The weakest side of his administration lay in the readiness with which he had recourse to the criminal law to defend himself against political adversaries. He was, indeed, constantly subjected to attacks in the Press, which were often unjust and sometimes unmeasured, but no man who takes part in public life is exempt from calumny. He was himself never slow to attack his opponents, both personally in the Parliament, and still more by the hired writers of the Press. None the less, to defend himself from attacks, he too often brought his opponents into the police court, and Bismarckbeleidigung became a common offence. Even the editor of Kladderadatsch was once imprisoned. He must be held personally responsible, for no action could be instituted without his own signature to the charge. We see the same want of generosity in the use which he made of attempts, or reputed attempts, at assassination. In 1875, while he was at Kissingen, a young man shot at him; he stated that he had been led to do so owing to the attacks made on the Chancellor by the Catholic party. No attempt, however, was made to prove that he had any accomplices; it was not even suggested that he was carrying out the wishes of the party. It was one of those cases which will always occur in political struggles, when a young and inexperienced man will be excited by political speeches to actions which no one would foresee, and which would not be the natural result of the words to which he had listened. Nevertheless, Bismarck was not ashamed publicly in the Reichstag to taunt his opponents with the action, and to declare that whether they would or not their party was Kuhlmann's party; "he clings to your coat-tails," he said. A similar event had happened a few years before, when a young man had been arrested on the charge that he intended to assassinate the Chancellor. No evidence in support of the charge was forthcoming, but the excuse was taken by the police for searching the house of one of the

Catholic leaders with whom the accused had lived. No incriminating documents of any kind were found, but among the private papers was the correspondence between the leaders in the party of the Centre dealing with questions of party organisation and political tactics. The Government used these private papers for political purposes, and published one of them. The constant use of the police in political warfare belonged, of course, to the system he had inherited, but none the less it was to have been hoped that he would have been strong enough to put it aside. The Government was now firmly established; it could afford to be generous. Had he definitely cut himself off from these bad traditions he would have conferred on his country a blessing scarcely less than all the others.

The opposition of the parties in the Reichstag to his policy and person did not represent the feelings of the country. As the years passed by and the new generation grew up, the admiration for his past achievements and for his character only increased. His seventieth birthday, which he celebrated in 1885, was made the occasion for a great demonstration of regard, in which the whole nation joined. A national subscription was opened and a present of two million marks was made to him. More than half of this was devoted to repurchasing that part of the estate at Schoenhausen which had been sold when he was a young man. The rest he devoted to forming an institution for the help of teachers in higher schools. A few years before, the Emperor had presented to him the Sachsen Wald, a large portion of the royal domains in the Duchy of Lauenburg. He now purchased the neighbouring estate of Friedrichsruh, so that he had a third country residence to which he could retire. It had a double advantage: its proximity to the great forest in which he loved to wander, and also to a railway, making it little more than an hour distant from Berlin. He was able, therefore, at Friedrichsruh, to continue his management of affairs more easily than he could at Varzin.

CHAPTER XVII.

RETIREMENT AND DEATH.

1887-1898.

Well was it for Germany that Bismarck had not allowed her to fall into the weak and vacillating hands of a Parliamentary government. Peace has its dangers as well as war, and the rivalry of nations lays upon them a burden beneath which all but the strongest must succumb. The future was dark; threatening clouds were gathering in the East and West; the hostility of Russia increased, and in France the Republic was wavering; a military adventurer had appeared, who threatened to use the desire for revenge as a means for his personal advancement. Germany could no longer disregard French threats; year by year the French army had been increased, and in 1886 General Boulanger introduced a new law by which in time of peace over 500,000 men would be under arms. Russia had nearly 550,000 soldiers on her peace establishment, and, against this, Germany only 430,000. They were no longer safe; the duty of the Government was clear; in December, 1886, they brought forward a law to raise the army to 470,000 men and keep it at that figure for seven years. "We have no desire for war," said Bismarck, in defending the proposal; "we belong (to use an expression of Prince Metternich's) to the States whose appetite is satisfied; under no circumstances shall we attack France; the stronger we are, the more improbable is war; but if France has any reason to believe that she is more powerful than we, then war is certain." It was, he said, no good for the House to assure the Government of their patriotism and their readiness for sacrifice when the hour of danger arrived; they must be prepared beforehand. "Words are not soldiers and speeches not battalions."

The House (there was a majority of Catholics, Socialists, and Progressives) threw out the bill, the Government dissolved, and the country showed its confidence in Bismarck and Moltke; Conservatives and National Liberals made a coalition, the Pope himself ordered the Catholics not to oppose the Government (his support had been purchased by the partial repeal of a law expelling religious orders from Prussia), and the Emperor could celebrate his ninetieth birthday, which fell in March, 1887, hopeful that the beneficent work of peaceful reform would continue. And yet never was Bismarck's resource so needed as during the last year in which he was to serve his old master.

First, a French spy was arrested on German soil; the French demanded his release, maintaining that German officers had violated the frontier. Unless one side gave way, war was inevitable; the French Government, insecure as it was, could not venture to do so; Bismarck was strong enough to be lenient: the spy was released and peace was preserved. Then, on the other side, the passionate enmity of Russia burst out in language of unaccustomed violence; the national Press demanded the dismissal of Bismarck or war;

the Czar passed through Germany on his way to Copenhagen, but ostentatiously avoided meeting the Emperor; the slight was so open that the worst predictions were justified. In November, on his return, he spent a few hours in Berlin. Bismarck asked for an audience, and then he found that despatches had been laid before the Czar which seemed to shew that he, while avowedly supporting Russia in Bulgarian affairs, had really been undermining her influence. The despatches were forged; we do not yet know who it was that hoped to profit by stirring up a war between the two great nations. We can well believe that Bismarck, in the excitement of the moment, spoke with an openness to which the Czar was not accustomed; he succeeded, however, in bringing about a tolerable understanding. The Czar assured him that he had no intention of going to war, he only desired peace; Bismarck did all that human ingenuity could to preserve it. By the Triple Alliance he had secured Germany against the attack of Russia. He now entered into a fresh and secret agreement with Russia by which Germany agreed to protect her against an attack from Austria; he thereby hoped to be able to prevent the Czar from looking to France for support against the Triple Alliance. It was a policy of singular daring to enter into a defensive alliance with Russia against Austria, at the same time that he had another defensive alliance with Austria against Russia. [13] To shew that he had no intention of deserting his older ally, he caused the text of the treaty with Austria to be published. This need no longer be interpreted as a threat to Russia. Then, that Germany, if all else failed, might be able to stand on her own resources, another increase of the army was asked for. By the reorganisation of the reserve, 500,000 men could be added to the army in time of war. This proposal was brought before the Reichstag, together with one for a loan of twenty-eight million marks to purchase the munitions of war which would be required, and in defence of this, Bismarck made the last of his great speeches.

It was not necessary to plead for the bill. He was confident of the patriotism of the House; his duty was to curb the nervous anxiety which recent events had produced. These proposals were not for war, but for peace; but they must indeed be prepared for war, for that was a danger that was never absent, and by a review of the last forty years he shewed that scarcely a single year had gone by in which there had not been the probability of a great European conflict, a war of coalitions in which all the great States of Europe would be ranged on one side or the other. This danger was still present, it would never cease; Germany, now, as before, must always be prepared; for the strength of Germany was the security of Europe.

"We must make greater exertions than other Powers on account of our geographical position. We lie in the middle of Europe; we can be attacked on all sides. God has put us in a situation in which our neighbours will not allow us to fall into indolence or apathy. The pike in the European fish-pond prevent us from becoming carp."

It was not their fault if the old alliance with Russia had broken down; the alliance with Austria still continued. But, above all, Germany must depend on her army, and then they could look boldly into the future. "It will calm our citizens if they think that if we are attacked on two sides we can put a million good soldiers on the frontier, and in a few weeks support them by another million." But let them not think that this terrible engine of war was a danger to the peace of Europe. In words which represent a profound truth he said: "It is just the strength at which we aim that makes us peaceful. That sounds paradoxical, but it is so. With the powerful engine into which we are forming the German army one undertakes no offensive war." In truth, when the army was the nation, what statesman was there who would venture on war unless he were attacked? "If I were to say to you, 'We are threatened by France and Russia; it is better for us to fight at once; an offensive war is more advantageous for us,' and ask for a credit of a hundred millions, I do not know whether you would grant it,—I hope not." And he concluded: "It is not fear which makes us lovers of peace, but the consciousness of our own strength. We can be won by love and good-will, but by them alone; we Germans fear God and nothing else in the world, and it is the fear of God which makes us seek peace and ensue it."

These are words which will not be forgotten so long as the German tongue is spoken. Well will it be if they are remembered in their entirety. They were the last message of the older generation to the new Germany which had arisen since the war; for already the shadow of death lay over the city; in the far South the Crown Prince was sinking to his grave, and but a few weeks were to pass before Bismarck stood at the bedside of the dying Emperor. He died on March 9, 1888, a few days before his ninety-first birthday, and with him passed the support on which Bismarck's power rested.

He was not a great man, but he was an honourable, loyal, and courteous gentleman; he had not always understood the course of Bismarck's policy or approved the views which his Minister adopted. The restraint he had imposed had often been inconvenient, and Bismarck had found much difficulty in overcoming the prejudices of his master; but it had none the less been a gain for Bismarck that he was compelled to explain and justify his action to a man whom he never ceased to love and respect. How beneficial had been the controlling influence of his presence the world was to learn by the events which followed his death.

That had happened to which for five and twenty years all Bismarck's enemies had looked forward. The foundation on which his power rested was taken away; men at once began to speculate on his fall. The noble presence of the Crown Prince, his cheerful and kindly manners, his known attachment to liberal ideas, his strong national feeling, the success with which he had borne himself on the uncongenial field of battle, all had made him the hope of the generation to which he belonged. Who was so well suited to solve the difficulties of internal policy with which Bismarck had struggled so long? Hopes never to be fulfilled! Absent from his father's deathbed, he returned to Berlin a crippled and dying man, and when a few weeks later his body was lowered into the grave, there were buried with him the hopes and aspirations of a whole generation.

His early death was indeed a great misfortune for his country. Not that he would have fulfilled all the hopes of the party that would have made him their leader. It is never wise to depend on the liberalism of a Crown Prince. When young and inexperienced he had been in opposition to his father's government—but his father before him had, while heir to the throne, also held a similar position to his own brother.

As Crown Prince, he had desired and had won popularity; he had been even too sensitive to public opinion. His, however, was a character that required only responsibility to strengthen it; with the burden of sovereignty he would, we may suppose, have shewn a fixity of purpose which many of his admirers would hardly have expected of him, nor would he have been deficient in those qualities of a ruler which are the traditions of his family. He was not a man to surrender any of the prerogatives or authority of the Crown. He had a stronger will than his father, and he would have made his will felt. His old enmity to Bismarck had almost ceased. It is not probable that with the new Emperor the Chancellor would long have held his position, but he would have been able to transfer the Crown to a man who had learnt wisdom by prolonged disappointment. How he would have governed is shewn by the only act of authority which he had time to carry out. He would have done what was more important than giving a little more power to the Parliament: he would at once have stopped that old and bad system by which the Prussian Government has always attempted to schoolmaster the people. During his short reign he dismissed Herr von Puttkammer, the Minister of the Interior, a relative of Bismarck's wife, for interfering with the freedom of election; we may be sure that he would have allowed full freedom of speech; and that he would not have consented to govern by aid of the police. Under him there would not have been constant trials for Majestätsbeleidigung or Bismarckbeleidigung. This he could have done without weakening the power of the Crown or the authority of the Government; those who know Germany will believe that it was the one reform which was still required.

The illness of the Emperor made it desirable to avoid points of conflict; both he and Bismarck knew that it was impossible, during the few weeks that his life would be spared, to execute so important a change as the resignation of the Chancellor would have been. On many points there was a difference of opinion, but Bismarck did not unduly express his view, nor did he threaten to resign if his advice were not adopted. When, for instance, the Emperor hesitated to give his assent to a law prolonging the period of Parliament, Bismarck did not attempt to control his decision. When Herr Puttkammer was dismissed, Bismarck did not remonstrate against an act which was almost of the nature of a personal reprimand to himself. It was, however, different when the foreign policy of the Empire was affected, for here Bismarck, as before, considered himself the trustee and guarantor for the security of Germany. An old project was now revived for bringing about a marriage between the Princess Victoria of Prussia and Prince Alexander of Battenberg. This had been suggested some years before, while the Prince was still ruler of Bulgaria; at Bismarck's advice, the Emperor William had refused his consent to the marriage, partly for the reason that according to the family law of the Hohenzollerns a marriage with the Battenberger family would be a mésalliance. He was, however, even more strongly influenced by the effect this would have on the political situation of Europe.

The foundation of Bismarck's policy was the maintenance of friendship with Russia; this old-established alliance depended, however, on the personal good-will of the Czar, and not on the wishes of the Russian nation or any identity of interests between the two Empires. A marriage between a Prussian princess and a man who was so bitterly hated by the Czar as was Prince Alexander must have seriously injured the friendly relations which had existed between the two families since the year 1814. Bismarck believed that the happiness of the Princess must be sacrificed to the interests of Germany, and the Emperor William, who, when a young man, had for similar reasons been required by his father to renounce the hand of the lady to whom he had been devotedly attached, agreed with him. Now, after the Emperor's death the project was revived; the Emperor

Frederick wavered between his feelings as a father and his duty as a king. Bismarck suspected that the strong interest which the Empress displayed in the project was due, not only to maternal affection, but also to the desire, which in her would be natural enough, to bring over the German Empire to the side of England in the Eastern Question, so that England might have a stronger support in her perennial conflict with Russia. The matter, therefore, appeared to him as a conflict between the true interests of Germany and those old Court influences which he so often had had to oppose, by which the family relationships of the reigning sovereign were made to divert his attention from the single interests of his own country. He made it a question of confidence; he threatened to resign, as he so often did under similar circumstances; he let it be known through the Press what was the cause, and, in his opinion, the true interpretation, of the conflict which influenced the Court. In order to support his view, he called in the help of the Grand Duke of Baden, who, as the Emperor's brother-in-law, and one of the most experienced of the reigning Princes, was the proper person to interfere in a matter which concerned both the private and the public life of the sovereign. The struggle, which threatened to become serious, was, however, allayed by the visit of the Queen of England to Germany. She, acting in German affairs with that strict regard to constitutional principle and that dislike of Court intrigue that she had always observed in dealings with her own Ministers, gave her support to Bismarck. The marriage did not take place.

Frederick's reign lasted but ninety days, and his son ruled in his place. The new Emperor belonged to the generation which had grown up since the war; he could not remember the old days of conflict; like all of his generation, from his earliest years he had been accustomed to look on Bismarck with gratitude and admiration. In him, warm personal friendship was added to the general feeling of public regard; he had himself learnt from Bismarck's own lips the principles of policy and the lessons of history. It might well seem that he would continue to lean for support on the old statesman. So he himself believed, but careful observers who saw his power of will and his restless activity foretold that he would not allow to Bismarck that complete freedom of action and almost absolute power which he had obtained during the later years of the old Emperor. They foretold also that Bismarck would not be content with a position of less power, and there were many ready to watch for and foment the differences which must arise.

In the first months of the new reign, some of Bismarck's old enemies attempted to undermine his influence by spreading reports of his differences with the Emperor Frederick, and Professor Geffken even went so far as to publish from the manuscript some of the most confidential portions of the Emperor's diary in order to shew that but for him Bismarck would not have created the new Empire. The attempt failed, for, rightly read, the passages which were to injure Bismarck's reputation only served to shew how much greater than men thought had been the difficulties with which he had had to contend and the wisdom with which he had dealt with them.

From the very beginning there were differences of opinion; the old and the new did not think or feel alike. Bismarck looked with disapproval on the constant journeys of the Emperor; he feared that he was compromising his dignity. Moltke and others of the older generation retired from the posts they filled; Bismarck, with growing misgivings, stayed on. His promises to his old master, his love of power, his distrust of the capacity of others, all made it hard for him to withdraw when he still might have done so with dignity. We cannot doubt that his presence was irksome to his master; his influence and authority were too great; before them, even the majesty of the Throne was dimmed; the Minister was a greater man than the Sovereign.

If we are to understand what happened we must remember how exceptional was the position which Bismarck now occupied. He had repeatedly defied the power of Parliament and shewn that he was superior to the Reichstag; there were none among his colleagues who could approach him in age or experience; the Prussian Ministers were as much his nominees as were the officials of the Empire. He himself was Chancellor, Minister-President, Foreign Minister, and Minister of Trade; his son was at the head of the Foreign Office and was used for the more important diplomatic missions; his cousin was Minister, of the Interior; in the management of the most critical affairs, he depended upon the assistance of his own family and secretaries. He had twice been able against the will of his colleagues to reverse the whole policy of the State. The Government was in his hands and men had learnt to look to him rather than to the Emperor. Was it to be expected that a young man, ambitious, full of spirit and self-confidence, who had learnt from Bismarck himself a high regard for his monarchical duties, would acquiesce in this system? Nay, more; was it right that he should?

It was a fitting conclusion to his career that the man who had restored the monarchical character of the Prussian State should himself shew that before the will of the King he, as every other subject, must bow.

Bismarck had spent the winter of 1889 at Friedrichsruh. When he returned to Berlin at the end of January, he found that his influence and authority had been undermined; not only was the Emperor influenced by other advisers, but even the Ministry shewed an independence to which he was not accustomed. The chief causes of difference arose regarding the prolongation of the law against the Socialists. This expired in 1890, and it was proposed to bring in a bill making it permanent. Bismarck wished even more than this to intensify the stringency of its provisions. Apparently the Emperor did not believe that this was necessary. He hoped that it would be possible to remove the disaffection of the working men by remedial measures, and, in order to discuss these, he summoned a European Congress which would meet in Berlin.

Here, then, there was a fundamental difference of opinion between the King of Prussia and his Minister; the result was that Bismarck did not consider himself able to defend the Socialist law before the Reichstag, for he could not any longer give full expression to his own views; the Parliament was left without direction from the Government, and eventually a coalition between the extreme Conservatives, the Radicals, and the Socialists rejected the bill altogether. A bitterly contested general election followed in which the name and the new policy of the Emperor were freely used, and it resulted in a majority opposed to the parties who were accustomed to support Bismarck. These events made it obvious that on matters of internal policy a permanent agreement between the Emperor and the Chancellor was impossible. It seems that Bismarck therefore offered to resign his post as Minister President, maintaining only the general control of foreign affairs. But this proposition did not meet with the approval of the Emperor. There were, however, other grounds of difference connected even with foreign affairs; the Emperor was drawing closer to England and thereby separating from Russia.

By the middle of March, matters had come to a crisis. The actual cause for the final difference was an important matter of constitutional principle. Bismarck found that the Emperor had on several occasions discussed questions of administration with some of his colleagues without informing him; moreover, important projects of law had been devised without his knowledge. He therefore drew the attention of the Emperor to the principle of the German and Prussian Constitutions. By the German Constitution, as we have seen, the Chancellor was responsible for all acts of the Ministers and Secretaries of State, who held office as his deputies and subordinates. He therefore claimed that he could require to be consulted on every matter of any importance which concerned any of these departments. The same right as regards Prussian affairs had been explicitly secured to the Minister-President by a Cabinet order of 1852, which was passed in order to give to the President that complete control which was necessary if he was to be responsible for the whole policy of the Government. The Emperor answered by a command that he should draw up a new order reversing this decree. This Bismarck refused to do; the Emperor repeated his instructions.

It was a fundamental point on which no compromise was possible; the Emperor proposed to take away from the Chancellor that supreme position he had so long enjoyed; to recall into his own hands that immediate control over all departments which in old days the Kings of Prussia had exercised and, as Bismarck said, to be his own Prime Minister. In this degradation of his position Bismarck would not acquiesce; he had no alternative but to resign.

The final separation between these two men, each so self-willed and confident in his own strength, was not to be completed by ceremonious discussions on constitutional forms. It was during an audience at the castle, that the Emperor had explained his views, Bismarck his objections; the Emperor insisted that his will must be carried out, if not by Bismarck, then by another. "Then I am to understand, your Majesty," said Bismarck, speaking in English; "that I am in your way?" "Yes," was the answer. This was enough; he took his leave and returned home to draw up the formal document in which he tendered his resignation. This, which was to be the conclusion of his public life, had to be composed with care; he did not intend to be hurried; but the Emperor was impatient, and his impatience was increased when he was informed that Windthorst, the leader of the Centre, had called on Bismarck at his residence. He feared lest there was some intrigue, and that Bismarck proposed to secure his position by an alliance with the Parliamentary opposition. He sent an urgent verbal message requiring the resignation immediately, a command with which Bismarck was not likely to comply. Early next morning, the Emperor drove round himself to his house, and Bismarck was summoned from his bed to meet the angry sovereign. The Emperor asked what had taken place at the interview with Windthorst, and stated that Ministers were not to enter on political discussions with Parliamentary leaders without his permission. Bismarck denied that there had been any political discussion, and answered that he could not allow any supervision over the guests he chose to receive in his private house.

"Not if I order it as your sovereign?" asked the Emperor.

"No. The commands of my King cease in my wife's drawing-room," answered Bismarck. The Emperor had forgotten that Bismarck was a gentleman before he was a Minister, and that a Prussian nobleman could not be treated like a Russian boyar. [14]

No reconciliation or accommodation was now possible. The Emperor did all he could to make it appear that the resignation was voluntary and friendly. He conferred on the retiring Chancellor the highest honours: he raised him to the rank of Field Marshal and created him Duke of Lauenburg, and publicly stated his intention of presenting him with a copy of his own portrait. As a soldier, Bismarck obediently accepted the military honour; the new title he requested to be allowed not to use; he had never been asked whether he desired it.

No outward honours could recompense him for the affront he had received. What profited it him that the Princes and people of Germany joined in unanimous expression of affection and esteem, that he could scarcely set foot outside his house for the enthusiastic crowd who cheered and followed him through the streets of Berlin? For twenty-four years he had been Prussian Minister and now he was told he was in the way. His successor was already in office; he was himself driven in haste from the house which so long had been his home. A final visit to the Princes of the Royal House, a last audience with the Emperor, a hasty leave-taking from his friends and colleagues, and then the last farewell, when in the early morning he drove to Charlottenburg and alone went down into the mausoleum where his old master slept, to lay a rose upon his tomb.

The rest he had so often longed for had come, but it was too late. Forty years he had passed in public life and he could not now take up again the interests and occupations of his youth. Agriculture had no more charms for him; he was too infirm for sport; he could not, like his father, pass his old age in the busy indolence of a country gentleman's life, nor could he, as some statesmen have done, soothe his declining years by harmless and amiable literary dilettanteism. His religion was not of that complexion that he could find in contemplation, and in preparation for another life, consolation for the trials of this one. At seventy-five years of age, his intellect was as vigorous and his energy as unexhausted as they had been twenty years before; his health was improved, for he had found in Dr. Schweninger a physician who was not only able to treat his complaints, but could also compel his patient to obey his orders. He still felt within himself full power to continue his public work, and now he was relegated to impotence and obscurity. Whether in Varzin or Friedrichsruh, his eyes were always fixed on Berlin. He saw the State which he had made, and which he loved as a father, subjected to the experiment of young and inexperienced control. He saw overthrown that carefully planned system by which the peace of Europe was made to depend upon the prosperity of Germany. Changes were made in the working of that Constitution which it seemed presumption for anyone but him to touch. His policy was deserted, his old enemies were taken into favour. Can we wonder that he could not restrain his impatience? He felt like a man who sees his heir ruling in his own house during his lifetime, cutting down his woods and dismissing his old servants, or as if he saw a careless and clumsy rider mounted on his favourite horse.

From all parts of Germany deputations from towns and newspaper writers came to visit him. He received them with his customary courtesy, and spoke with his usual frankness. He did not disguise his chagrin; he had, he said, not been treated with the consideration which he deserved.

He had never been accustomed to hide his feelings or to disguise his opinions. Nothing that his successors did seemed to him good. They made a treaty with England for the arrangement of conflicting questions in Africa; men looked to Bismarck to hear what he would say before they formed their opinion; "I would never have signed the treaty," he declared. He quickly drifted into formal opposition to the Government; he even made arrangements with one of the Hamburg papers that it should represent his opinions. He seemed, to have forgotten his own principle that, in foreign affairs at least, an opposition to the policy of the Government should not be permitted. He claimed a privilege which as Minister he would never have allowed to another. He defied the Government. "They shall not silence me," he said. It seemed as though he was determined to undo the work of his life. Under the pretext that he was attacking the policy of the Ministers, he was undermining the loyalty of the people, for few could doubt that it was the Emperor at whom the criticisms were aimed.

In his isolation and retirement, the old uncompromising spirit of his ancestors once more awoke in him. He had been loyal to the Crown—who more so?—but his loyalty had limits. His long service had been one of personal and voluntary affection; he was not a valet, that his service could be handed on from generation to generation among the assets of the Crown. "After all," he would ask, "who are these Hohenzollerns? My family is as good as theirs. We have been here longer than they have." Like his ancestors who stood out against the rule of the Great Elector, he was putting personal feeling above public duty. Even if the action of the new Government was not always wise, he himself had made Germany strong enough to support for a few years a weak Ministry.

More than this, he was attempting to destroy the confidence of the people in the moral justice and necessity of the measures by which he had founded the Empire. They had always been taught that in 1870 their country had been the object of a treacherous and unprovoked attack. Bismarck, who was always living over again the great scenes in which he had been the leading actor, boasted that but for him there would never have been a war with France. He referred to the alteration in the Ems telegram, which we have already narrated, and the Government was forced to publish the original documents. The conclusions drawn from these disclosures and others which followed were exaggerated, but the naïve and simple belief of the people was irretrievably destroyed. Where they had been taught to see the will of God, they found only the machinations of the Minister. In a country where patriotism had already taken the place of religion, the last illusion had been dispelled; almost the last barrier was broken down which stood between the nation and moral scepticism.

Bismarck's criticism was very embarrassing to the Government; by injuring the reputation of the Ministry he impaired the influence of the nation. It was difficult to keep silence and ignore the attack, but the attempts at defence were awkward and unwise. General Caprivi attempted to defend the treaty with England by reading out confidential minutes, addressed by Bismarck to the Secretary of the Minister for Foreign Affairs, in which he had written that the friendship of England and the support of Lord Salisbury were more important than Zanzibar or the whole of Africa. He addressed a circular despatch to Prussian envoys to inform them that the utterances of Prince Bismarck were without any actual importance, as he was now only a private man. This only made matters worse; for the substance of the despatch quickly became known (another instance of the lax control over important State documents which we so often notice in dealing with German affairs), and only increased the bitterness of Bismarck, which was shared by his friends and supporters.

For more than two years the miserable quarrel continued; Bismarck was now the public and avowed enemy of the Court and the Ministry. Moltke died, and he alone of the great men of the country was absent from the funeral ceremony, but in his very absence he overshadowed all who were there. His public popularity only increased. In 1892, he travelled across Germany to visit Vienna for his son's wedding. His journey was a triumphal progress, and the welcome was warmest in the States of the South, in Saxony and Bavaria. The German Government, however, found it necessary to instruct their ambassador not to be present at the wedding and to take no notice of the Prince; he was not even granted an audience by the Austrian Emperor. It was held necessary also to publish the circular to which I have already referred, and thereby officially to recognise the enmity.

The scandal of the quarrel became a grave injury to the Government of the country. A serious illness of Bismarck caused apprehension that he might die while still unreconciled. The Emperor took the opportunity, and by a kindly message opened the way to an apparent reconciliation. Then a change of Ministry took place: General Caprivi was made the scapegoat for the failures of the new administration, and retired into private life, too loyal even to attempt to justify or defend the acts for which he had been made responsible. The new Chancellor, Prince Hohenlohe, was a friend and former colleague of Bismarck, and had in old days been leader of the National party in Bavaria. When Bismarck's eightieth birthday was celebrated, the Emperor was present, and once more Bismarck went to Berlin to visit his sovereign. We may be allowed to believe that the reconciliation was not deep. We know that he did not cease to contrast the new marks of Royal favour with the kindly courtesy of his old master, who had known so well how to allow the King to be forgotten in the friend.

As the years went on, he became ever more lonely. His wife was dead, and his brother. Solitude, the curse of greatness, had fallen on him. He had no friends, for we cannot call by that name the men, so inferior to himself, by whom he was surrounded—men who did not scruple to betray his confidence and make a market of his infirmities. With difficulty could he bring himself even to systematic work on the memoirs he proposed to leave. Old age set its mark on him: his beard had become white; he could no longer, as in former days, ride and walk through the woods near his house. His interest in public affairs never flagged, and especially he watched with unceasing vigilance every move in the diplomatic world; his mind and spirit were still unbroken when a sudden return of his old malady overtook him, and on the last day of July, 1898, he died at Friedrichsruh.

He lies buried, not among his ancestors and kinsfolk near the old house at Schoenhausen, nor in the Imperial city where his work had been done; but in a solitary tomb at Friedrichsruh to which, with scanty state and hasty ceremony, his body had been borne.

FOOTNOTES:

[1]

There seems no authority for the statement that the Bismarcks had sprung from a noble Bohemian family.

[2]

It is to this visit that a well-known anecdote refers; having landed at Hull one Sunday morning, he was walking along the streets whistling, when a chance acquaintance of the voyage asked him to desist. Disgusted, he left the town. The story, as generally told, says that he went to Edinburgh; we can have no doubt that Scarborough was meant.

[3]

Life of Herr v. Thadden-Triglaff, by Eleanor, Princess of Reuss.

[4]

This trait is confirmed by Busch, who in his record of the conversations of Bismarck observes that with one or two exceptions he seldom had a good word to say for his colleagues.

[5]

I take the metaphor from Gerlach, but the English language does not allow me to adopt the whole.

[6]

Kohl prints a memorandum of this year (1861) which probably is that sent to Herr von Below; in it the ideas of the letter are developed at greater length and the language is more cautious; Bismarck recommends in it a representation of the people at the Diet, but points out that under present circumstances the consent of the Diet could not be attained; the plan to which he seems to incline is that of a separate union between some of the States; exactly the plan which Radowitz had followed and Bismarck had ten years before so bitterly opposed.

[7]

Speech of January 28, 1886.

[8]

The complication of offices became most remarkable when Bismarck in later years undertook the immediate direction of trade. He became Minister of Finance for Prussia; and we have a long correspondence which he carries on with himself in his various capacities of Prussian Minister, Prussian representative in the Council, and Chancellor of the Empire.

[9]

Sybel states that this was not the case.

[10]

Some of the more exaggerated statements were contradicted at the time, apparently by Prince Radziwill, but in the excitement of the moment no one paid attention to this.

[11]

Comte Hérisson d'Hérisson, Journal d'un officier d'ordonnance.

[12]

The Ghibellines were expelled from Italy in 1267, when Conradin of Hohenstaufen was beheaded by Charles of Anjou.

[13]

Our knowledge of this treaty is still very incomplete; even the date is not certain, but it seems most probable that it was executed at this time. Neither Bismarck's own memoirs nor Busch's book throw any light upon it.

[14]

It must be remembered that our knowledge of these events is imperfect and probably inaccurate; it is at least one-sided. It comes entirely from the published statements of those who gained their information directly or indirectly from Bismarck.

17853452R10222

Printed in Great Britain
by Amazon